DEVELOPMENTAL MOVEMENT EXPERIENCES FOR CHILDREN

DEVELOPMENTAL MOVEMENT EXPERIENCES FOR CHILDREN

DAVID L. GALLAHUE
Indiana University

Macmillan Publishing Company
New York

Collier Macmillan Publishers
London

Macmillan Publishing Company
866 Third Avenue, New York, New York 10022
Collier Macmillan Canada, Inc.

Library of Congress Cataloging in Publication Data:

Gallahue, David L.
    Developmental movement experiences for children.

    Includes bibliographies and index.
    1. Movement education.   2. Motor ability in children.   I.   Title.

GV452.G34   372.8'6   81-16424
ISBN 0-02-340330-6   AACR2

Printed in the United States of America

Printing   3 4 5 6   Year   8 9 0

ISBN 0-02-340330-6

For Ellie, David Lee, Jennifer, and Al
"The Sunshine of My Life"

To be a child
   is to know the fun of living.
To have a child
   is to know the beauty of life.
To teach a child
   is to know the joy of giving.
To love a child
   is to know love fulfilled.

—The Author—

PREFACE

This text, *Developmental Movement Experiences for Children,* has been evolving in my mind for the past several years. As with many other physical educators, I have not been content to view the process of educating children physically merely as a matter of playing games or dancing dances in hopes that somehow they will magically develop the movement abilities necessary for their play, sports, and daily living. Nor have I been content to take the view of a strict adherent to movement education philosophy, focusing exclusively on the movement concepts of effort, space, and relationships. I have opted instead for a blend of the traditional and newer movement education positions, viewing them here as a *means* to the more inclusive end: that of developing and refining fundamental movement and sport skill abilities. Therefore, this text is intended for the teacher and the student who views physical education from a developmental standpoint and uses movement activities as a means of developing and refining movement abilities. It will be valuable to early childhood educators, elementary classroom teachers, and physical education teachers who wish to utilize a developmental skill theme approach to help improve childrens' movement abilities.

The text is written from a "cookbook" approach and is intended to complement the companion text entitled, *Understanding Motor Development in Children* (D.L. Gallahue, New York: John Wiley, 1982). The text has been divided into five distinct sections, a brief description of each section follows.

SECTION ONE   BACKGROUND

This section contains a brief overview of the potential outcomes of a quality movement program, a curricular model for teaching developmental physical education, and suggestions for effective teaching by skill themes. These chapters provide the background information for the sections that follow.

Chapter 1, "Movement with Meaning," focuses on the potential outcomes of quality physical education. The view is taken that although definite results can be achieved in the cognitive and affective development of the child through movement, the development and refinement of movement abilities and physical abilities is still our primary concern.

Chapter 2, "Fundamental Movement and Physical Abilities of Children," offers a developmental overview of the acquisition of locomotor, manipulative, and stability abilities in children. The components of physical fitness and motor fitness are also briefly discussed.

Chapter 3, "Developmental Physical Education: A Curricular Model," presents a curricular model that outlines the developmental approach to physical education. Much of this chapter has been taken from the companion text mentioned above and forms the basis for the developmental skill theme approach presented in Sections Two, Three, and Four.

Chapter 4, "Planning, Organizing, and Implementing Developmental Skill Themes," should help you get started. It provides a variety of practical ideas for planning and organizing your program around skill themes and actually implementing the skill theme approach.

SECTION TWO   FUNDAMENTAL LOCOMOTOR SKILL THEMES

The skill themes that have been selected for inclusion in Chapters 5 through 8 represent the primary fundamental locomotor movements that children need to master. Each of these fundamental movements form the basis for a variety of sport skill movements. The grouping of Walking and Running; Jumping and Hopping; Skipping, Sliding, and Galloping; and Leaping and Climbing is not arbitrary. These fundamental movements compliment one another and at the same time offer variety to the lesson. You may, however, wish to group them differently, or deal with them separately. Either method should work equally well as long as the focus of the lesson is on improvement beyond the current level of ability of the individual or group.

Chapter 9 provides a variety of locomotor game activities. This chapter is intended to provide you with additional appropriate movement experiences for children. The listing of activities is in no way complete and should be supplemented with additional experiences.

SECTION THREE   FUNDAMENTAL MANIPULATIVE SKILL THEMES

The fundamental manipulative skill themes presented in Chapters 10 through 14 do not represent all of the fundamental manipulative movements that children need to develop. Space limitations only permitted the inclusion of eight. These were selected because of their wide use in sports and similarity to other manipulative movements.

The grouping of Throwing and Catching, Kicking and Trapping, Dribbling and Volleying, and Striking and Ball Rolling is, again, not arbitrary. Skill themes involving throwing and catching, and kicking and trapping fit together as naturally as salt and pepper. Dribbling and volleying were grouped together because both involve giving force to an object—one in a downward direction (hand dribble) and the other in an upward direction. Striking and ball rolling may seem like strange partners but both involve giving force to an object, though one uses a sudden explosive action (sometimes involving the use of an implement) and the other does not. Of course, you may choose to group skill themes together any way you wish, or deal with them separately.

SECTION FOUR   FUNDAMENTAL STABILITY SKILL THEMES

Chapters 15 through 18 represent only a few of the skill themes that may be included under the heading of stability. These have been selected because they are most crucial to the developing child. In fact, static and dynamic balance permeates all movement whether it be locomotive, manipulative, or stability. Body Rolling and Dodging have been included as skill themes because of their close link with a variety of sport activities. Chapter 18 provides a wide variety of Individualized Stability Activities.

SECTION FIVE   SKILL THEME INTEGRATION

Chapters 19 through 21 provide a variety of movement experiences that may be effectively integrated with the skill themes presented in the preceding three sections. Although some may prefer to consider rhythmic activities and perceptual-motor activities as separate units, these types of movement activities are generally most effectively learned when integrated with fundamental movement skill themes. The chapters in this section contain only a sampling of the vast array of Rhythmic, Perceptual-Motor and Perceptual activities that are possible to integrate with movement skill themes. Remember also that the primary focus of the movement lesson is on developing and refining movement abilities. Incorporation of the movement experiences contained in these chapters should serve to enhance your skill themes, not replace them. However, you may wish to develop specific rhythmic, perceptual-motor, and perceptual skill themes for children who are experiencing difficulties in these areas *in addition* to your regular program.

As with any project of this nature there are many people to thank for contributions both direct and indirect. I am especially indebted to Ken Gustin for his excellent stroboscopic photography throughout the text, and Bob Koslow for his photographic contributions. Laura Shipley deserves special recognition for her patience in deciphering my scribbling and typing the manuscript. I also wish to thank my many friends and colleagues all over the world for their many contributions through the years. A special thanks is once again extended to my wife, Ellie, for exercising so much patience and recognizing my need to write. Also hugs and kisses to David Lee and Jennifer for permitting me to be their dad and to teach and observe them as they develop and refine their movement abilities.

COMPANION TEXT

Gallahue, David L.: *Understanding Motor Development in Children,* New York: Wiley, 1982.

This text is designed for the undergraduate or graduate student taking a first course in the study of the growth and motor development of children. It has been written in a practical, easy-to-understand, and easy-to-use manner so that it may be of significant value to early childhood, elementary, and physical education teachers. Each chapter contains an introduction to the specific topic, followed by a research-based discussion. The summary and chapter highlights at the end of each chapter provide a condensed overview and delineation of the major points discussed earlier. The critical readings at the end of each chapter are for the student desiring further information on the subject. Each chapter contains tables and figures, line drawings, and photographs designed to provide the reader with a clearer understanding of the process of motor development from birth to childhood.

COMPANION FILM

THE PROGRESSIVE DEVELOPMENT OF MOVEMENT ABILITIES IN CHILDREN

(15 minutes, sound, color)

This film, developed by the author and Marika Botha, and produced and directed by Ken Gustin, was made possible through a grant from Indiana University and John Wiley & Sons, Inc. The film depicts the development of children's movement abilities, ranging from the first reflexive movements of newborns and the rudimentary movements of infants to the fundamental and sport skill abilities of children and adolescents. Based on the research information and theoretical model presented in the text, the film is an excellent device for introducing the topic of motor development to students, parents, and professional groups.

The film is available for rental ($15.00*) or purchase ($120.00*) from:

Indiana University
Audio Visual Center
Student Services Building, Room 008
Bloomington, Indiana 47405

*Current costs; prices are subject to change.

CONTENTS

SECTION TWO   FUNDAMENTAL LOCOMOTOR SKILL THEMES

SECTION THREE FUNDAMENTAL MANIPULATIVE SKILL THEMES

SECTION One

BACKGROUND

1

Movement with Meaning

Parents and teachers have become increasingly aware of the importance of providing children with meaningful movement experiences. There is a growing realization among educators that the so-called play experiences engaged in by preschool and elementary school children play an important role in *learning to move and learning through movement*. For children, movement is at the very center of their life. It permeates all facets of their development, whether in the motor, cognitive, or affective domains of human behavior. In this chapter we will take a cursory look at the contribution that movement can make to each of these domains. The reader is referred to the companion text entitled *Understanding Motor Development in Children* for an in-depth study.

PSYCHOMOTOR DEVELOPMENT

The primary contribution of movement programs for children is in the development of psychomotor competencies. Psychomotor development is at the very heart of the physical education program and should be viewed as an avenue by which both cognitive and affective competencies can also be enhanced. Psychomotor development refers to *learning to move* with control and efficiency through space. It is often referred to simply as motor development (the terms will be used interchangeably) and is subdivided here into two aspects, namely *movement abilities* and *physical abilities*.

3

With preschool and elementary school children the term "movement abilities" refers to the development and refinement of a wide variety of fundamental movements. These movement abilities are developed and refined to a point that children are capable of operating with considerable ease and efficiency within their environment. As they mature, the fundamental movement abilities that were developed when they were younger are applied to a wide variety of games and sports that, hopefully, are engaged in as a part of their daily life experiences. The fundamental movement abilities of striking an object in an underhand, sidearm, or overarm pattern, for example, are elaborated upon and found in numerous sport and recreational pursuits such as golf, tennis, and baseball.

The term "physical abilities" refers to the young child's ever-increasing ability to function and operate within the environment with regard to his or her level of physical fitness and motor fitness. Children's physical abilities are influenced by a variety of health- and performance-related factors that in turn influence their movement abilities.

The joy of efficient movement.

Movement Abilities

Movement behavior may be categorized into three broad and sometimes overlapping categories. These categories represent the primary focus of the motor development specialist when working with children in a physical education program. The first and most basic of these movement categories is referred to as stability. _Stability abilities_ are those developing patterns of movement that permit children to gain and maintain a point of origin for the explorations that they make through space. Stability abilities are sometimes referred to as nonlocomotor movements because they involve such stationary activities as bending, stretching, twisting, and turning. They also include activities in which a _premium_ is placed on maintaining equilibrium such as with inverted supports (tip-up, tripod, or headstand) and rolling movements (forward, backward, or sideward rolls).

At the time when stability abilities are developing, fundamental locomotor abilities are also being enhanced. _Locomotion_ involves projection of the body into external space by altering its location in either a vertical or horizontal plane. Such activities as running, jumping, skipping, and galloping are commonly thought of as locomotor in nature. It is through locomotion that children are able to effectively explore the world about them.

The third aspect of developing movement abilities in children involves the development of fundamental manipulative abilities. _Gross motor manipulation_ involves imparting force to objects such as in throwing, striking, kicking and volleying, and receiving force from objects as with catching and trapping. It is through the manipulation of objects that children are able to come into actual physical contact with objects in their world.

Phases of Motor Development.* The movement education of preschool and primary-grade children involves the development of fundamental locomotor, manipulative, and stability movement abilities. Upon closer examination of movement behavior throughout the life cycle, we find that these three categories permeate human movement from infancy through adulthood. That is, locomotor, manipulative, and stability movement activities are experienced at all levels in the total life experience which may be classified motorically into developmental phases and stages. These developmental stages correspond roughly with the phases of development outlined in the following paragraphs (see Figure 1.1).

The _reflexive movements_ of the fetus and newborn represent the first phase of motor development. Reflexive behaviors are subcortically controlled. They precede and operate concurrently with the development of _rudimentary movement abilities._ Rudimentary movements begin developing in the infant from shortly after birth to

---

*For a detailed discussion of the movement abilities of young children and the phases of motor development, see D. L., Gallahue, _Understanding Motor Development in Children_ (New York: John Wiley, 1982).

AGE PERIODS OF MOTOR DEVELOPMENT

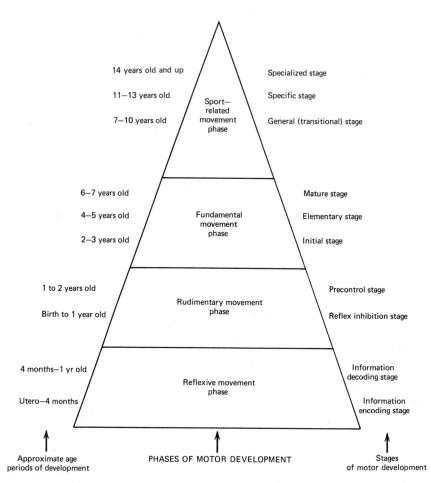

Figure 1.1 Age periods of motor development.

approximately 2 years of age. They involve locomotor activities such as creeping, crawling, and walking. They include manipulative experiences such as reaching for, grasping, and releasing objects and also involve the stability movements of gaining control of the head, neck, and trunk along with learning how to sit and stand unaided.

The third phase of motor development is the *fundamental movement* phase. This phase was discussed briefly in the preceding paragraphs and is the primary concern of this book. Developing fundamental movement abilities involves progressing from the *initial stage* to the *elementary* and finally the *mature stage* in attaining mechanically mature levels of performance in a variety of basic movements. This phase begins around the second year of life and continues through the preschool years and primary grades to about age 7.

Boys and girls in the intermediate grades (third, fourth, and fifth grades) are generally considered to be in middle childhood. This stage of development gives rise to the fourth phase of motor development, namely the *sport related movement* phase and its three corresponding stages: the general (or transitional), specific, and specialized stages. *General movement abilities* closely resemble the fundamental movement abilities of the preceding phase because they involve many of the same movements. The difference, however, lies in the fact that these fundamental movements are now elaborated upon, more highly developed, and approached as sport skills that are applied to a wide variety of lead-up activities for individual, dual, and team sports.* The fundamental movement of striking, for example, is now approached as the sport skill of striking a softball, golf ball, or tennis ball and applied to lead-up games such as fungo, low-hole golf, and tennis volley rather than the *official* sport.

The *specific movement abilities* stage corresponds with the developmental stage of later childhood and preadolescence (sixth, seventh, and eighth grades). This stage is similar to the previous one except that the child is developmentally more mature and more capable of coping with the physical and psychological demands brought about through greater emphasis on form, skill, and accuracy in the performance of more advanced lead-up games and the official sport itself.

The final stage of motor development is the *specialized movement abilities* stage beginning around high school and continuing through adulthood. Specialized skills involve application of the knowledges gained in the preceding phases to a selected few lifetime activities that are engaged in on either a recreational or competitive level on a regular basis. One of the primary goals of education is to develop individuals to a point that they become happy, healthy, contributing members of society. We must not lose sight of this lofty but worthy goal and proceed to view the hierarchical development of movement abilities as stepping stones to the specialized movement skill level. We must view children as *children* and structure meaningful movement experiences appropriate for their particular developmental level. Only when we recognize that the progressive development of movement abilities in a developmentally appropriate sequence is imperative to the balanced motor development of children will we truly be contributing to the total development of each individual. Specialized skill development can and should play a role in our lives, but it is unfair to children to require that they specialize in one or

---

*The term ''sport skills'' is used throughout in the broad sense of the term and includes dance, recreational activities, and cooperative activities as well as traditional competitive sports.

Developing rudimentary stability abilities.

two skill areas at the expense of developing their abilities and appreciations for many other areas.

The reader is cautioned to view the age ranges for each phase of motor development in general terms only. Children will often be seen to function at different phases depending on their experiential background and hereditary makeup. For example, it is entirely possible for a 10-year-old to function at the specialized movement skill phase in stability activities involving gymnastic-type movements but only at the rudimentary or fundamental movement phase in a variety of manipulative or locomotor activities involving such activities as throwing, catching, or running. Although we should continue to encourage this precocious behavior in gymnastics, we should also be very concerned that the child catches up to his or her age mates in the other areas and develops at least an acceptable level of proficiency in them// We must, therefore, refer to the phases of motor development as convenient guidelines of where the *majority* of children are functioning at a given point in time. Rigid adherence to the age classifications is unwise and in direct conflict with the principle of individual differences.//

Physical Abilities

The physical development aspects of the psychomotor domain may be classified as either *physical fitness* or *motor fitness* (see Figure 1.2). These terms, however, are elusive and difficult to define to the mutual satisfaction of experts in the field.

Physical Fitness. Fitness is a relative term that may refer to such things as spiritual, emotional, and social fitness as well as physical fitness. As a result, the concept of "total fitness" has developed over the years and is probably best exemplified by Mathews' statement that "a child who is fit enjoys robust health, a fine looking physique, a satisfactory level of social and emotional adjustment and a proficiency in the basic skills of movement."[1] Agreement on a suitable definition of physical fitness is difficult and is generally done so in broad terms because the level of fitness required of one individual may not be the same as that required of another. Hence, physical fitness is generally considered to be the ability to perform one's daily tasks without undue fatigue. It also is a state in which ample reserves of energy should be available for recreational pursuits and to meet emergency needs. Muscular strength, muscular endurance, circulatory–respiratory endurance, and muscular flexibility are generally considered to be the components of physical fitness.

Motor Fitness. The concept of motor ability or "motor fitness," as it is often termed, is also an elusive one that has been studied extensively over the past several

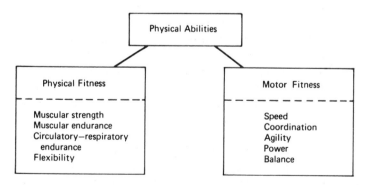

Figure 1.2 The physical fitness and motor fitness components of physical ability.

[1]Mathews, D.K. *Measurement in Physical Education* Philadelphia: Saunders, 1973, p. 5.

years and is classified by some experts as being a part of physical fitness. Hockey's statement probably best summarizes the debate:

> Many factors associated with the development of skill have erroneously been referred to as physical fitness components. It should be kept in mind that only factors that relate to the development of health and increase the functional capacity of the body should be classified as physical fitness components. Those that are necessary for skillful performance of an activity should be classified as motor ability components.[2]

Motor fitness is generally thought of as one's performance abilities as influenced by the factors of speed, agility, balance, coordination, and power.

The generality and specificity of one's motor abilities has been debated and researched for years with the bulk of recent research evidence in favor of its specificity. For years many physical educators somehow let themselves believe that motor abilities were general in nature; as a result, the term *"general* motor ability" came into vogue. It was assumed that because an individual excelled in a certain sport, corresponding ability would be automatically carried over to other activities. Although this often does occur, it is probably due to the individual's personal motivation, numerous activity experiences, and several specific sport aptitudes rather than transfer or carryover of skills from one activity to another. In an effort to avoid confusion between the terms "motor ability" and "general motor ability" we will instead refer to the factors of speed, agility, balance, coordination, and power as elements of *motor fitness*.

COGNITIVE DEVELOPMENT

Another important outcome of a well-rounded movement education program for children is the enhancement of fundamental cognitive concepts. Throughout the history of humankind, philosophers, psychologists, and educators have indicated that a relationship exists between the functioning of the body and the mind. From the Greek philosophers of Socrates and Plato to the educational theorists of the twentieth century there has been a great deal of philosophical support. The fact is, however, that little had been done of an experimental or practical nature prior to the 1960s to put this philosophical construct into operation. A look at psychology, education, and child growth and development textbooks prior to this time makes this point abundantly clear. Topics were generally segregated or categorized under distinctly separate chapter headings with little consideration given to the interrelations between motor and cognitive functioning. Not until the growth of popularity of the works of Jean Piaget has there been a shift in favor of recognizing the importance of movement in the development of both psychomotor and cognitive aspects of the child's behavior. Piaget, a developmental psychologist, emphasized

---

[2]Hockey, R.V. *Physical Fitness* St. Louis; C. V. Mosby, 1973, p. 6.

the tremendous importance of movement as an information-gathering device for children to learn about themselves and their world. Physical educators, and special educators have since been quick to capitalize on this point and have developed a series of motor-training programs designed to enhance children's cognitive abilities.

The movement experiences of preschool and primary-grade children can be effectively used as a medium for *learning through movement*. Educators now recognize that important perceptual−motor skills and fundamental academic concepts can be effectively dealt with in a movement education program. This is not meant to imply that movement is the primary or sole mode by which cognitive abilities can or should be developed. It is, however, meant to say that movement can, through good teaching, be effectively used as a tool for enhancing children's cognitive awareness of themselves and the world around them. The proper use of the "teachable moment" along with the emphasis placed on the development of cognitive concepts of *why, what, how,* and *when* in relation to one's movement can play an important role in helping children get ready for learning by supplementing and reinforcing information that is dealt with in the traditional setting of the nursery school or classroom.

There are two primary aspects of cognitive development that may be dealt with effectively through the movement education portion of the child's day. The first of these aspects is the various perceptual−motor concepts involving the development of body awareness, spatial awareness, directional awareness, and establishment of an effective time−space orientation. The second aspect of cognitive development involves the development and reinforcement of increased understandings and appreciations of fundamental academic concepts involving science, mathematics, the language arts, and social studies through the medium of movement. The bulk of available evidence indicates that both types of cognitive concepts, whether perceptual−motor or academic in nature, may be enhanced through active involvement in carefully selected and directed movement activities. It should be noted, however, that there is little support for the notion that increased movement abilities will have a correspondingly positive affect on the native intelligence of children. The use of movement as a method of enhancing cognitive development is *not* a panacea. Only through the combined and coordinated efforts of parents, classroom teachers, and the physical education teacher will positive inroads be made into the development of cognitive abilities.

Perceptual−Motor Abilities

The process of interacting with our environment is a combination of perceptual and motor processes, which are not independent of one another, as is often assumed. The dash that appears in the term "perceptual−motor signifies the *interdependence* of one on the other. This becomes apparent when we recognize that efficient and effective movement is dependent on accurate perceptions of ourselves and our world

Developing concepts of "in," "on," "through" with inner tubes.

and that the development of one's perceptual abilities is dependent, in part, on movement.

The development of perceptual—motor abilities is a process of both maturation and experience, and as a result all children develop at their own individual rate. Not all children are at the same ability level upon entering school, and although nothing can be done about the maturational component of this process, parents and teachers can have an important influence on the experience component.

The development of perceptual—motor abilities involves the establishment and refinement of kinesthetic sensitivity to one's world through movement. This kinesthetic sensitivity involves the development and refinement of an adequate *space* structure and *temporal* (time) structure. All movement occurs in space and involves an element of time, and the development of these structures is basic to efficient functioning in a variety of other areas. In order to enhance children's knowledge of their spatial world we should involve them in movement activities designed to contribute to their body awareness, directional awareness, and spatial awareness. The temporal world of children may be correspondingly enhanced through activities that involve synchrony, rhythm and the sequencing of movements. Selected visual, auditory, and tactile abilities may also be reinforced through movement in a variety of carefully selected activities (see Figure 1.3).

Academic Concept Readiness

Movement activities for children can enhance the understanding of fundamental academic concepts when they are integrated with material dealt with during the academic portion of the day. Several textbooks have presented in operational terms how specific types of activity might be effectively used to enhance the acquisition of language-arts competencies, basic mathematical operations, and social studies and science concepts. There are a variety of indirect and direct reasons why this occurs. Among them is the fact that active participation is fun. It is often a more natural approach that more closely approximates the needs and interests of children. Active participation in a game in which academic concepts are being dealt with makes it difficult for children's attention to be diverted by extraneous stimuli. Also, a large proportion of today's children place a high negative value on academic understandings but have a high positive regard for physical abilities. Using active games as a learning medium tends to pair pleasurable and highly regarded activity with that which may not be as highly valued, and thus tends to give more pleasure to the practice of the academic skill. Lastly, active learning through movement

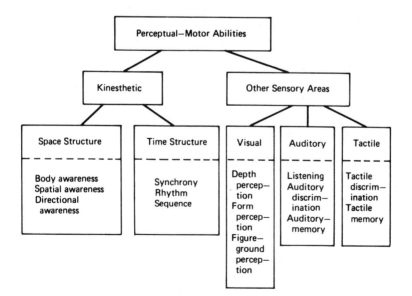

Figure 1.3 The sensory components of perceptual-motor development.

activities enables children to deal in concrete terms with their world rather than in the abstract.

Children generally regard movement as fun and do not equate it with the routine "work" of the classroom. It should be noted, however, that *not all* children benefit best in the enrichment of their academic abilities through active participation in movement activities. On the contrary, there is an overwhelming amount of evidence that indicates that the traditionally silent and relatively immobile form of thought is quite effective for many individuals. The point to be made here is that *some* children benefit greatly from a program that integrates movement activities with academic concept development and that *most* children will probably realize at least some improvement.

AFFECTIVE DEVELOPMENT

A third important but often overlooked outcome of a good physical education program is enhancement of the affective domain. Affective development involves dealing with children's increasing ability to act, interact, and react effectively with other people as well as with themselves. It is often referred to as "social—emotional development," and its successful attainment is of crucial importance to children. For without sufficient social and emotional competencies, children will encounter continual difficulty in relating effectively to their peers, adults, and even themselves. A good or poor parent, an affluent or culturally deprived environment, and the quality and quantity of stimulation given children will largely determine whether they view their world as one that they can control or as one that controls them.

The movement experiences engaged in by children play an important role in their perception of themselves as individuals as well as how they are able to relate to their peers and utilize their free time. Astute parents and teachers recognize the vital importance of balanced social—emotional growth. They understand the developmental characteristics of children and gather these necessary understandings of their behavior in at least the following two areas: (1) self-concept and (2) peer relations and play. This knowledge enables them to encourage and structure meaningful movement experiences that strengthen children's social—emotional growth and are in accordance with their developmental needs, interests, and capabilities.

Self-concept

Children are active, energetic, and emerging beings. They are engrossed in play and utilize play experiences as a means of finding out more about themselves and their bodies. The important beginnings of self-concept or "self-esteem," as it is often termed, is formed in the preschool years. Young children generally view themselves on one end of two extremes in all that they do. Their egocentric nature does not permit them to view themselves objectively in light of their particular strengths and weaknesses. They are unable to fully grasp the concept that one's abilities to do things lie somewhere *between* these self-limiting poles. The "right-wrong," "good-bad" world that children live in plays a key role in how they view themselves. Since their world is one of play and vigorous activity, the successes and failures that they experience play an important role in the establishment of a stable self-concept. If children experience repeated failure in their play world and are unable to perform the fundamental movement tasks of early childhood, they are likely to encounter difficulties in establishing a stable positive concept of themselves.

Based on this knowledge it becomes important for parents and teachers to structure meaningful movement experiences that are within children's developmental capabilities. Ones that reduce the failure potential, thereby enhancing the success potential. It is not enough to say that "failure is a fact of life" or that "if one does not know failure one cannot appreciate success." We must be ever mindful that children are developmentally unable to utilize such logic due to their egocentric nature. The possibility and risk of failure must be *gradually* introduced to children in a manner that is educationally appropriate. We must endeavor to instill the noble concept that each person is a unique individual with a variety of limitations as well as capabilities. Positive feelings toward oneself will help form the basis for developing this concept.

Movement experiences that permit exploration and problem solving on the part of children are very worthwhile. They permit children to solve movement problems or challenges within the limits of their own abilities and do not require the emulation of a predetermined criterion of performance. In this way each child is permitted to achieve a measure of success bounded only by the limits of his or her capabilities.

Movement experiences that have an adventure or "pseudo-danger" element to them are of value in enhancing children's self-concept. Activities such as those that permit children to climb trees or a jungle gym, balance several feet off the ground on a rope ladder or balance beam, or crawl through a homemade tunnel all incorporate an element of adventure in which children must overcome their natural fears and uncertainties to accomplish a "dangerous" task. The feelings of exhilaration and self-satisfaction with accomplishing such a task helps to promote an "I can" attitude within children and enhance their self-esteem.

Peer Relations and Play

While children are engaged in learning about themselves and their world they are also involved in learning how to interact with their peers. Children gradually move through various stages in the establishment of successful relations with members of their peer group. The first is the egocentric stage, in which they literally view themselves as the center of the universe during the first 2 years of life. The

Time to relax and enjoy.

egocentric child is content to play alone with very limited contact with other children. The second stage is that of parallel play. Three- and 4-year old children exhibit behavior characteristic of this stage, in which they are content to play alongside other children but do not enter into group activities for extended periods of time. At about age 5 years, children enter the group-play stage. This stage is characterized by the ability to play in small groups for increasing periods of time followed by the ability to play in large groups and in team-type efforts by age 7 or 8 years.

Movement serves as a primary vehicle by which children progress through each of the play stages. The wise parent and teacher will recognize that wholesome peer relations are a developing phenomena. They will be careful to view children's difficulty with sharing, playing together, and concern for others' feelings as factors that must be dealt with understandingly in light of each child's developmental level. Through wise guidance, movement can be used as an effective tool in helping children develop each of these abilities.

The world of children is a play world. Play serves as a primary vehicle by which they learn about themselves and the world about them. If asked "what did you do today" young children characteristically respond by saying "play." Care must be taken not to view such a response as a frivolous remark or unnecessary part of their daily life. Play must be viewed in the perspective that it is the work of children. That is, through play, whether individual or group, active or quiet, children develop fundamental understandings of the world in which they live.

The development of fundamental movement abilities contributes to children's use of leisure time. The ability to perform a wide variety of locomotor, manipulative, and stability-type movements in an acceptable manner enables children to pursue a variety of play-type activities. Children who do not move well are hindered in their pursuit of leisure-time activities that involve the use and development of their movement abilities. As a result, a negative cycle that witnesses poor movement abilities being formed due to lack of instruction, opportunity, or encouragement is established. The constructive use of leisure time can be enhanced through the possession of efficient movement abilities. Although gross motor activities are only one way of engaging in leisure they are important ones for most children and adults.

Summary

The movement activities engaged in by children play a very important role in the development of their psychomotor, cognitive, and affective abilities. Children are involved in the important and exciting task of *learning to move* effectively and efficiently through their world. They are developing a wide variety of fundamental movement abilities, enhancing their physical abilities, and learning to move with joy and control. Children also *learn through movement*. Movement serves as a vehicle by which they explore all that is around them. It aids in developing and

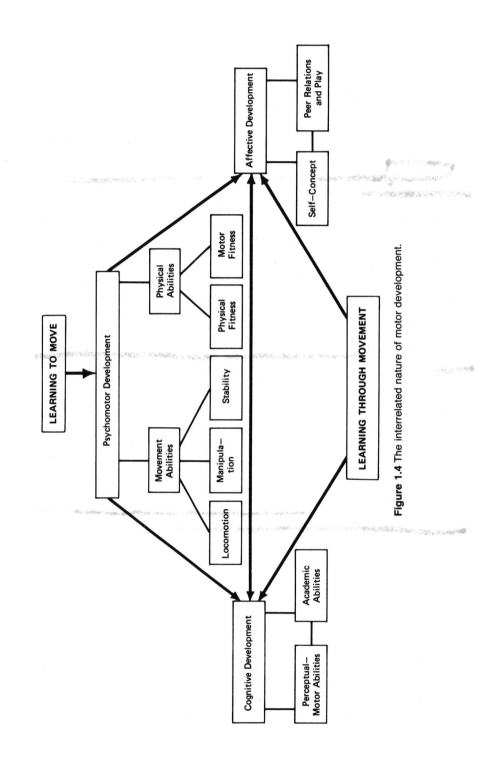

Figure 1.4 The interrelated nature of motor development.

reinforcing a variety of perceptual-motor and academic concepts. It also serves as a medium for encouraging affective development in which effective and efficient movement contributes to enhancing a positive self-concept, wholesome peer relations, and the worthy use of leisure time through constructive play. Figure 1.4 provides an overview of the interrelated nature of the psychomotor, cognitive, and affective domains as applied to movement.

Educators and parents are beginning to realize that reciting the alphabet, being able to count to 100, and writing one's name are not the important learning tasks for young children. Readiness for learning is more than parroting facts and figures, it is a state of developmentally integrated maturity rather than the ability to memorize isolated facts. Children who have developed the following abilities are well on their way to success in school:

1. To love themselves and value their existence as human beings.
2. To possess the fundamental motor and perceptual abilities necessary for cognitive and motor learning.
3. To be able to interpret the meanings of other people's behavior as well as their own.
4. To understand the difference between thoughts and actions and to recognize that feelings are harmless to others.
5. To be able to communicate feelings and emotions as well as thoughts and ideas with words.
6. To wonder and inquire.
7. To be able to risk failure as a necessary part of learning.
8. To understand that complicated questions do not have simple answers in a complex and inconsistent world.
9. To have a mind of their own and to be able to make decisions.
10. To trust their environment and the people in it and to know when to ask for help.

SUGGESTED READINGS

AAHPER *Echoes of Influence for Elementary School Physical Education,* Washington, D.C., 1977.

Gallahue, D.L., *Understanding Motor Development in Children,* New York, John Wiley, 1982.

Pangrazi, R.P. and V.P. Dauer, *Movement in Early Childhood and Primary Education,* Minneapolis, Burgess, 1981.

Schurr, E.L., *Movement Experiences for Children: A Humanistic Approach to Elementary School Physical Education,* Englewood Cliffs, New Jersey, Prentice-Hall, 1980.

2

Fundamental Movement and Physical Abilities of Children

In recent years there has been growing interest in the motor development of children. No longer are educators content with the vague notion that children somehow magically increase their abilities to function motorically as they advance in age. Physicians, physiologists, physical educators, and educators in general are becoming increasingly aware of the need for accurate information concerning the course of motor development in children and its influence on the developing child.

Several questions must be answered before sound motor development programs can be formulated.

1. What principles of motor development affect the motor learning of children?
2. What are the influences of maturation and experience on motor development?
3. When is the optimum time to introduce various skills?
4. What is the role of physical fitness and motor fitness in motor development?

Clarification of these questions is needed in order to develop a more comprehensive understanding of children and their needs. If we fail to answer these questions, we run the risk of repeating many of the same mistakes made by curriculum developers who in the past often took existing high-school curricula and "watered them down" to fit the needs of junior-high and elementary-school children.

FUNDAMENTAL MOVEMENT ABILITIES

The process of motor development is dependent on a variety of developmental principles, involving factors such as the direction and the rate of growth, differentiation and integration of muscle systems, readiness for learning, individual differences, phylogenetic and ontogenetic behaviors, and the effects of both maturation and experience. We must be aware of the tremendous complexity of the

Rope jumping is an excellent conditioning and coordination activity that can be enjoyed by both boys and girls.

process of motor development and view our role objectively as a catalyst in this process, attempting to affect change through the interjection of developmentally appropriate movement experiences. We cannot justify the view that free play, or recess time, provides ample opportunity and motivation for children to develop and refine their movement abilities.

The development and refinement of a wide variety of fundamental movement abilities is of great importance. Children need to learn more about their bodies. They need to learn how to effectively gain and maintain their equilibrium in relationship to constant alternations in the force of gravity. They must learn how to move effectively through space using a variety of efficient patterns. Children need to learn how to relate with other objects in their environment and to be able to give and receive force from these objects. It is also important that they become adaptable and flexible in these movement responses rather than exhibit rigid or inflexible behaviors.

The process of developing movement abilities is one in which gradual shifts or increments in the child's level of functioning occur in the stability, locomotor, and manipulative categories of movement behavior. During infancy, children gain the very simplest controls over their movements in order that they may survive at the lowest level of motoric functioning. Preschool and primary-grade children are involved in developing and refining fundamental movement abilities. Fundamental movement abilities are those basic movements of which all that we do are composed. The many complex movements found in sport and dance are no more than more highly elaborated forms of these fundamental movements developed and combined with one another at a more sophisticated level of functioning (see Figure 2.1). As was pointed out earlier in Chapter 1, fundamental movement abilities continue to be elaborated upon, more highly refined, and applied to increasingly complex patterns of movement as the individual develops.

For many years we have made the assumption that children develop mature patterns of movement through the process of maturation only. It is true that various elements of numerous movement patterns can be expected to be present by certain general age periods. It is, however, erroneous to conclude that the maturational factor alone will ensure the development of mature patterns of movement that may be elaborated upon and more highly developed without the benefit of experience. A wide variety of meaningful movement experiences are necessary to help each child refine her or his movements to a point where they are fluid and adaptable to a wide variety of movement situations. Then, and only then, should the individual be exposed to the more complex sport-type experiences. Witness, for example, the comments of children when the boys say, "she throws and runs just a like a girl" or when the girls say, "boys can't jump rope or play hopscotch." Do comments like these really mean that girls cannot learn how to throw and run efficiently, or that boys cannot learn how to jump rope or play hopscotch proficiently? Certainly not. This situation is merely a reflection of cultural factors that often influence the different types of *experience* that boys and girls are encouraged to take part in.

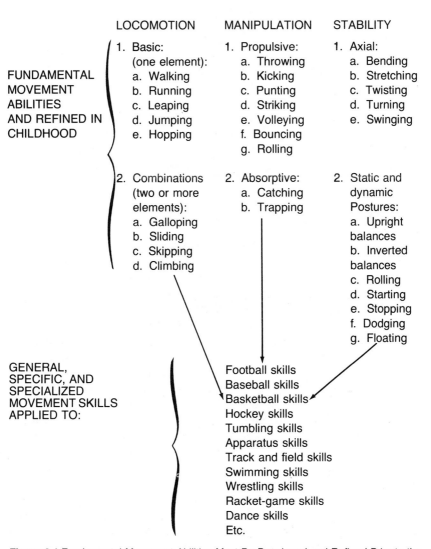

Figure 2.1 Fundamental Movement Abilities Must Be Developed and Refined Prior to the Introduction Of Sport Skills

There are few physiological differences in the early years between boys and girls that would inhibit them from developing and refining efficient movement in those skills often thought to be the exclusive domain of the opposite sex.

Children need to be exposed to a wide variety of fundamental movements and encouraged to refine these basic patterns of movement. Maturation alone will not account for the development of mature efficient patterns of movement. Meaningful movement experiences are of vital importance to children. These are the years when children are learning to move.

Although they are valuable, we must extend ourselves beyond the notion that swings and slides, along with free play and recess time, are all that is needed for children's optimum and balanced motor development. A portion of each day should be spent in some form of guided movement experiences that encourage the child to develop and refine the many important movement abilities used throughout life. Tables 2.1, 2.2, and 2.3 present a list of some rudimentary and fundamental movement abilities and the approximate age at which they begin to emerge in children. These tables should serve as indications of when children are *generally* maturationally ready to benefit from guided movement experiences.

PHYSICAL ABILITIES OF CHILDREN

The physical fitness and motor fitness of children should be of great concern to all parents and teachers and not just the physical educator and physician. The fitness level of boys and girls in our North American society is of great concern to many. This concern was highlighted by a test of minimum muscular efficiency (the Kraus-Weber test) that was administered to several thousand American and European children. The results of this 1954 experiment indicated that the performance of American children was significantly poorer that that of their European counterparts. In fact, over 55 percent of the Americans failed the test, as compared to less than 10 percent of the European youth.[1] Although the comparison has been criticized for several reasons, it pointed out the important fact that American children are often found to be in poor physical condition.

As a result of the Kraus–Hirschand study, the President of the United States at that time, Dwight D. Eisenhower, established the President's Council on Youth Fitness in 1956. This council was established in an effort to promote the upgrading of the physical fitness of our children. Since that time the President's Council and others concerned with the fitness level of our youth have made many important contributions toward that goal. The AAHPER (American Alliance for Health, Physical Education, and Recreation) Physical Fitness Test was developed for boys and girls in the fourth grade and above. The importance of gaining and maintaining a higher level of fitness has been promoted by the President's Council through publications, newspaper articles, and television spots. The importance of movement, motor development, and good physical education programs as a means of enhancing the fitness level of children has also been promoted.

The fact remains, however, that a great many of our children are still unfit. There are two factors that have contributed greatly to this state of affairs. First, the

[1]Kraus, H. and Hirschland, R.P. "Minimum Muscular Fitness Tests in Children," *Research Quarterly 25*, 178, 1954.

Table 2.1 Sequence of Emergence of Selected Locomotor Abilities

Movement Pattern	Selected Abilities	Approximate Age of Onset
Walking		
Walking involves	Rudimentary upright unaided gait	13 months
placing one foot in	Walks sideways	16 months
front of the other	Walks backward	17 months
while maintaining	Walks upstairs with help	20 months
contact with the	Walks upstairs alone—follow step	24 months
supporting surface	Walks downstairs alone—follow step	25 months
Running		
Running involves a	Hurried walk (maintains contact)	18 months
brief period of no	First true run (nonsupport phase)	2–3 years
contact with the	Efficient and refined run	4–5 years
supporting surface	Speed of run increases	5 years
Jumping		
Jumping takes three	Steps down from low objects	18 months
forms: (1) jumping	Jumps down from object with both feet	2 years
for distance; (2)	Jumps off floor with both feet	28 months
jumping for height;	Jumps for distance (about 3 feet)	5 years
and (3) jumping	Jumps for height (about 1 foot)	5 years
from a height. It		
involves a one- or		
two-foot takeoff		
with a landing on		
both feet		
Hopping		
Hopping involves a	Hops up to three times on preferred foot	3 years
one-foot takeoff	Hops from four to six times on same foot	4 years
with a landing on	Hops from eight to ten times on same foot	5 years
the same foot	Hops distance of 50 feet in about 11 seconds	5 years
	Hops skillfully with rhythmical alteration	6 years
Galloping		
The gallop	Basic but inefficient gallop	4 years
combines a walk	Gallops skillfully	6 years
and a leap with the		
same foot leading		
throughout		
Skipping		
Skipping combines	One-footed skip	4 years
a step and a hop in	Skillful skipping (about 20 percent)	5 years
rhythmic alteration	Skillful skipping for most	6 years

Table 2.2 Sequence of Emergence of Selected Manipulative Abilities

Movement Pattern	Selected Abilities	Approximate Age of Onset
Reach, Grasp, Release		
Reaching, grasping, and releasing involve making successful contact with an object, retaining it in one's grasp and releasing it at will	Primitive reaching behaviors	2−4 months
	Corralling of objects	2−4 months
	Palmar grasp	3−5 months
	Pincer grasp	8−10 months
	Controlled grasp	12−14 months
	Controlled releasing	14−18 months
Throwing		
Throwing involves inparting force to an object in the general direction of intent	Body faces target, feet remain stationary, ball thrown with forearm extension only	2−3 years
	Same as above but with body rotation added	3.6−5 years
	Steps forward with leg on same side as the throwing arm	5−6 years
	Mature throwing pattern	6.6 years
	Boys exhibit more mature pattern than girls	6 years and over
Catching		
Catching involves receiving force from an object with the hands, moving from large to progressively smaller balls	Chases ball; does not respond to aerial ball.	2 years
	Responds to aerial ball with delayed arm movements	2−3 years
	Needs to be told how to position arms	2−3 years
	Fear reaction (turns head away)	3−4 years
	Basket catch using the body	3 years
	Catches using the hands only with a small ball	5 years
Kicking		
Kicking involves imparting force to an object with the foot	Pushes against ball. Does not actually kick it.	18 months
	Kicks with leg straight and little body movement (kicks *at* the ball)	2−3 years
	Flexes lower leg on backward lift.	3−4 years
	Greater backward and forward swing with definite arm opposition	4−5 years
	Mature pattern (kicks *through* the ball)	5−6 years
Striking		
Striking involves sudden contact to objects in an overarm, sidearm, or underhand pattern	Faces object and swings in a vertical plane	2−3 years
	Swings in a horizontal plane and stands to the side of the object.	4−5 years
	Rotates the trunk and hips and shifts body weight forward. Mature horizontal patterns	5 years 6−7 years

Stability is the most basic aspect of movement behavior and is developed through practice.

Table 2.3 Sequence of Emergence of Selected Stability Abilities

Movement Pattern	Selected Abilities	Approximate Age of Onset
Dynamic Balance		
Dynamic balance involves maintaining one's equilibrium as the center of gravity shifts	Walks 1-inch straight line	3 years
	Walks 1-inch circular line	4 years
	Stands on low balance beam	2 years
	Walks on 4-inch wide beam short distance	3 years
	Walks on same beam, alternating feet	3−4 years
	Walks on 2- or 3-inch beam	4 years
	Performs basic forward roll	3−4 years
	Performs mature forward roll	6−7 years
Static Balance		
Static balance involves maintaining one's equilibrium while the center of gravity remains stationary	Pulls to a standing position	10 months
	Stands without handholds	11 months
	Stands alone	12 months
	Balances on one foot 3−5 seconds	5 years
	Supports body in basic inverted positions	6 years
Axial Movements		
Axial movements are static postures that involve bending, stretching, twisting, turning, and the like	Axial movement abilities begin to develop early in infancy and are progressively refined to a point where they are included in the emerging manipulative patterns of throwing, catching, kicking, striking, trapping, and other activities	2 months− 6 years

impact of the importance and need for enhancing physical fitness has been centered on children in middle childhood through adolescence (fourth grade through high school) and into adulthood. Little attention has been paid to the fitness needs of children during the preschool and primary-grade years. As a result our knowledge of the fitness of young children is very limited. This has given rise to the second factor, namely the child's "heart myth" and other basically false assumptions concerning the fitness of children.

The child's heart myth has made the assumption that there is a discrepancy in the development of the heart and blood vessels in children and as a result vigorous exercise should be avoided at the risk of "straining" the heart. This widely believed myth has been disproven by Karpovich,[2] Astrand,[3] and others and is reflected in

[2]Karpovitch, P.V. "Textbook Fallacies Regarding the Development of the Child's Heart," *Research Quarterly 8*, 1937.

[3]Astrand, P. *Experimental Studies of Working Capacity in Relation to Sex and Age,* Copenhagen: Munksgoaard, 1952.

Upper arm and shoulder girdle strength can be enhanced through use of the horizontal ladder.

Corbin's statement that "barring injury, a healthy child cannot physiologically injure his heart permanently through physical exercise."[4] Other assumptions, namely that children play all day and get plenty of vigorous activity, no longer hold true. Vigorous exercise and activity have been shown to be important factors in normal healthy growth.

Physical Fitness

A review of the literature on fitness reveals a marked lack of information on children under 8 years of age. The nature of most tests of physical fitness requires the individual to go "all out" and perform at his or her maximum. Anyone familiar with children will readily recognize the difficulty of the situation. The problems lie in: (1) being able to sufficiently motivate the youngsters for maximum performance, (2) accurately determining if a maximum effort has been achieved, and (3) overcoming the fears of anxious parents. Muscular strength, muscular endurance, circulatory–respiratory endurance, and flexibility are generally considered to be the components of physical fitness. Each is briefly discussed in the following paragraphs and summarized in Figure 2.2

Muscular strength is the ability of the body to exert a maximum force against an external object on the body. In its purest sense it is the ability to exert *one* maximum effort. Children engaged in daily active play are doing much to enhance their leg strength by running and tricycling. Their arm strength is developed through such activities as lifting and carrying large toys, handling tools, and swinging on the monkey bars. Strength is measured by use of a dynamometer or tensiometer. These instruments are calibrated and designed to measure grip strength, leg strength, or back strength.

Muscular endurance is the ability to exert force against an external object on the body for several repetitions. Muscular endurance is similar to muscular strength in the activities performed but differs in the emphasis. Strength-building activities require overloading the muscle or group of muscles to a greater extent than endurance activities. Endurance-building activities have less of an overload on the muscles but require a greater number of repetitions. Boys and girls performing several sit-ups, pull-ups, or push-ups are performing muscular-endurance activities. The daily play routine of children when viewed in toto is an excellent example of endurance. Most of us would find it extremely difficult to match the endurance of an energetic child in terms of relative body proportions.

When we speak of *relative* endurance we are referring to the child's fitness level adjusted for body weight. It stands to reason that the adult's gross level of fitness is greater than that of children, but when we divide one's body weight into the total fitness score we find that the differences are much less pronounced.

[4]Corbin, C.B. *Becoming Physically Educated in the Elementary School,* Philadelphia: Lea and Febiger, 1976, p. 22.

MUSCULAR STRENGTH

The ability to perform one maximum effort

MUSCULAR ENDURANCE

The ability to perform a movement task over an extended period of time.

CIRCULATORY RESPIRATORY ENDURANCE

The ability of the heart, lungs and vascular system to function efficiently at a high rate for an extended period of time.

FLEXIBILITY

The range of motion of the various joints of the body.

Figure 2.2 The health related components of physical fitness.

Circulatory–respiratory endurance is an aspect of muscular endurance specific to the heart, lungs, and vascular system. It refers to the ability to perform numerous repetitions of an activity requiring considerable use of the circulatory and respiratory systems. To date little research has been conducted in this important area with preschool or primary-grade children. It is difficult to accurately measure the volume of oxygen utilized in aerobic (stress producing activities requiring considerable consumption of air) activities without the use of sophisticated scientific equipment. We may assume, however, that the aerobic working capacity of an individual begins to develop as early as the preschool years and is dependent in part on the lifestyle of the individual child. Activities such as running, peddling a bicycle, and swimming should be a part of the daily life experiences of children.

Flexibility is the fourth and final area of physical fitness to be considered. Flexibility is joint-specific and can be improved with practice. Flexibility is the ability of the various joints of the body to move through their full range of motion. Most children are involved in numerous flexibility-developing activities. Their constant bending, twisting, turning, and stretching, along with the natural elasticity of their bodies, accounts for much of their flexibility. We need only to look at the contorted positions that children sit in while watching television or listening to a story to realize that they have a good deal of flexibility in the hip and knee-joint area. All too often, however, the range of motion diminishes in later childhood and adolescence due to lack of activity.

Motor Fitness

Much has been said and done concerning the motor performance of the skilled performer and athlete. The literature is replete with information dealing with the performance levels, mechanics, and physiological capabilities of adolescents and adults, but relatively little work has been done with children. The situation is much the same as with physical fitness and only recently have investigators begun to more closely analyze the motor abilities of young children. The tests available have not been rigorously standardized and are inadequately constructed. The need for tests and scales of motor abilities has increased over the past several years because of the increasing interest in the relationship of motor performance to learning and other factors. Although the available tests of motor ability are inadequate in several ways, they do, upon further standardization and modification in the testing and scoring criteria, offer great potential.

Motor fitness is considered to be one's quality of performance of a movement task. The child that displays skill in activities such as bicycling, swimming, throwing, catching, and climbing is said to possess good motor fitness. The components of motor fitness are briefly discussed in the following paragraphs and diagrammed in Figure 2.3.

Coordination is the ability to integrate separate motor systems with varying sensory modalities into efficient movement. The harmonious working together of

COORDINATION

The rhymthmical integration of motor and sensory systems into a harmonious working together of the body parts.

SPEED

The ability to move from one point to another in the shortest time possible over a short distance.

AGILITY

The ability to move from point to point as rapidly as possible while making successive movements in different directions.

POWER

The ability to perform one maximum explosive force.

BALANCE

The ability to maintain one's equilibrium in relationship to the force of gravity in both static and dynamic movement situations.

Figure 2.3 The components of motor fitness.

the synchrony, rhythm, and sequencing aspects of temporal awareness are the predecessors of coordinated movement. Various parts of the body may be involved, such as eye–foot coordination as in kicking a ball or walking upstairs. Eye–hand coordination is evident in fine motor activities such as bead stringing, tracing, and modeling clay and gross motor activities such as catching, striking, or volleying a ball.

Speed is the ability to move from one point to another in the shortest time possible. It is influenced by one's reaction time (the amount of time elapsed from the signal "go" to the first movements of the body) and movement time (the time elapsed from the initial movement to completion of the activity). Reaction time is generally considered to be innate but movement time may be improved with practice. In children we may witness their speed of movement in such activities as crawling, running, climbing, and playing tag.We may foster its natural development by providing plenty of opportunity and open space in which to run and play.

Agility is the ability to change the direction of the body accurately while it is moving from one point to another as fast as possible. It is the ability to make quick and accurate shifts in body position and direction of movement. Agility may be enhanced in young children through participation in tagging and dodging activities. Performing through mazes and obstacle courses are also aids to agility development.

Power is the ability to perform one maximum effort in as short a period as possible. It is sometimes referred to as "explosive strength" and represents the combination of strength times speed. This combination of strength and speed is exhibited in children by jumping, striking, and throwing for distance. The speed of contraction of the muscles involved, as well as the strength and coordinated use of these muscles, determines the degree of power.

Balance is a complex quality of motor fitness. It is influenced by vision, the inner ear, cerebellum, proprioceptors, and the skeletal muscles. Balance is the ability to maintain one's equialibrium in relation to the force of gravity. It is the ability to make minute alterations in one's body position when it is placed in various positions of balance. Balance may be subdivided into *static* and *dynamic* balance. Static balance is the ability to maintain one's equilibrium in a fixed position, such as when standing on one foot or on a balance board. Dynamic balance is the ability to maintain one's equialibrium while the body is in motion.Walking on a balance beam and bouncing on a trampoline are examples of dynamic balance activities.

In actuality all movement involves an element of either static or dynamic balance, because balance is a basic aspect of all movement. As such it is very important for children to begin developing their balancing abilities at an early age.

Summary

The motor development of children represents *one* aspect of the total developmental process. It is intricately interrelated with both the cognitive and affective domains of human behavior. The importance of optimum motor development in children must not be minimized or thought of as being of secondary importance to these other developmental processes. The unity of man clearly demonstrates the integrated development of the mind and the body and the many subtle interrelationships of each.

Principles of motor development emerge from the study of children as they grow. These principles are general in nature and illustrate the gradual progression from relatively simple levels of functioning to more complex levels. Each of these principles are affected by the combined influences of maturation and experience.

Maturation and experience influence the development of movement abilities. An adequately developed movement pattern is one which is adaptable, flexible, and useable in a wide range of environmental situations. Developing the many movement abilities characteristic of the preschool and elementary years contributes markedly to the physical abilities of children. The physical fitness and motor fitness of today's children are of great concern to many because of the frequent lack of opportunity and/or motivation to be physically active. The motor development program in the home, nursery school, or elementary school must provide many opportunities for large muscle activity and strive to increase the children's level of motivation for vigorous activity.

SUGGESTED READINGS

Corbin, C.B. (ed.), *A Textbook of Motor Development*, Dubuque, Iowa,Wm. C. Brown, 1980.

Cratty, B. J., *Perceptual and Motor Development of Infants and Children*, New York, Macmillan, 1979.

Espenschade, A.S. and H.M. Eckert, *Motor Development*, Columbus, Ohio, Charles E. Merrill, 1979.

Gallahue, D.L.: *Understanding Motor Development in Children*, New York, JohnWiley, 1982.

McClenaghan, B.A. and D.L. Gallahue, *Fundamental Movement: A Developmental and Remedial Approach*, Philadelphia,W.B. Saunders, 1978.

Sinclair, C.B., *Movement of the Young Child: Ages Two to Six*, Columbus, Ohio, Charles E. Merrill, 1972.

CHAPTER 3

Developmental Physical Education: A Curricular Model

If the phases and stages of motor development presented in Chapter 1 are to have any real meaning, we should be able to construct a curricular model congruent with these phases. This curricular model should be able to serve as a "blueprint for action." In other words, it should make up the basic structure around which the daily lesson is planned and carried out by the teacher in the gymnasium or on the playing field. What has been discussed in the preceding chapters is of little value if we can not bring order to it and make practical application to the lives of children. The value of theory and research that fails to foster models for implementation is limited at best. Similarly, curricular models not based on sound research and theory are little better. It is, therefore, the intent of this chapter to propose a developmentally based curricular model for implementing the physical education program during the preschool and elementary school years.

CURRICULAR MODELS IN PHYSICAL EDUCATION

Curricular rationales take many forms. Bain[1] has identified six curricular rationales that are in use today by physical education teachers: (1) movement forms, (2) movement analysis, (3) human movement disciplines, (4) developmental stages, (5)

---

[1] Bain, L. "Status of Curriculum Theory In Physical Education," *Journal of Physical Education and Recreation*, 49: 25, 1978.

motor learning tasks analysis, and (6) student motives and purposes. The movement analysis and developmental stage models are most often found at the elementary school level and are the most common choices for curriculum development. These two approaches were debated by Tanner[2] and Gallahue[3] and summarized in an article by Ward and Werner[4].

The developmental model is defined as that approach to physical education which aims to educate children in the use of their bodies so that they can move more efficiently and effectively in a wide variety of fundamental movements and be able to apply these basis abilities to a wide variety of movement skills that may or may not be sport related. At the heart of the developmental model is the focus on developmentally appropriate movement experiences that promote increased skill development at all levels. Games, sports, dances, and the like serve as a vehicle for improving skill.

The movement analysis approach to physical education is defined as "that approach to physical education which teaches children to move skillfully with a knowledge of how they move and a meaningfulness in their movement". The movement analysis model is exemplified by movement education programs that place emphasis on understanding and application of the movement concepts originally proposed by Laban. These movement concepts are important but like the content areas of physical education should serve as a vehicle by which developmentally appropriate movement abilities are developed and refined. The developmental model for teaching physical education presented here attempts to recognize the validity of both the developmental stage and movement analysis curriculum rationales. It places the child at the center of the curricular process rather than content areas or movement concepts.

In order to facilitate presentation of the developmental model we will first review the three categories into which movement may be classified and the appropriate movement skill themes that may be extracted from each category. Then we will discuss the three major content areas of physical education and the three movement concepts of movement education. We will then look at the stages in the process of motor learning and the implications for emphasizing indirect or direct methods of teaching. A developmental model will be presented for both the preschool and primary grades, and the upper elementary and middle school grades.

[2]Tanner, P. "Movement Education: A Total Program of Elementary School Physical Education," in *Proceedings of the Contemporary Elementary School Physical Education Conference*, Georgia State University, Atlanta, Georgia, 1979.

[3]Gallahue, D.L. "Movement Education: Its Place In The Elementary School Physical Education Program," *Proceedings of the Contemporary Elementary School Physical Education Conference*, Georgia State University, Atlanta, Georgia, 1979.

[4]Ward, D. and Werner, P. "Analysis of Two Curricular Approaches In Physical Education", *Journal of Physical Education and Recreation*, 52:60−63, 1981.

CATEGORIES OF MOVEMENT AND MOVEMENT SKILL THEMES

The categories of movement as they relate to motor development have been discussed extensively. Briefly, a category of movement is a classificatory scheme based on common underlying principles of movement. Although others have used the term "nonlocomotor" rather than "stability" as a category of movement. I have chosen to give recognition to the term "stability" as a movement category. Doing so is not arbitrary nor without support from others. Smith and Smith[5]; Gallahue, Werner, and Luedke[6]; and more recently Riggs[7] have all chosen to classify movement behavior into the categories of locomotion, manipulation, and stability. These three categories serve as the organizing centers of the developmental physical education curriculum during the preschool and elementary school years and serve as the basis for the formation of movement skill themes (see Tables 3.1 and 3.2).

A developmental skill theme is a particular fundamental movement or sport skill around which a specific lesson or series of lessons is organized. In the developmental curriculum a category of movement serves as the organizing center of each unit of the curriculum while skill themes serve as the organizing centers of the daily lesson plan. Each category of movement is briefly reviewed in the following paragraphs with a few examples of possible skill themes.

Stability

Stability refers to the ability to maintain one's balance in relationship to the force of gravity even though the nature of the application of the force may be altered or parts of the body may be placed in unusual positions. The classification of stability extends beyond the concept of balance and includes various axial movements and postures in which a premium is placed on controlling one's equilibrium. Stability is the most basic form of human movement. It is basic to all efficient movement and permeates both the category of locomotion and manipulation. Bending, stretching, pivoting, dodging, and walking on a balance beam are all examples of skill themes that may be incorporated into the daily lesson plan at the fundamental or sport skill phase of development.

Locomotion

Locomotion refers to changes in the location of the body relative to fixed points on the ground. To walk, run, hop, jump, slide, or leap is to be involved in locomotion. The movement classification of locomotion develops in conjunction with stability

[5]Smith, K.V. and Smith, W.M. *Perception and Motion: An Analysis of Space Structured Behavior,* Philadelphia: W.B. Saunders, 1972.

[6]Gallahue, D.L., Werner, P.H., and Luedke, G.C. *A Conceptual Approach To Moving & Learning* New York: Wiley, 1975.

[7]Riggs, M.L. *Jump To Joy,* Englewood Cliffs, N.J.: Prentice-Hall, 1980.

Table 3.1 Fundamental Movement Skill Themes

Fundamental Stability Movements Stressed	Fundamental Locomotor Movements Stressed	Fundamental Manipulative Movements Stressed
Bending	Walking	Throwing
Stretching	Running	Catching
Twisting	Jumping	Kicking
Turning	Hopping	Trapping
Swinging	Skipping	Striking
Inverted supports	Sliding	Volleying
Body rolling	Leaping	Bouncing
Landing	Climbing	Ball rolling
Stopping		Punting
Dodging		
Balancing		

but not apart from it. Fundamental aspects of stability must be mastered before efficient forms of locomotion may take place. The vertical jump, rebounding, and high jumping are examples of skill themes that may be incorporated into the daily lesson plan at the fundamental or sport skill phase of development.

Manipulation

Manipulation is concerned with giving force to objects and absorbing force from objects by use of the hands or feet. The tasks of throwing, catching, kicking, trapping, and striking are included under the category of manipulation. Manipulation also refers to the fine motor controls required for tasks such as buttoning, cutting, printing, and writing. The scope of this book, however, is limited to the gross motor aspects of manipulation. Generally speaking, fundamental large muscle manipulative abilities tend to develop somewhat later than fundamental stability and locomotor abilities. This is due, in part, to the fact that most manipulative movements incorporate elements of both stability and locomotion. Throwing a ball, passing a football, and pitching a baseball, are examples of skill themes within the manipulative catagory of movement.

CONTENT AREAS OF PHYSICAL EDUCATION

Fundamental movements and sport skills within the categories of movement outlined above may be developed and refined through the three major content areas of physical education: *games and sports, rhythms,* and *self-testing* activities. The learning of particular games, rhythms, or self-testing activities is a *means* of developing stability, locomotor, and manipulative abilities appropriate to the developmental level of the child. Teachers must not lose sight of this goal. Every activity used in the program should be selected with a conscious awareness that it

Table 3.2 Selected Sport Skill Themes*

Sport Skill Themes	Locomotor Skills Stressed	Manipulative Skills Stressed		Stability Skills Stressed	
Basketball sport skills	Running Sliding Leaping Jumping	Passing Catching Shooting Dribbling Rebounding	Tipping Blocking	Selected axial movements Pivoting Blocking Dodging Cutting Guarding Picking Faking	
Combative sport skills	Stepping Sliding Hopping Leaping	Dexterity (fenc- ing) Striking (kendo)		All axial movement skills Dodging & feinting Static balance skills Dynamic balance skills	
Dance skills	Running Leaping Jumping Stepping	Hopping Skipping Sliding	Tossing Catching	All axial movements Static balance postures Dynamic balance postures	
Disc sport skills	Stepping Jumping Running		Tossing Catching	All axial movement skills Static balance postures Dynamic balance postures	
Football sport skills	Running Sliding Leaping	Jumping	Passing Catching Carrying	Kicking Punting Centering	Blocking Pivoting Tackling Dodging
Gymnastic skills	Running Jumping Skipping	Leaping Hopping Landing			Inverted supports Rolling, landing All axial movements Static balance tricks Dynamic balance tricks

Category					
Implement striking sport skills (tennis, squash, raquet-ball, hockey, lacrosse, golf)	Running Sliding Leaping Skating Walking		Forehand Backhand Striking Driving Putting Chipping	Lob Smash Drop Throwing Catching Trapping	Dynamic balance Turning Twisting Stretching Bending Dodging Pivoting
Skiing sport skills	Stepping Walking Running Sliding		Poling		All axial movements Dynamic balance skills Static balance skills
Soccer sport skills	Running Jumping Leaping Sliding		Kicking Trapping Juggling Throwing Blocking	Passing Dribbling Catching Rolling	Tackling Marking Dodging Feinting Turning
Softball/baseball skills	Running Sliding Leaping	Jumping	Throwing Catching Bunting	Pitching Batting	Selected axial movements Dynamic balance skills Dodging
Target sport skills			Aiming Shooting		Static balance skills
Track & field skills	Running Hopping Jumping	Horizontal jumping Leaping Starting	Shot put Discus Javelin Throwing	Hammer Pole vault Baton passing	All axial movements Dynamic balance skills
Volleyball sport skills	Running Sliding Sprawl Roll	Jumping Dive	Serving Volleying Bump	Dig Spike Dink Block	Dynamic balance skills Selected axial movements

Source: (Compiled by P527 Class, Summer 1981)

can contribute to developing and refining certain movement abilities. For children, their primary objective may be fun, but serious teachers of movement have as their objectives learning to move and learning through movement. The possibility of fun as the motivation to learn is a by-product of any good educational program and is an important objective. This point cannot be overemphasized, but when fun becomes the primary objective of the program for the teacher, then it ceases to be a physical education program and becomes a recreation period.

Games and Sports

Games and sports are used as a means of enhancing movement abilities appropriate to the child's developmental level. They are often classified into three subcategories that proceed from the simple to the complex in the following manner:

1. Low organized games and relays
2. Lead-up games
3. Official sports

Rhythms

Rhythms are an important content area of the movement program. They are generally categorized into four subcontent areas:

1. Rhythmic fundamentals
2. Creative rhythms
3. Folk and square dance
4. Social dance

Self-testing

Self-testing (or individualized movement as it is often called) is the third major content area of the program. This area represents a wide variety of activities in which children work at their own pace and can improve their performance through their own individual efforts. Individualized movement activities may be classified in a variety of ways. The following is a common classification scheme for typical self-testing activities.

1. Fundamental movement activities.
2. Sport skill activities
3. Physical fitness activities
4. Stunts
5. Tumbling
6. Small (hand) apparatus
7. Large apparatus

Achieving effectiveness and efficiency in each of the three categories of movement at either the fundamental or the sport skill phase is the primary reason for incorporating games, rhythms, and self-testing activities in the program. The degree to which this is achieved is dependent on the particular developmental level of the children and the teacher's expertise in structuring developmentally appropriate movement experiences. Games, rhythms, and self-testing activities serve only as the *vehicle* by which these experiences are applied.

MOVEMENT CONCEPTS OF MOVEMENT EDUCATION

Fundamental movements and sport skills within the three categories of movement may be elaborated upon and dealt with in terms of movement concepts. The development of particular movement concepts namely, *effort, space,* and *relationships* is the central focus of many movement education programs and is omitted from most "traditional" physical education programs. In a developmental curriculum movement concepts are included and represent an emphasis to the program along with the three content areas discussed in the preceding section. The primary focus of the developmental curriculum is on fundamental movement and sport skill development through implementation of skill themes. These skill themes are applied to the understanding and application of movement concepts and the content areas of physical education.

A brief explanation of the three movement concept areas in relationship to movement skill development follows.

Effort

The concept of effort deals with *how* the body moves. Children during the preschool and primary grade years need to learn about the concept of effort. Effort may be subdivided into three categories with possibility for a wide variety of movement experiences combined with locomotor, manipulative, and stability movements:

1. *Force:* Refers to the degree of muscular tension required to move the body or its parts from place to place or to maintain its equilibrium. Force may be heavy or light or fall somewhere in between these two extremes.
2. *Time:* Refers to the speed at which movement takes place. A movement may be fast or slow, gradual or sudden, erratic or sustained.
3. *Flow:* Refers to the continuity or coordination of movements. A movement may be smooth or jerky, free or restricted.

Space

The concept of space deals with *where* the body moves. During the young years, a child needs to understand where his or her body can move in space as well as how it

Exploring the concept of effort.

can move. The following movement concepts of space can be directly related to all locomotor manipulative and stability movements.

1. *Level:* Refers to the height at which a movement is performed. A movement may be performed at a high, medium, or low level.
2. *Direction:* Refers to the path of movement. Movement may occur in a forward, backward, diagonal, up, down, left, or right direction, or it may be in a straight/curvy, or zig zag pattern.
3. *Range:* Refers to relative *location* of ones body (self-space/general space) and how various *extensions* of the body (wide/narrow, far/near, long/short, large/small) are used in movement.

Relationships

The concept of relationships deals with both *how and where* the body moves in harmony with objects and other people. The concept of relationships is important for children to understand and experience through the medium of movement.

1. *Objects:* Refers to stationing oneself in different positions to objects. Object relationships may be over/under, near/far, on/off, behind/in front,

Exploring the concept of space.

alongside, front/back, underneath/on top, in/out, between/among, and others.

2. *People:* Refers to moving in various forms *with* people. People relationships include solo, partner, group, and mass movement.

LEVELS OF MOTOR SKILL LEARNING

The content areas and the movement concepts discussed above may be implemented in a variety of ways. The teacher must, however, be aware that individuals tend to pass through typical learning levels as they develop and refine new movement skills. These levels are based on two developmental concepts. First, that the acquisition of movement abilities progresses from the simple to complex. Second, that children proceed gradually from general to specific in the development and refinement of their abilities. Based on these two concepts and fortified with the models by Gentile[8] and Lawther[9] it is possible to view learning a skill as a phenomenon that occurs in levels in the following manner.

1. Exploration
2. Discovery

[8]Gentile, A. "A Working Model of Skill Acquisition With Application To Teaching," *Quest*, 17:3−23, 1972.

[9]Lawther, J.D. *The Learning and Performance of Physical Skills,* Englewood Cliffs, N.J.: Prentice-Hall, 1977.

Experimenting with the concept of relationships.

> **3.** Combination
> **4.** Selection
> **5.** Refined performance (see Figure 3.1)

When involved in developing new stability, locomotor, or manipulative skills that are to be used in game, rhythm, or self-testing activities, we all generally go through the following sequence of learning experiences:

1. We *explore* the movements involved in the task in relative isolation to one another. The learner does not have control of movement but gets used to the task and forms a gross general framework of the pattern or skill.

2. We *discover* ways and means of executing each of these movements better through indirect means such as the observation of others performing, pictures, films, or books. During this aspect of achieving a gross general framework, the learner begins to gain control and coordinate the task. It becomes relatively automatic.

3. We *combine* the isolated movements with others and experiment with them in various ways. This is a practice stage in which separate tasks are integrated, elaborated upon, and begun to be utilized in varying ways.

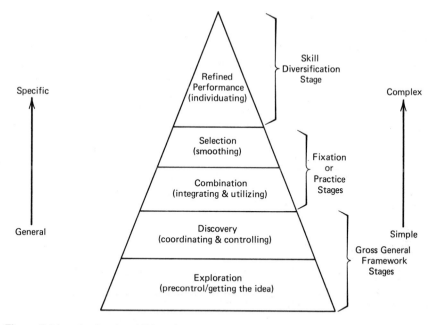

Figure 3.1 Levels of motor skill learning.

4. We *select* "best" ways of combining each of these movements through a variety of lead-up games and informal means of competition and presentation. This aspect of practice is more specific and detailed than the previous stage with more attention given to smoothing out the whole of several skill-related tasks.

5. We *refine* the selected movements to a high degree and perform the particular activity through formal or informal means of competition, or through leisure-time pursuits. This is often called the automatic or skill diversification stage, and is rarely reached in elementary or middle school physical education classes.

This sequential progression of skill learning is similar for adolescents and adults as it is for children, although it may not be as readily apparent. This is because the adolescent and adult are generally at the sport skill phase and may spend less time with exploration, discovery, and the combination of new skills, and more time in the selection and performance aspects of the sequence. Preschool and primary grade children at the fundamental movement pattern phase of development spend a great deal of time exploring, discovering, and combining new movements and less time with the selection of best ways of moving and the refined performance of activities.

Intermediate grade children typically at the general movement skill level spend the bulk of their time combining skills and less time with all others. Those at the specific movement skill level spend the greater portion of their time involved with more direct forms of combination and selecting best ways of executing skills. Those at the specialized level are involved primarily in refined performance activities and continuing to select best ways of moving.

The teacher who is aware that the *emphasis* given to certain types of movement experiences is dependent upon the child's level of development, will structure the environment and utilize teaching approaches that provide appropriate types of learning. Figure 3.2 illustrates how teachers may utilize various forms of indirect and direct teaching approaches that are best suited to the developmental level of their students in order to facilitate the development of fundamental and sport skill abilities.

Facilitating Exploration

Exploration represents the first level of the skill learning hierarchy (Figure 3.2). In order to take advantage of this level the teacher utilizes indirect teaching approaches that encourage exploration. The movement exploration technique of teaching movement is thought by many to help children enhance knowledge of their body and its potential for movement in space. Children are encouraged to explore and experiment with the movement potentials of their bodies. Accuracy and skill in performance are not stressed. This is accomplished by the teacher refraining from establishing a model of performance for the particular movement being explored. Instead, the children are presented with a series of movement questions or challenges posed by the teacher and given an opportunity to solve these problems as they see fit. Any *reasonable* solution to the problem is regarded as correct. At this time, there is no single "best" method of performance that the teacher attempts to elicit from the children. The teacher is more concerned with their creative involvement in the learning process.

Movement exploration experiences are not particularly concerned with the product of the movement act other than acceptable execution of fundamental movements. However, the process of learning that children are involved in during the act is of vital importance. In other words, the teacher is not particularly concerned about the ball going into the hoop, David jumping a certain distance, or the form with which Jennifer executes a handstand. Instead, the teacher is interested in students achieving some degree of success within the level of their own particular abilities. The teacher also places importance and value on the ability to think and act as an individual.

This is not to imply that success or goal-directed behavior is not important. On the contrary, movement exploration techniques are particularly appropriate for young children because they structure the environment for success simply by considering all reasonable solutions to the problems posed by the teacher as correct.

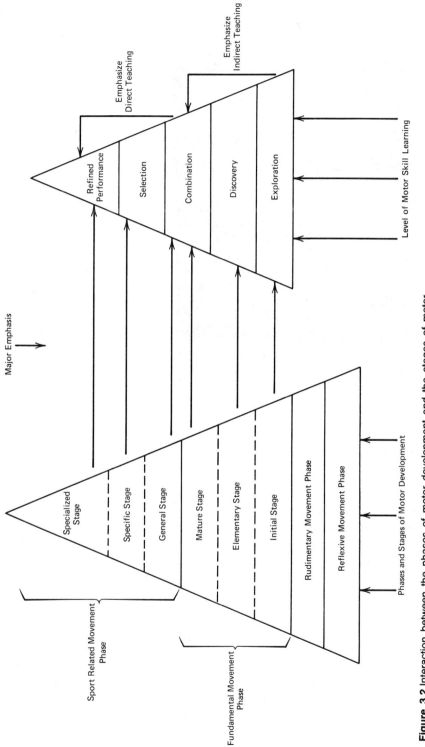

Figure 3.2 Interaction between the phases of motor development and the stages of motor learning.

Exploration on the inner tubes.

Success and goal directed behavior is an individual standard that does not require children to emulate a model of performance or to compete with their peers, but permits success within the limits of the child's own abilities. In doing so, the child is continually encouraged to explore and experiment with endless variations that influence the performance of all locomotor, manipulative, and stability movements in both the content areas (games, rhythms, and self-testing activities) and the movement concept areas (effort, space, and relationships).

Faciliating Discovery

Discovery represents the second classification of the learning hierarchy. Movement experiences that incorporate discovery may be included into the lesson by the teacher in an indirect manner similar to the use of movement exploration techniques. The directed discovery or limitation method of teaching is often used when the child is in the process of discovery. The use of this technique requires that the teacher not establish a model for "correct" performance at the outset of the experience. Problems are stated in the form of questions or challenges that are posed

The observation phase is an important aspect in the process of discovery.

by the teacher. These questions result in emphasis being placed on movement pattern development rather than on skill development. Both the movement exploration and the limitation methods utilize problem-solving techniques as a common tactic in developing the child's movement abilities. Gilliom[10] has defined problem solving as:

> original thinking, an individual's technique of productive thinking, his techniques of inquiry, which is characterized by (1) a focus on an incomplete situation, (2) the freedom to inquire, and (3) the desire to put together something new to him, on his own, to make the incomplete situation into a complete one.

It is the method employed by the child in the solution of the problems posed by the teacher that causes exploration and guided discovery to be considered separately

---

[10]Gilliom, B.C. *Basic Movement Education for Children: Rationale and Teaching Units,* Reading, Massachusetts: Addison–Wesley, 1970, (P. 21).

here. The limitation or guided discovery technique incorporates an observation phase into the total experience, instead of not establishing a model of performance and accepting all solutions as correct as with movement exploration. The observation phase takes the form of observing the solutions of fellow students, the teacher, or individuals on film in relation to the problem presented. Only after the students have had an opportunity to solve the problem within the limits of their own understanding and ability is the observation phase utilized.

Instead of problems being entirely open-ended, as with movement exploration, there is a gradual funneling of questions in such a manner that they lead the children to "discovering" for themselves how to perform the particular movement under consideration. There is no single best way to move at this stage of development, and it allows for the performance of several "best" ways. At the end of the process of attempting solutions to the problem at hand, the children have an opportunity to evaluate their interpretations in light of the solutions of others. They are then given an opportunity to reassess their solutions in light of the performance of others (see Figure 3.3).

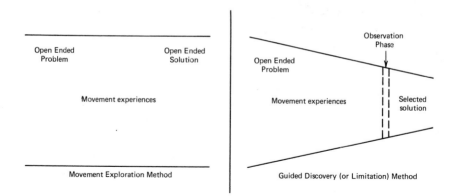

Figure 3.3 Differences between movement exploration and the guided discovery (limitation method) teaching techniques, both of which utilize indirect methods.

Facilitating Combination

Combination represents a transitional category in the hierarchical sequence of learning experiences. Movement experiences that utilize a combination of movement patterns or skills are incorporated into the lesson by the teacher through the use of both indirect and direct styles of teaching (see Figure 3.4).

Indirect combination is a logical extension of the movement exploration and guided discovery approaches. These experiences differ only in that activities involving stability, locomotion, and/or manipulation are combined through the

Riding a bicycle requires the coordinated combination of several fundamental movement abilities.

problem-solving approaches used at the exploration and discovery stages of learning.

Direct combination experiences follow a more traditional approach to developing and refining combinations of stability, locomotor, and/or manipulative movements. Direct or traditional teaching approaches, as they are often called, involve establishing a model for correct performance through explanation and demonstra-

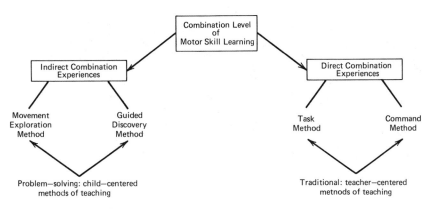

Figure 3.4 At the combination level of motor skill learning the teacher often utilizes both indirect and direct methods of teaching.

tion of the skills to be learned before they are practiced by the students. The children then duplicate the movement characteristics of the model as nearly as possible within the limits of their abilities in a short practice session or drill. The class is generally stopped and the model is presented again along with general comments concerning problems that the class as a whole may be encountering. The class is then involved in an activity that incorporates these skills. The teacher circulates among the students and stops to aid those individuals who may still be having difficulty executing the skills with a general level of proficiency. Direct combination experiences differ from indirect experiences primarily in that they require a model for performance to be established before the movement experience begins while the other does not. The task and the command styles of teaching as proposed by Mooston[11] are two of the most commonly used teacher directed methods.

Facilitating Selection

Selection represents the fourth level of the learning hierarchy. In order to take advantage of this level of experience the teacher aids the students in making

The teacher aids in helping students select the most efficient ways of performing.

[11]Mooston, M. *Teaching Physical Education,* Columbus, Ohio: Charles E. Merrill, 1981.

conscious decisions concerning best methods of performing the numerous combinations of stability, locomotor, or manipulative skills. Rather than merely refining combinations of fundamental movements, children at both the general and specific sport skill stages begin to select preferred ways of moving in a wide variety of sport, game, and dance activities. Selection experiences follow the same direct progression of explanation, demonstration, and practice, followed by general and specific correction and drill that is used with direct combination experiences. Selection-type experiences, however, utilize more advanced activities than those found in the combination stage. These experiences generally take the form of advanced lead-up activities to dual, team, and individual sports rather than low organized games and sport skill practice. Lead-up activities combine two or more selected skills into an approximation of the official sport. Advanced lead-up activities used during this period incorporate numerous elements of the official sport. They are modified primarily in terms of the time, equipment, and facilities required and are a close approximation of the final desired combination of specialized movement skills that would be performed in the official sport.

Facilitating Refined Performance

Refined performance is the fifth and final level of the learning hierarchy. Individuals at this stage are ready to pit their skills and abilities against those of others. Refined performance experiences have no place in a developmentally sound physical education curriculum for the preschool and elementary school child and must not be confused with appropriate forms of informal and low level competition. Refined performance as used here refers to the actual implementation of activities from the selection stage in interscholastic, intercollegiate, intramural, or informal recreational activities. As the performance becomes more refined, greater stress is placed on accuracy and form in performing in a single "best" way.

To be involved in the movement experiences that stress refined performance is to be at the specialized skill stage of development. The job of the preschool and elementary school teacher is to provide children with a series of experiences that contribute to fundamental movement pattern and general sport skill development that forms the basis for specialized skill development in later years.

A DEVELOPMENTAL CURRICULAR MODEL

Unfortunately, programs stressing specialized skill development for young children abound throughout North America. Specialized skill development places primary emphasis on refined performance and little emphasis on the other aspects of the learning sequence outlined on the preceeding pages. There is nothing inherently wrong with skill specialization, but we must ask ourselves if skill specialization in the preschool and elementary school is really in the best interests of most children.

Refined performance is the final level of the motor skill learning hierarchy.

If it is considered to be in the child's best interest, it should serve only to *supplement* the regular program in the form of after-school activities. Specialized skill development should never overshadow, replace, or serve as the primary purpose of the regular physical education program. The regular program in the nursery and elementary school should stress the development and refinement of fundamental movement patterns and a wide variety of sport skills rather than dealing with specialized skill development through refined performance experiences.

We must involve children in a series of coordinated movement experiences that go beyond the learning of isolated skills and the in-school playing of specific sports that they would probably learn on their own through some form of organized activity outside of the school such as the YMCA, YWCA, Boys' or Girls' Clubs, or the Police Athletic League. Broer[12] aptly stated that:

> If physical education is to make a real contribution to the total education of each student it must do more than give him a few isolated skills, most of which can be used only in specific recreational situations.

The developmental model of physical education is based on the proposition that the development of children's movement abilities occurs in distinct but often overlapping *phases* (reflexes, rudimentary movement abilities, fundamental movement patterns, and sport related abilities) in each of the *categories of human movement* (stability, locomotion, and manipulation) and that this is achieved through participation in *skill themes* that are applied to the various *content areas* of physical education (self-testing, games and sports, and rhythmics) and *movement concepts* of movement education (effort, space, and relationships) at the appropriate *level of skill learning* (exploration, discovery, combination, selection, or refined performance) that are recognized through the implementation of various *indirect* (movement exploration and guided discovery), and *direct* (command and task) teaching approaches (see Figure 3.5).

Preschool and Primary Grades

Developmental teaching recognizes that preschool and primary grade children are involved in developing and refining fundamental movement patterns in the three categories of movement. These categories serve as the organizing centers of the curriculum and formation of skill themes at this level. This can be done because each pattern of movement found under these three categories can be dealt with in relative isolation of one another (see Figure 3.1). These fundamental movements serve as the basis for sport skill movements. They are developed and refined at the

---

[12]Broer, M.: *Efficiency In Human Movement*, Philadelphia. W.B. Saunders, 1973, (P. 8).

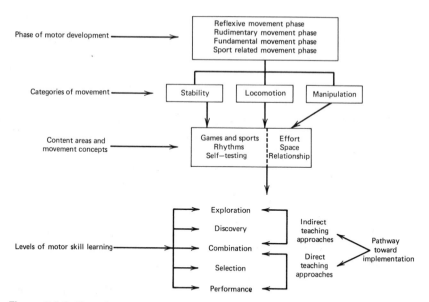

Figure 3.5 Outline of a sequentially based model for the motor development and physical education of the individual.

exploration, discovery, and combination stages of learning *primarily* through indirect styles of teaching that make use of games, rhythms, and self-testing activities and the application of effort, space, and relationship concepts to aid in their development (see Figure 3.6).

Upper Elementary and Middle School

When the developmental model is applied to the upper elementary and middle school grades the focus of the curriculum changes from the fundamental movement phase to the sport-related movement phase of development. During this phase of development, children are constantly combining various stability, locomotor, and manipulative patterns of movement in a wide variety of sport skills. Because of this it becomes impossible to implement movement skill themes that focus on only one category of movement. Instead, at this level, skill themes are viewed in the context of the sport area to which they are being applied. The game of softball, for example, becomes a *sport skill theme* and involves combinations and elaborations of fundamental manipulative abilities (throwing, catching, striking), locomotor abilities (base running and sliding) and stability abilities (twisting, turning, and stretching). The teacher at this level places attention on developing sport skills related to a particular sport skill theme. This is applied to the various content areas and *knowledge concepts* (rules, strategies, understandings, and appreciation) of

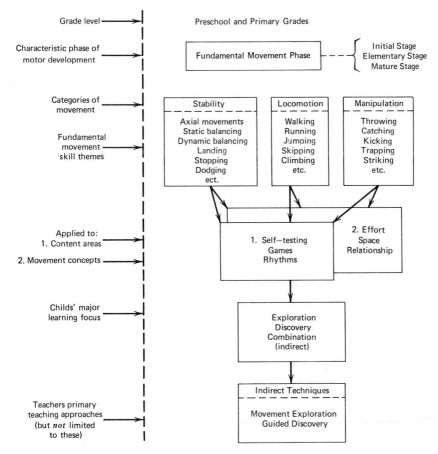

Figure 3.6 Implementing the developmental model at the preschool and primary grade level.

physical education. The teacher recognizes that the children's major learning focus at this level is on the combination of skills and selection of "best" ways of performing, therefore, the teacher utilizes direct teaching methods as his or her *primary* approach to teaching (see Figure 3.7).

Summary

For too many years teachers of physical education, as well as the general population, have had only a vague notion of why the balanced motor development and movement education of children is important. The developmental model

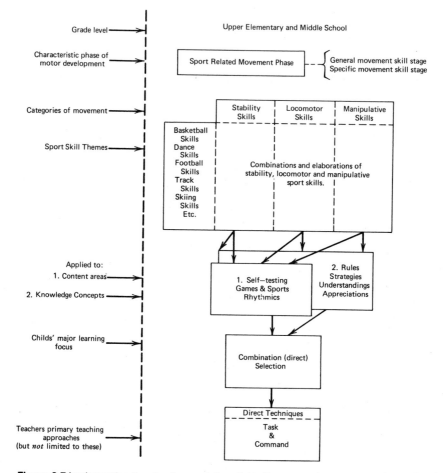

Figure 3.7 Implementing the developmental model in the upper elementary grades and middle school.

presented here is based on the phases and stages of motor development. Movement experiences and teaching methodologies are utilized that recognize the developmental level of the child. The utilization of games, rhythms, and self-testing activities as well as concepts of effort, space, and relationships are viewed as a means of achieving increased skill rather than an end in themselves. The vital importance of learning to move is too critical to be left to chance or the whims of untrained people. The individual with knowledge of (1) the phases of motor development, (2) how children learn, and (3) how to implement developmentally appropriate and existing programs for children, can serve a vital role in developing children's movement and physical abilities.

SUGGESTED READINGS

Bruner, J.S., "The Act of Discovery," *Harvard Educational Review,* 31, 1, 1961.

Melograno, V., *Curriculum Designing for Physical Education: Self-Directed Learning Modules,* Dubuque, Iowa: Kendall/Hunt, 1981.

Mooston, M. *Teaching Physical Education,* Columbus, Ohio: Charles E. Merrill, 1981.

Ward, D. and P. Werner, "Analysis of Two Curricular Approaches in Physical Education," *Journal of Physical Education and Recreation,* 1981.

CHAPTER 4

Planning, Organizing, and Implementing Developmental Skill Themes

The theme approach to teaching has become popular in recent years throughout education. Basically, a theme is an organizing center around which the lesson or unit of study is focused. Rather than centering on a particular content area (that is, games and sports, rhythmics, or self testing activities) and certain activities within that content area, a developmental skill theme centers on certain movement skills that are to be developed and refined as the major focus of the physical education lesson. Therefore, children who are at the fundamental movement phase of development are involved in a variety of skill themes designed to advance them to a more mature stage. Boys and girls who have reached the sport skill phase of development are involved in combining and applying their fundamental movement abilities to a number of sport skill activities.

The focus of the developmental skill themes found in Sections II, III, and IV is on fundamental movements. The information contained in this chapter provides ideas on how to utilize the developmental skill theme approach and how to incorporate it into existing programs.

Planning

A crucial element to the success of any educational program is planning. Without careful planning, the physical education class ends up being little more than a glorified recess period. Experience has shown that teachers who fail to plan are

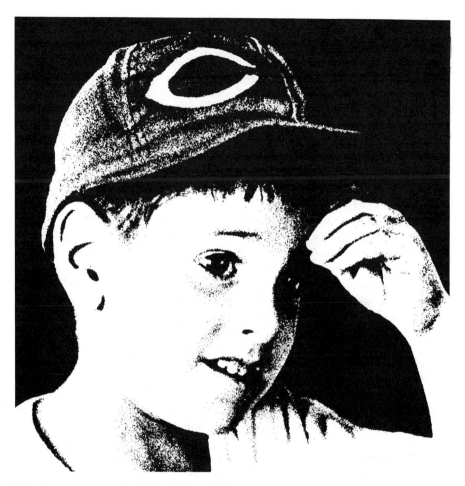

The planning process should be child centered.

really in essence planning to fail. They delude themselves with the notion that they are too competent, too busy, or somehow above planning. As a result they invariably run into difficulties and a series of disasters that are unnecessary, unfulfilling, and educationally unsound. The following represents a five step approach to planning and implementing the physical education program. It is presented in detail here and again in outline form at the beginning of each chapter in Sections Two, Three, and Four as a reminder to make the best use of the limited time available.

Preplanning

The first step in the curricular process is to develop a scope and sequence chart. Basically a scope and sequence chart is a blueprint for action. It provides a general overview of the school year (scope) and an idea of the progression involved from year to year (sequence). The scope and sequence chart is the end result of one's preplanning procedures which include inventorying the facilities, equipment, and supplies that are available as well as determining the number of times classes meet per week, and the length of each class period. This important general information along with other considerations such as class size and alternative facilities during inclement weather provide information necessary to develop a general blueprint for the school year. The exact amount of time to be spent on any one skill theme should remain somewhat flexible. Two to four class periods on some themes is appropriate, returning to them later on in the school year. Or you may wish to spend as long as four weeks on a specific theme. The long term plan should be geared to the developmental needs and interests of your students and will require specific appropriate adjustments.

It is suggested that near-equal balance be given to skill themes during the course of the school year. The specific amount of time spent on particular skill themes will change as the abilities of individuals or the class change. I have found it helpful to children over the years to focus more heavily on stability skill themes during the intitial stage and gradually reduce this amount as they progress on to the elementary and mature stages of fundamental movement ability. I have also found it helpful to increase the emphasis on some skill themes, namely in the manipulative areas, and to remain constant in others as children progress from stage to stage. Figure 4.1 provides a brief overview of the suggested *approximate* amount of time to be spent on the skill themes contained in the following Sections with suggestions for changes in emphasis in terms of percentages as the child progresses from stage to stage. These percentages should serve only as general indicators of the ebb and flow of skill theme emphasis. Actual percentages may vary greatly depending on the abilities of the individual child as well as the group.

Observing and Assessing

After the initial preplanning has been completed, it is necessary to observe the students and informally assess where they are at the present time in their movement abilities. Each of the chapters in Sections Two, Three, and Four provide a description of the typical characteristics of several movement skills at the initial, elementary, and mature stages of development. It will be helpful to read these carefully and study the accompanying stroboscopic photographs that visually portray each stage. After carefully studying this information, informally assess your students' abilities in one or two movement skills. Based on this observational

	Initial Stage	Elem. Stage	Mature Stage
Locomotor Skill Themes			
Walking and Running	10%	10%	10%
Jumping and Hopping	10	10	10
Skipping, Sliding and Galloping	5	5	5
Leaping and Climbing	5	5	5
Manipulative Skill Themes			
Throwing and Catching	10	10	15
Kicking and Trapping	10	10	10
Dribbling and Volleying	5	5	10
Striking and Rolling	5	5	10
Stability Skill Themes			
Dynamic and Static Balance	25	20	10
Body Rolling	10	10	5
Dodging	5	10	10
	100%	100%	100%

Figure 4.1 The approximate time percentages devoted to specific skill themes during the school year will vary according to the developmental level of the class.

assessment you can classify individuals or the group as being generally at the initial, elementary, or mature stage of development for the specific patterns being observed. With this information specific plans for lessons can be made and care can be taken to utilize methods and techniques designed to move the class to more advanced stages. Each of the skill themes presented in the following chapters contain a *Developmental Activities Teaching Progression Chart*. By merely referring to this chart, you can locate appropriate activities geared to the assessed level of development.

It is crucial to the developmental skill theme approach that observation and assessment occur *before* beginning the planning and implementing phase. In the past teachers have often been guilty of planning and implementing lessons and entire programs on age related criteria. Although it is true that the level of development of one's movement abilities are age related, they are *not* age dependent. Therefore, we must not assume that all 3- and 4-year-olds are at the initial stage, all 5- and 6-year-olds at the elementary stage and all 7- and 8-year-olds at the mature stage, even though there is a tendency to improve with age. Diagnostic teaching requires that we carefully observe and assess the entry level of the learner prior to formulating and implementing specific strategies to advance the learner to the next level or stage of development.

Planning and Implementing

Once the entry level of the students has been determined, it becomes a matter of devising and implementing specific means by which improvement will be fostered. Each of the chapters in Sections Two, Three, and Four contain parts entitled *Teaching Tips* and *Concepts Children Should Know*. These should help you get started. It is helpful at this time to develop a unit plan for the theme you are preparing to present. Figure 4.2 provides a sample outline of a theme unit designed for nine lessons. The lessons may be presented in a single unit or dispersed over a longer period of time. Your choice will depend on the age level of the children and the specific theme being presented.

When planning a daily lesson it is important to determine what the specific skill objectives of that lesson are. These may be succinctly stated in a few words or presented in elaborate behavioral terms. Personally, I am not convinced of the necessity of elaborate systems for stating objectives and writing them out for each lesson. I do not know of any experienced teacher who does utilize an elaborate system even though we stress its importance in almost all methods classes. Experienced and successful teachers do, however, always have in mind what the objective of their lesson is even though it may not be carefully written out or stated in behavioral terms. Objectives are important. It is the elaborate and detailed nature of stating them (which is often advocated) that is of questionable value.

Once the objectives of the lesson have been determined it will be necessary to focus on the actual content of the lesson itself. The lesson generally consists of four parts: *Introduction, Review, Body,* and *Summary* (see Figure 4.3). The introductory portion of the lesson is short, lasting from five to seven minutes. It is designed to get the children organized and involved in a vigorous activity quickly. The introductory activity may serve as a warm-up or as a lead-in activity for the lesson to follow. The keys to successful introductory activities are total participation, vigorous activity, and ease of organization. Also, the introductory activity often serves as an important way of ''burning off'' excess energy thus enabling the children to focus their attention on the lesson to come.

The review is the second part of the lesson. It generally lasts from five to ten minutes and provides a brief time to focus on the highlights of the previous lesson. Lengthy explanations and discussions of the previous lesson should be avoided. Rather, an appropriate activity coupled with strategic teacher comments should be the major aspect of this portion of the lesson. Remember, the reason for review is to help the child make the link between the material that was covered in the previous lesson and that which will be presented as new material in the present lesson.

The body of the lesson is the central focus of the lesson. It has the greatest amount of time devoted to it and serves as the core of the entire lesson. The body of the lesson may range from fifteen to twenty-five minutes in length, depending upon the total time alotted, and contains the new material to be taught that day and the application of that material to appropriate activities. The body of the lesson centers

CLASS _____ GRADE _____
LENGTH OF LESSON _____ LENGTH OF THEME _____
MEETINGS PER WEEK _____
SKILL THEME _____
STAGE: INITIAL ELEMENTARY MATURE
DESIRED OUTCOMES

	Day 1	Day 2	Day 3
OBJECTIVES:			
INTRODUCTORY ACTIVITY			
REVIEW ACTIVITY			
BODY			
SUMMARY			
	Day 4	Day 5	Day 6
OBJECTIVES:			
INTRODUCTORY ACTIVITY			
REVIEW ACTIVITY			
BODY			
SUMMARY			
	Day 7	Day 8	Day 9
OBJECTIVES:			
INTRODUCTORY ACTIVITY			
REVIEW ACTIVITY			
BODY			
SUMMARY			

Equipment Needed _____

Figure 4.2 Outline For A Developmental Skill Theme Unit

INTRODUCTION:

Begin the lesson with an easy to organize, active, maximum participation activity to be used as a warm-up activity, or lead-in to the body of the lesson.	5−7 minutes

REVIEW:

Briefly go over the main points of the previous lesson using a specific activity and key teaching phrases.	5−10 minutes

BODY:

A. Utilize a variety of exploratory guided discovery or skill development activities focusing on improvement.	10−20 minutes
B. Implementation: Incorporate the new skill into an appropriate individualized activity or low level game activity.	5−10 minutes

SUMMARY:

A. Review: Briefly review the highlights of the day's lesson.	3 minutes
B. Dismissal: Rather than letting children run to the doors, provide a fun, novel, and challenging dismissal activity.	2 minutes
	30−50 minutes total

Figure 4.3. Time Frame For A Typical Lesson

on a variety of problem solving experience and/or skill drill activities depending on the developmental level of the class. Children at the fundamental movement pattern level will benefit from a variety of exploratory, guided discovery, and skill development activities. (A suggested progression of activities are contained with each skill theme presented in Sections II, III, and IV). The body of the lesson may also involve skill implementation through a variety of individualized or game activities. (Chapters 9, 14, and 18 contain a variety of individualized and game activities for reinforcing locomotor, manipulative, and stability abilities, respectively.) However, care should be taken to focus on the problem-solving aspect of the skill with efforts concentrated on progressing to higher stages of ability rather than the playing of games. Only after the skill has been reasonably mastered should it be incorporated into game-type activities.

The summary is the last part of the lesson. It is an important aspect even though it may last only two or three minutes. The summary provides the instructor with an opportunity to bring closure to the lesson by helping the children recall what was worked on during the lesson and why they took part in the activities. This also permits time to highlight what will be presented in the next lesson and to arrange for orderly dismissal.

Evaluating and Revising

Each of the steps outlined above is important to the successful execution of the daily lesson. Care should be taken to plan all aspects carefully in order to maximize the impact of the lesson. The effectiveness of your lessons should be periodically evaluated and adjustments made in the methods, techniques, and approaches used to convey the skill theme. Without periodic evaluation it is impossible to know what has been achieved in terms of improved abilities and to plan effectively for subsequent lessons. Therefore it is suggested that the teacher informally assess pupil progress on a regular basis. This may be done by using the information found in the Summary of each Chapter in Section II, III, and IV. At the preschool and elementary school level, the key to successful evaluation is to keep it simple. There is no need for elaborate diagnostic procedures. As long as you are familiar with the characteristics of the initial, elementary, and mature stages of a skill theme, simple observational assessment will suffice in most cases. Based on your informal evaluation of the progress or lack of progress of individuals or the class, you will need to make modifications in your remaining lessons. It is easy to see that the process of constantly monitoring pupil progress provides the teacher with information necessary for planning effective, challenging, and developmentally appropriate lessons. Figure 4.4 provides an overview of the cyclic nature of the steps in the planning process.

Moving On

Probably the most crucial but least scientific aspect of the entire planning procedure is to know when to move on to another skill theme. It is impossible to provide anything more than general guidelines as to how much time should be spent on a particular skill theme. No two groups, classes, or individuals are exactly alike and therefore no universal formula of number of lessons, number of minutes, or percentage can be provided. Experienced teachers, however, seem to sense when it is time to move to another theme. Some of the clues that they use are:

1. The percentage of children within the class who have achieved the objectives of the unit.
2. The percentrage of children who have shown a reasonable degree of improvement beyond their entry level.
3. The interest that the children display in the lessons.
4. The amount of time the children spend on the task.

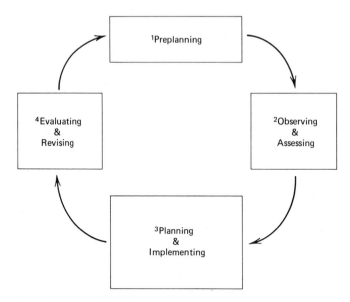

Figure 4.4 Steps in the planning processes.

Ideally, the teacher wants all children to achieve a 100 percent success rate throughout the entire curriculum. This, however, is not possible given the normal variation in natural abilities, learning styles, and other factors. However, the experienced teacher continues to strive for 100 percent success being fully aware that she/he will have to individualize teaching in order to maximize this elusive goal. Also the leader will not be discouraged with less than perfection. She/he will adopt an attitude that success is equal to improvement, and that improvement is relative to the individual's entry level and the movement challenges presented. For example, if the children are assessed at the onset of the unit to be at the initial level in volleying and striking and they have "only" achieved the elementary level after several lessons, there has been improvement even though the mature level has not been reached. Also, the teacher can structure her/his movement challenges in such a way as to minimize or maximize success. A high success rate is desirable but the movement challenges must be structured in such a way that they are challenging but not overwhelming. Therefore, the teacher needs to carefully and continually observe and refocus the lesson in order to achieve a balance between success, challenge, and failure.

Subtle clues of frustration, boredom, inattention, and general off-task activity are good indicators that it is time to refocus your lessons or move on to another skill theme. As a general rule of thumb, it is better to spend two or three lessons on a skill theme with young children returning to it once or twice during the school year rather than focusing all your attention on it at any one time. Older children tend to benefit from longer periods of time on particular skill themes but it is suggested that you not spend beyond a maximum of eight to ten lessons on any one or two themes at one time. Remember, however, to be flexible and responsive to the needs of your students.

The successful teacher recognizes the need for a scope and sequence chart that provides a blueprint for the physical education program. The successful teacher also recognizes the need for observational assessment, and detailed planning but is never constrained by these plans. A constant process of evaluating and reassessing pupil progress, interest, and needs enables the successful teacher to be flexible and to be able to refocus lessons in order to create the most effective learning environment.

ORGANIZING

A variety of activity formations are used in the gymnasium and on the playground. Each is used for specific purposes. Use of the proper activity formations can enhance the limited time that you have. Avoid selecting activities that require frequent formation changes. The most commonly used formations are diagrammed and described below:

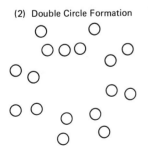

(1) Single Circle Formation

1. Used for circle games and dances

2. Used for parachute activities

3. Good formation for discussions

4. Keep groups small for maximum participation (8 to 10 maximum)

5. Stand at the edge of the circle when talking, never in the center

(2) Double Circle Formation

1. Used for circle parte

1. Used for circle partner activities

2. Used for numerous circle dances and mixers

3. Used for some circle games

4. Use mark on the floor to designate places

5. Change partners often

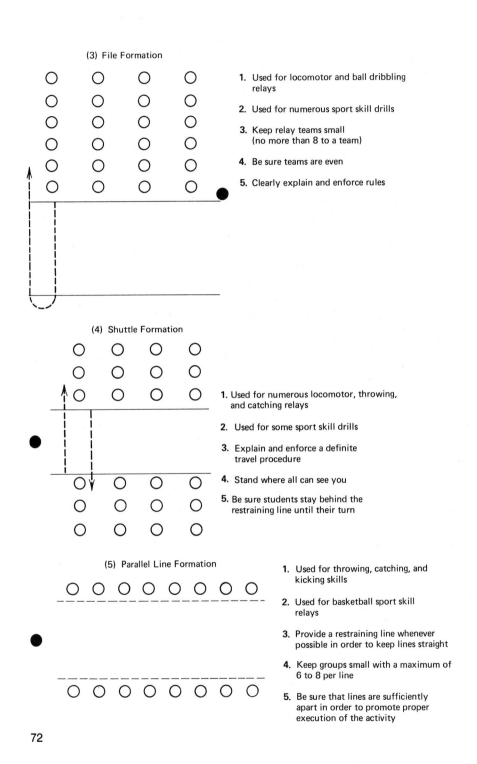

(3) File Formation

1. Used for locomotor and ball dribbling relays

2. Used for numerous sport skill drills

3. Keep relay teams small (no more than 8 to a team)

4. Be sure teams are even

5. Clearly explain and enforce rules

(4) Shuttle Formation

1. Used for numerous locomotor, throwing, and catching relays

2. Used for some sport skill drills

3. Explain and enforce a definite travel procedure

4. Stand where all can see you

5. Be sure students stay behind the restraining line until their turn

(5) Parallel Line Formation

1. Used for throwing, catching, and kicking skills

2. Used for basketball sport skill relays

3. Provide a restraining line whenever possible in order to keep lines straight

4. Keep groups small with a maximum of 6 to 8 per line

5. Be sure that lines are sufficiently apart in order to promote proper execution of the activity

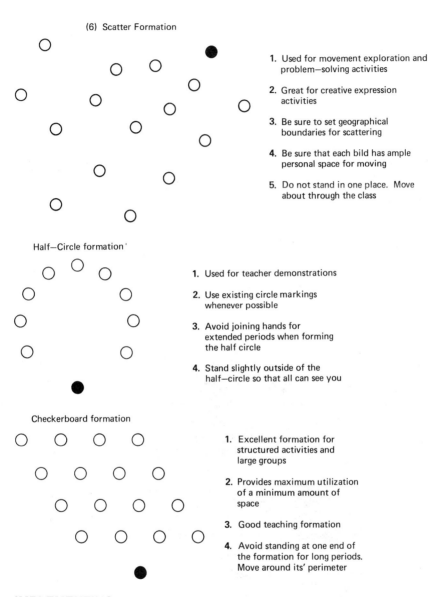

(6) Scatter Formation

1. Used for movement exploration and problem—solving activities

2. Great for creative expression activities

3. Be sure to set geographical boundaries for scattering

4. Be sure that each bild has ample personal space for moving

5. Do not stand in one place. Move about through the class

Half—Circle formation '

1. Used for teacher demonstrations

2. Use existing circle markings whenever possible

3. Avoid joining hands for extended periods when forming the half circle

4. Stand slightly outside of the half—circle so that all can see you

Checkerboard formation

1. Excellent formation for structured activities and large groups

2. Provides maximum utilization of a minimum amount of space

3. Good teaching formation

4. Avoid standing at one end of the formation for long periods. Move around its' perimeter

IMPLEMENTING

The following is a list of recommendations for implementing the skill theme approach in the actual lesson. A careful reading of these suggestions and incorporation of them in your lessons will help maximize your teaching effectiveness.

1. Keep verbalization to a minimum.

2. Don't begin until everyone is listening.
3. Stand where everyone can see and hear you.
4. Do not "talk down" to students, but use a vocabulary that is understandable to them.
5. Do not attempt to emulate the pupils' height when talking or working with them.
6. Summarize, using key words or phrases.
7. Analyze intitial performance of the task. Comment on general problems, assist individually with specific problems.
8. When asking for questions from the class, be specific in nature.
9. Place emphasis on the techniques employed during demonstrations rather than on the results.
10. Constantly observe and evaluate your pupils' performance. Alter your approach and emphasis to meet the pupils' needs.
11. Encourage self-evaluation of progress by students.
12. Utilize the final few mintues for review, self-evaluation, and planning with the children for the next lesson.

Discipline is sometimes necessary.

13. Evaluate the lesson yourself in terms of achievement of your specific objectives.
14. Be thoroughly prepared. Overplan, and know exactly what you intend to do from minute to minute and how you plan to do it.
15. Be cheerful and show a genuine interest in your students but do not become ''buddy-buddy'' with them or ''one of the gang.''
16. Have a thorough knowledge of the activity to be taught before introducing it.
17. Have on hand and readily available all necessary equipment and other required materials.
18. Keep all students actively participating throughout the period whenever possible.
19. Help students achieve proficiency in skill by devoting sufficient time to practice in skills.
20. Provide opportunities for the atypical child to engage in and derive satisfaction from participation in appropriate activities.
21. Change the activity or provide a short rest period when there are signs of fatigue after participation in vigorous activities.
22. Modify rules and sizes of activity areas according to the needs determined by the abilities and sizes of the class members.
23. Develop a spirit of fun and pleasure during activities.
24. Treat all students fairly, recognize individual differences, and avoid embarassing those who have made mistakes.
25. Offer as many varied activities as time, space, and equipment will allow. An activity should be continued long enough for students to become skilled.
26. Develop necessary skills before trying the activity or game.
27. Integrate isolated skills into a game when possible.
28. Build skill upon skill.
29. Warm-up activities should pertain to the skills being used in the class.
30. Never let an activity drag.When the children begin to lose interest, use a variation or change the activity.
31. Use sparingly those activities which provide activity for only a few.
32. Employ teaching techniques which will help each child learn something new every day.
33. Analyze classes that did not go well; realize the reason may be your fault more often than not.
34. Correlate your activities with other school subjects.
35. Arrange activities to provide continuous advancement throughout the entire school year with definite objectives for each skill level.
36. Be observant of individual differences. Structure lessons so that all will achieve a reasonable degree of success and at the same time feel challenged by the lesson.

SUMMARY

A developmental skill theme approach can be easily incorporated into the physical education curriculum. At the preschool and primary grade level the focus of developmental skill themes is on enhancing fundamental movement abilities. Children that have achieved the mature stage in a variety of fundamental movements are ready to begin focusing on developmental skill themes at the sport skill phase of development. The scope of this text is limited to fundamental movement skill themes and the information contained in each of the following chapters are dedicated to that end. With careful planning, organizing, and implementation of the developmental skill themes that follow, you will be doing much to aid children in the optional development of their fundamental movement abilities.

SUGGESTED READINGS

Graham G., and others, *Children Moving: A Reflective Approach to Teaching Physical Education,* Palo Alto, California: Mayfield, 1981.

Hoffman, H. A., and others, *Meaningful Movement for Children: A Developmental Theme Approach To Physical Education,* Boston: Allyn and Bacon, 1981.

Logsdon, B. J., and others, *Physical Education For Children: A Focus On The Teaching Process,* Philadelphia: Lea and Febiger, 1977.

Morris, G. S. D., *Elementary Physical Education: Toward Inclusion,* Salt Lake City, Utah: Brighton Publishing Company, 1980.

Two

FUNDAMENTAL LOCOMOTOR SKILL THEMES

CHAPTER 5

Walking and Running

The walking and running patterns begin developing early in the young child. Around the first birthday the infant achieves an upright gait and begins to walk. Skill in walking develops rapidly until about age six at which time it resembles the adult pattern in many ways. Care, however, must be taken to monitor the child's walking posture and to provide movement experiences that help him or her focus on the proper walking pattern.

By 18 months, the child is attempting to run but no flight phase is apparent. The initial attempts at running resemble a fast walk. A flight phase marking the onset of true running generally appears between the second and third birthday. With proper amounts of practice, encouragement, and instruction, the running pattern should continue to improve and be at the mature stage by age seven.

In order to make the best use of your time when working on walking and running, you may find the following sequence of preplanning, observing and assessing, planning and implementing, and evaluation and revision helpful:

1. *Preplanning:* Determine when and for approximately how long you wish to focus on walking and running as a skill theme.
2. *Observing and Assessing:* Study the verbal descriptions and visual descriptions provided for each stage of the walking and running pattern (see pages 80–82, and 83–85). Then informally assess the walking and running abilities of the class or of individual children, making an effort to determine if their movements are typically at the initial, elementary, or mature stages.

3. *Planning and Implementing:* Study the Teaching Tips and Concepts Children Should Know found on pages 82−83, and 85−87. Based on this information and your informal assessment, select appropriate movement activities from the Developmental Activity Teaching Progression Chart for walking and running located on page 87.

4. *Evaluation and Revision:* Informally reassess walking and running performance in terms of improvement or lack of improvement. You may wish to utilize the questions found in the Summary on page 92. Modify your plans and movement activities to more closely suit specific individual and group needs.

WALKING

Developmental Sequence Checklist

Initial Stage:
- Difficulty maintaining upright posture
- Unpredictable loss of balance
- Rigid, halting leg action
- Short steps
- Flat-footed contact
- Toes turn outward
- Wide base of support
- Flexed knee at contact followed by quick leg extension
- Arms held up for balance

Elementary Stage:
- Gradual smoothing out of pattern
- Step length increased
- Heal-toe contact
- Arms down to the sides with limited swing
- Base of support within the lateral dimensions of the trunk
- Out-toeing reduced or eliminated
- Increased pelvic tilt
- Apparent vertical lift

Mature Stage:
- Reflexive arm swing
- Narrow base of support
- Relaxed elongated gait
- Little vertical lift
- Definite heel-toe contact

Visual Description Checklist

Initial Stage:

Elementary Stage:

Mature Stage:

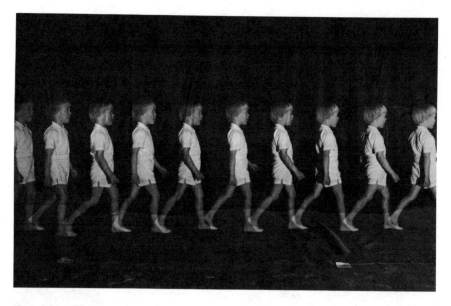

Teaching Tips

Common Problems

- Walking on the toes
- Walking with the toes turned in ("pigeon-toed")
- Walking with the toes turned outward ("duck-footed")
- Poor rhythmical coordination and alteration of the arms and legs
- Poor posture and body alignment
- Excessive vertical lift
- Wide base of support
- Head forward
- Too much side to side swinging of the arms

Recommendations

- Provide activities that stress keeping the trunk erect.
- Utilize mirrors when possible.
- Provide a visual model of good walking posture.
- Work for ability to walk with attention focused on other activities.
- Include leg and foot strengthening activities in the program.

- Use "stepping stones" or small carpet squares to emphasize pointing the toes straight ahead.
- Stress pushing off from the toes.
- Stress walking lightly with the head up and arms swinging freely.

Concepts Children Should Know

Skill Concepts

- Many elements of walking are similar to running except one foot is always in contact with the ground.
- When you walk, keep your head up and your trunk straight.
- Check your feet once in a while to be sure that your toes are pointed straight ahead.
- When you walk, your heel is the first part of your foot to contact the ground and your toes are the last to leave.
- Your arms should swing opposite the action of your legs in a relaxed, rhythmical manner.

Movement Concepts

- You can walk in many different directions at different speeds and different levels.
- You can look happy or sad, healthy or sick when you walk.
- You can walk in different pathways, and with objects or with people.
- When you carry an object, your walking pattern should be modified to suit the object.
- Your walking pattern can be adjusted in many ways to suit your needs.

RUNNING

Developmental Sequence Checklist

Initial Stage:
- Leg swing is short, limited
- Stiff, uneven stride
- No observable flight phase
- Incomplete extension of support leg
- Stiff, short swing; varying degrees of elbow flexion
- Legs tend to swing outward horizontally
- Swinging leg rotates outward from the hip
- Swinging foot toes outward
- Wide base of support

Elementary Stage: —Stride length, swing, and speed increase
                     —Limited but observable flight phase
                     —Support leg extends more completely at takeoff
                     —Arm swing increases
                     —Horizontal swing is reduced on backswing
                     —Swinging foot crosses midline at height of recovery to rear

Mature stage: —Length of stride is at its maximum: speed of stride is fast
                     —Definite flight phase
                     —Support leg extends completely
                     —Recovery thigh is parallel to ground
                     —Arms swing vertically in opposition to the legs
                     —Arms are bent in approximate right angles
                     —Little rotary action of recovery leg and foot

Visual Description Checklist

Initial Stage:

Elementary Stage:

Mature Stage:

Teaching Tips

Common Problems

- Inhibited or exaggerated arm swing
- Arms crossing the midline of the body
- Improper foot placement
- Exaggerated forward trunk lean
- Arms flopping at the sides or held out for balance
- Twisting of the trunk
- Arhythmical action
- Landing flat-footed
- Flipping the foot or lower leg either in or out

Recommendations

- Determine the characteristic stage in running ability.
- Plan activities designed to move the child to the next stage.
- Include plenty of activities involving movement exploration at the initial stages of learning.
- Work for good listening skills while running.

—Use the commands "freeze" and "melt" to develop listening skills.

—Stress not bumping into others.

—Stress stopping without sliding on the knees.

—When playing tagging games, teach proper tagging, no pushing.

—Incorporate activities that gradually increase aerobic capacity.

—Provide a wide variety of running activities.

Concepts Children Should Know

Skill Concepts

—Keep your head up.

—Lean into your run *slightly*.

—Lift your knees.

—Bend your elbows and swing the arms freely.

—Contact the ground with your heels first.

—Push off from the balls of your feet.

—Run lightly.

—Running is basic to the successful playing of numerous games and sports.

Movement Concepts

-You can run at many different speeds and levels.

-You can land heavily or lightly.

-Your run can be smooth or jerky.

-You can run in many different directions and paths.

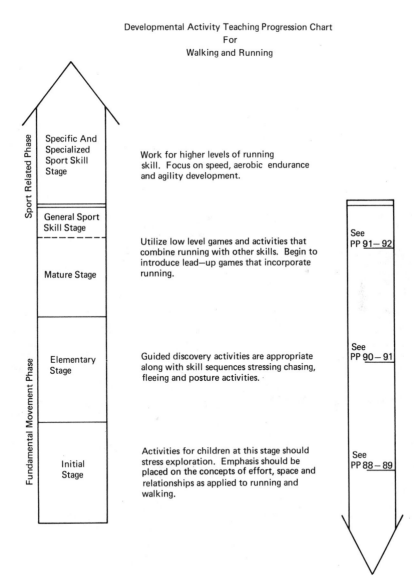

Developmental Activity Teaching Progression Chart
For
Walking and Running

Sport Related Phase	Specific And Specialized Sport Skill Stage	Work for higher levels of running skill. Focus on speed, aerobic endurance and agility development.	
	General Sport Skill Stage	Utilize low level games and activities that combine running with other skills. Begin to introduce lead-up games that incorporate running.	See PP 91-92
Fundamental Movement Phase	Mature Stage		
	Elementary Stage	Guided discovery activities are appropriate along with skill sequences stressing chasing, fleeing and posture activities.	See PP 90-91
	Initial Stage	Activities for children at this stage should stress exploration. Emphasis should be placed on the concepts of effort, space and relationships as applied to running and walking.	See PP 88-89

—You can run short distances or long distances, alone, or with others.

—Your running form should be altered as your speed changes.

—Your running pattern will be altered when you carry an object.

—Running requires a flight phase.

Exploratory Activities

The purpose of incorporating exploratory activities in movement lessons focusing on walking and running is to provide the individual at the initial or elementary stage in these patterns an opportunity to come to grips with the gross general framework of these skills. These activities are intended to help children get in touch with their bodies and to experiment with the multitude of variations in effort, space, and relationships that can be experienced. Combinations can be successfully included after the gross general framework idea has been established and the child is at the mature stage in walking and running.

The following is a sampling of exploratory activities to be included in the movement lesson.

Walking is an important fundamental movement used for a lifetime.

WALKING AND RUNNING

Can you run/walk—

Effort	Space	Relationships
Force	*Level*	*Objects*
—like a pixy?	—very tall?	—on the line?
—like an elephant?	—very small?	—across the line?
—on your tip toes?	—at a high level?	—under the bars?
—flat-footed?	—at a low level?	—behind the chair?
—as if you were	—at a medium level?	—around the chair?
floating?	—fast or slow at a high	—over the hoop?
—as if you weighed a	level?	—through the hoop?
million pounds?	—smoothly at a high	—carrying a ball?
—as softly as you can?	level?	—carrying a suitcase?
—as hard as you can?		—with boots on?
	Direction and Path	
Time	—forward?	*People*
—as fast you can?	—backward?	—all by yourself?
—as slow as you can?	—to the left-right?	—in front of a partner?
—starting slow and	—diagonally?	—behind a partner?
showing form?	—and change direction	—beside a partner?
—alternating fast and	once?	—holding a partner's hand?
slow?	—and change direction	—with the class?
	three times?	—without touching anyone?
Flow	—in a straight line?	—with two others?
—as smoothly as you can?	—in a curvy line?	—in formation?
—with jerky	—in a zig zag line?	
movements?	—in a pattern (show	
—like a machine?	shapes)?	**Combinations**
—like a robot?		An infinite variety of
—like a deer?	*Range*	exploratory experiences can be
—like a football player?	—in your own space?	devised simply by combining
—without using your	—throughout the room?	various effort, space and
arms?	—as far as you can?	relationship challenges.
	—and not bump anyone?	
	—with your feet wide?	
	—with big steps?	
	—with tiny steps?	

Guided Discovery Activities

The sampling of guided discovery activities that follow are designed to permit the child to experiment with a variety of movement challenges designed to lead to the mature patterns of walking and running. A problem-solving approach is used, but emphasis now begins to be placed on the proper mechanics of walking and running.

Walking

1. First have the children explore several of the variations of walking found on the previous page.
2. Then begin to place limiations on their responses to the challenges you present. For example:

Arm action—

   a. Stand tall and walk forward. Now swing your arms freely as you walk. What happens with big arm swings? With short? Why?
   b. How does it feel when you walk with your arms held at your side? Is the length of your stride affected by the use or nonuse of your arms?

Trunk action—

   c. Walk with an eraser balanced on your head. Try to cause others to drop their eraser while walking, but without touching. Play eraser tag. Why is it harder to balance your eraser when walking fast?
   d. Walk to the beat of the drum. What happens to your walking when the drum speeds up? Slows down? Walk in time to the music. March to the music. How is marching different from walking? How is it the same?

Total—

   e. What should you try to remember when you walk? (feet, arms, trunk, head)

3. Finally, have the children combine walking with different activities in an effort to achieve a more natural and automatic pattern. For example:
   a. Walk around the room while counting to 100.
   b. Walk around the room while talking to a friend.
   c. Freeze! How are your feet placed? Is your trunk straight?
   d. Walk forward while bouncing and catching a ball.
   e. Walk forward while carrying a heavy object.
   f. How is your walking pattern altered? Why?

Running

1. Have the children first explore the numerous variations of running found on page 89.
2. Then begin to put limitations on the possible responses to the movement challenges you present. For example:

General—   **a.** Run around the gym in a clockwise direction, counter-clockwise.

Arm action—   **b.** Run as fast as you can one time around the gym. What do your arms do? Do they move fast or slowly?

                        c. When you run slowly, do your arms move fast or slowly? Why?

                        d. How do you swing your arms when you run? Do they cross your chest, or do they stop before crossing?

                        e. Run with your arms crossing your chest. Now try it without crossing. Which is best? Why?

Leg action—   **f.** What part of your foot lands first when you are running as fast as you can? What about when you are jogging at a slower pace?

                        g. Run uphill. Run downhill. How does your stride change? Why does it change?

Trunk Action—   **h.** Lean as far forward when you run. Now try to stay very straight. Now try something in between. Which feels the best for you? Why?

Total—   **i.** Show me how you would run a five-mile race? How would you run a mile race, a quarter mile, fifty yards?

                        j. Why is your run slightly different for each distance?

                        k. Can you run to the rhythm made by the drum?

                        l. What happens to your run when the beat speeds up or slows down?

3. Now combine running with other activities in order to achieve a more "automatic" pattern.

    a. Can you tag someone lightly while running?

    b. Can you dodge someone who is trying to tag you?

    c. Run barefooted. Now try it with your street shoes. Now with your gym shoes. How does it feel? Which way is most comfortable? Safest?

    d. Run on different surfaces. How does it affect your running pattern? Why?

Skill Development Activities

After the fundamental movements of walking and running have been mastered to a reasonable degree and the child exhibits these patterns in their mature form, it is time to begin focusing on skill combinations and further refinement. In order to do this you will find it helpful to:

1. Return to the exploratory activities found on page 89 and devise experiences that focus on more extensive combinations of effort, space, and relationships.

2. Incorporate a variety of additional problem-solving activities into the lesson.
3. Incorporate a variety of chasing, fleeing, and tagging games into the lesson such as those found in Chapter 9.
4. Begin focusing on the application of walking and running skills into a variety of relay- and track-related activities such as:
   a. running relays
   b. shuttle relays
   c. dashes
   d. middle distance running
   e. distance running

The use to which mature walking and running patterns are put will depend primarily on the needs, interests, and developmental levels of the children being served.

SUMMARY

During the course of implementing a walking/running skill theme you will want to evaluate progress. Observational assessment in a game of tag or informal play situation should be adequate. If you are unable to answer "yes" to each of the following questions, in terms of individual class members as well as the entire group, you will need to make modifications in your lessons to suit the specific needs of your students:

Walking/Running:	Yes	No	Comments
1. Are the children able to walk/run from point to point with good postural control?			
2. Are they able to make smooth transitions in direction, level, and speed?			
3. Can they run about the gym or play-yard without bumping into each other?			
4. Can they utilize the walking and running patterns in conjunction with other basic skills?			
5. Do they walk and run without undue attention focused on the process?			
6. Are their movements relaxed, fluid, and rhythmical?			
7. Are there observable improvements in their walking and running abilities?			

The movement patterns of walking and running are basic to our everyday activities. It is essential that they be developed to the mature level. A variety of exploratory and guided discovery activities can aid in this process. Once the mature pattern has been obtained these skills may be utilized in a variety of game, sport, and dance situations. Practice in running and walking will enhance one's performance abilities. Speed and endurance will continue to improve with practice and will enable the individual to utilize these abilities in a variety of sport skills.

CHAPTER 6

Jumping and Hopping

Jumping and hopping are fundamental movement patterns that are used in a variety of sport, recreational, and daily living experiences. Jumping and hopping may take many forms all of which involves a take-off, flight phase, and landing. A jump differs from a hop in that a jump involves taking off on one or both feet and landing on both feet while a hop involves taking off on one foot and landing on the same foot. Jumping may occur in a roughly horizontal plane, in a vertical plane or from a height. Hopping may occur in place, or it may occur over a roughly horizontal plane.

In order to make the best use of your time when focusing on jumping and hopping as a skill theme, you will find it helpful to make use of the following sequence of events:

1. *Preplanning:* Determine when and for about how long you wish to focus on jumping and hopping as a skill theme.
2. *Observing and Assessing:* Study the verbal and visual descriptions provided for each stage of the three jumping patterns and one hopping pattern found on the following pages. Then informally assess the jumping and hopping abilities of the class or of individual children. Determine if their actions are typically at the initital, elementary, or mature stages.

94

3. *Planning and Implementing:* Study the Teaching Tips and Concepts Children Should Know found on pages 97−98, 102−103, and 106−107. Based on this and your assessment information, select appropriate activities from the Developmental Activity Teaching Progression Chart for jumping and hopping located on pages 112, 114−117.

4. *Evaluation and Revision:* Continually reassess jumping and hopping performance in terms of improved mechanics. You may wish to use the questions found in the Summary on page 121 as a guide. Modify your lessons to more closely suit specific individual and group needs.

Horizontal Jumping

Developmental Sequence Checklist

Initial Stage:
−Limited arm swing; the arms do not initiate the jumping action
−During flight, the arms move in a sideways-downward or rear-ward-upward arm action to maintain balance
−The truck moves in a vertical direction; little emphasis upon the length of jump
−Preparatory crouch is inconsistent in terms of leg flexion
−Has difficulty using both feet
−Extension of the ankles, knees, and hips at takeoff is limited
−Body weight falls backward at landing

Elementary Stage:
−Arms initiate jumping action
−Arms remain toward the front of body during preparatory crouch
−Arms move out to the side to maintain balance during flight
−Preparatory crouch is deeper and more consistent
−Extension of the knees and hips is more complete at takeoff
−Hips are flexed during flight and the thighs are held in a flexed position

Mature Stage:
−The arms move high and to the rear during the preparatory crouch
−During takeoff, the arms swing forward with force and reach high
−Arms are held high throughout the jumping action
−Trunk is propelled at approximately a forty-five degree angle
−Major emphasis is on horizontal distance
−Preparatory crouch is deep and consistent
−Complete extension of ankles, knees, and hips at takeoff
−Thighs are held parallel to the ground during flights; lower leg hangs vertically
−Body weight at landing moves forward

Visual Description Checklist

Initial Stage:

Elementary Stage:

Mature Stage:

Teaching Tips

Common Problems

- Poor preliminary crouch
- Inability to take-off with both feet simultaneously
- Restricted movements of the arms or legs
- Poor angle of take-off
- Loss of balance in the air
- Failure to extend fully upon takeoff
- Landing with one foot at a time
- Falling backward upon landing

Recommendations:

- Start with exploratory activities and progress to more directed techniques as skill develops.
- Avoid jumping in socks or gym shoes with poor traction.
- Use carpet squares as a challenge to jump over.
- Place emphasis on coordinated use of the arms and legs.

—Children like to measure the length of their jump. This is a good time to reinforce measuring with a yardstick or meter stick.

—See if children can jump a distance equal to their height.

—Try jumping from different surfaces. Discuss differences.

Concepts Children Should Know

Skill Concepts

—Crouch halfway down.

—Swing your arms back, then forward forcefully.

—Explode forward from a coiled position.

—Push off with your toes leaving the ground last.

—Stretch and reach forward.

—Bring your knees to your chest as you prepare to land.

—Your heels contact first upon landing.

—"Give" with your landing and fall forward.

Movement Concepts

—You can land heavy or light, but it is best to land lightly.

—If you swing your arms fast you will travel farther than if you swing them slowly.

—Your jump can be smooth or jerky, free or bound.

—You can jump in different directions and at different levels.

—You can combine your jump with other movements.

—You can jump in place, for height, for distance, or from a height.

—A jump requires taking off and landing on one or both feet.

—Jumping with objects will alter your pattern.

VERTICAL JUMPING

Developmental Sequence Checklist

Initial Stage: —Inconsistant preparatory crouch
                              —Difficulty taking off with both feet
                              —Poor body extension upon take-off
                              —Little or no head lift
                              —Arms tend to remain at side
                              —Little height is achieved

Elementary Stage:
— Exceeds ninety degree angle on preparatory crouch
— Exaggerated forward lean during crouch
— Takes off with both feet
— Trunk does not fully extend during flight phase
— Arms attempt to aid balance in flight but often unequally
— Noticable horizontal displacement upon landing

Mature Stage:
— Preparatory crouch with knee flexed from sixty to ninety degrees
— Forceful extension at the hips, knees, and ankles
— Simultaneous coordinated upward arm lift
— Upward head tilt with eyes focused on the target
— Full body extension
— Elevation of reaching arm by shoulder girdle tilt combined with downard thrust of non-reaching arm at the peak of flight

Visual Description Checklist

Initial Stage:

Elementary Stage:

Mature Stage:

Teaching Tips

Common Problems:

- —Inhibited or exaggerated crouch
- —Failure to extend the body, legs, and arms forcefully
- —Swinging the arms backward rather than upward
- —Flexion at the knees upon take-off
- —Arms out to the side for balance
- —Failure to lift with the head and extend at the shoulder
- —Landing with insufficient crouch

Recommendations

- —Some children may be "earthbound" and may require special assistance.
- —Stress coordinated action of legs and arms.
- —Require children to stretch and reach with the arms and head as they jump.
- —Use plenty of exploratory activities at the initial stage, progressing to more directed techniques later on.
- —Try jumping on different surfaces. Inner tubes, mattresses, and trampolines all provide exciting experiences.
- —Have children chalk their fingers to mark their jumps.
- —Have children jump and place a piece of tape to mark their jump.
- —Have children jump up and grab an object.

Concepts Children Should Know

Skill Concepts

- —Crouch about halfway down for your take off and landing.
- —"Explode" upward.
- —Forcefully swing and reach upward with your arms.
- —Stretch, reach, and look upward.
- —Extend at the shoulder of your reaching arm.
- —This jumping pattern is used in rebounding and the lay-up shot in basketball as well as the block and spike in volleyball.

Movement Concepts

- You must time your jump so that all body parts work together.
- You can jump high or low and with or without use of your arms.
- You jump highest if you use your arms.
- Your movements must be quick and forceful for the highest jumps.
- You can jump while holding objects but your height will be less.
- You can jump only as high as the force of gravity will let you.
- Vertical jumping requires a two-footed take-off in an upward direction and landing on both feet.

JUMPING FROM A HEIGHT

Developmental Sequence Checklist

Initial Stage
- One foot leads upon takeoff
- No flight phase
- Lead foot contacts lower surface prior to trailing foot leaving upper surface
- Exaggerated use of arms for balance
- Little flexion at knees upon landing

Elementary Stage:
- Two foot take-off with one foot lead
- Flight phase, but lacking in control
- Arms used ineffectively for balance
- One foot landing followed by immediate landing of trailing foot
- Inhibited or exaggerated flexion at knees and hip upon landing

Mature Stage:
- Two foot take-off
- Controlled flight phase
- Both arms used efficiently out to the sides to control balance as needed
- Feet contact lower surface simultaneously with toes touching first
- Feet land shoulder width apart
- Flexion at the knees and hip is congruent with the height of the jump

Visual Sequence Checklist

Initial Stage:

Elementary Stage:

Mature Stage:

Teaching Tips

Common Problems

- —Inability to take off with both feet
- —Exaggerated or inhibited body lean
- —Loss of control while in the air
- —Failure to land at the same time on both feet
- —Landing flatfooted
- —Failure to give sufficiently upon impact
- —Loss of balance upon landing

Recommendations

- —Start with a low height and gradually work up.
- —Place a mat on the floor.
- —Spot all jumping carefully.
- —Encourage exploration then gradually focus on the skill element.
- —Begin with single task skills, then combine two or three tasks (jump, clap your hands, land, and roll forward).
- —Stress proper landing techniques.
- —Emphasize control while in the air.
- —Provide different levels for different abilities.
- —Keep equipment well spaced for safety reasons.

Concepts Children Should Know

Skill Concepts

- —Push off with both feet.
- —Your toes are the last thing to leave the ground.
- —Lean forward slightly.
- —Move your arms forward or sideward in unison for balance.
- —Keep your legs shoulder width apart in preparation for landing.
- —Give at the ankles, knees, and hip joint upon landing.
- —Jumping from a height and landing is used in your play activities and in numerous sports.

Movement Concepts

- You can land either heavily or lightly.
- Your jump can be from many different heights.
- The extent of your crouch upon landing is based on the height of your jump.
- You can jump in many different directions going forward, backward, or to the side.
- Your jump should be smooth but can be jerky and awkward.
- Your jump can be far or near, high or low.
- You can jump and land with objects but must make adjustments.
- Jumping from a height requires taking off and landing on both feet.

HOPPING

Developmental Sequence Checklist

Initital Stage:
- Non-support leg flexed ninety degrees or less
- Non-support thigh is roughly parallel to the contact surface
- Body upright
- Arms flexed at elbows and held slightly to the side
- Little height or distance generated in a single hop
- Balance lost easily
- Limited to one or two hops

Elementary Stage:
- Non-support leg flexed
- Non-support thigh at forty-five degrees to contact surface
- Slight forward lean with the trunk flexed at the hip
- Non-support thigh flexes and extends at the hip to produce greater force
- Force is absorbed upon landing by flexing at the hip and the supporting knees
- Arms move vigorously up and down bilaterally
- Balance poorly controlled
- Generally limited in the number of consecutive hops that can be performed

Mature Stage:
- Non-support leg flexed at ninety degrees or less
- Non-support thigh lifts with vertical thrust of support foot
- Greater body lean
- Rhythmical action of non-support leg (pendulum swing) aiding in force production
- Arms move together in rhythmical fashion lifting as the support foot leaves the contact surface
- Arms not needed for balance but used for greater force production

Visual Sequence Checklist

Initial Stage:

Elementary Stage:

Mature Stage:

Teaching Tips

Common Problems

- Hopping flatfooted
- Exaggerated movements with the arms
- Exaggerated movement of the free leg
- Exaggerated forward lean
- Poor control of balance
- Failure to synchronize leg and arm action
- Inability to keep free leg from contacting floor (loss of balance)
- Inability to hop on either leg

Recommendations

- Provide activities that make use of hopping on the left foot and on the right foot.
- Begin with exploratory activities and progress to more directed experiences
- Work for rhythmical flow in hopping.

—Stress rhythmical alteration of the feet.

—Do not emphasize hopping for speed or distance too early.

—Work for control then gradually stress force.

Concepts Children Should Know

Skill Concepts

—Take off and land on the same foot.

—Lift your arms slightly as you spring up from your hop.

—Push off from your toes and land on the balls of your foot.

—Land softly

—Hopping is used in combination with jumping in the triple jump and the ballestra in fencing.

—Hopping is used in many dance steps including the polka, mazurka, and the schottische.

Jumping from a height and landing in control is an important fundamental movement ability.

Movement Concepts

- —You can land heavily or lightly when you hop.
- —You can hop in place or move in different directions.
- —You can hop at different speeds.
- —You can hop at different heights and levels.
- —You can hop over objects and in different pathways.
- —You can hop smoothly and freely or it can be bound and jerky.
- —You can hop with one foot or the other.
- —You can alternate hopping feet.
- —Hopping requires a takeoff and a landing on one foot.

Exploratory Activities

The primary purpose for exploration of jumping and hopping is to provide the child with ample opportunities to experiment with and explore various elements of effort, space, and relationships. Exploratory activities permit the individual an opportunity

Jumping over objects can be a challenging task.

Developmental Activity Teaching Progression Chart
For
Jumping and Hopping

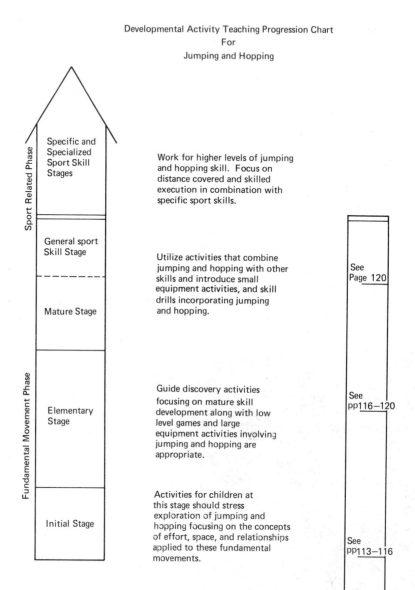

Specific and Specialized Sport Skill Stages — Work for higher levels of jumping and hopping skill. Focus on distance covered and skilled execution in combination with specific sport skills.

General sport Skill Stage / Mature Stage — Utilize activities that combine jumping and hopping with other skills and introduce small equipment activities, and skill drills incorporating jumping and hopping.

Elementary Stage — Guide discovery activities focusing on mature skill development along with low level games and large equipment activities involving jumping and hopping are appropriate.

Initial Stage — Activities for children at this stage should stress exploration of jumping and hopping focusing on the concepts of effort, space, and relationships applied to these fundamental movements.

Sport Related Phase

Fundamental Movement Phase

See Page 120

See pp116–120

See pp113–116

to "get the feel" of these movements and to develop an understanding of the movement concepts implied by them. Not all of the activities suggested on the following pages are suitable for those at the initial stages of jumping and hopping. Be selective in the use of these suggestions remembering that they are only a sampling and that many are appropriate for higher skill levels. Once the mature level has been achieved it may be wise to go back and experiment with the numerous combinations of effort, space, and relationships that are possible with jumping and hopping.

HORIZONTAL JUMP

Can you jump—

Effort	Space	Relationships
Force	*Level*	*Objects*
—as quietly as possible?	—from as small a	—over the box?
—as loudly as possible?	position as you can?	—across the rope?
—alternating loud and	—from as big of a	—through the hoop?
soft jumps?	position as you can?	—like a frog, or a rabbit?
—like a pixy?	—and stay under my	—while holding this ball?
—like a giant?	hand?	
		People
Time	*Direction*	—with a partner?
—very fast?	—forward/backward?	—as far as your partner?
—very slowly?	—sideways?	—over your partner?
—alternating fast and	—in a straight line?	—at the same time as your
slow jumps?	—several times in a zig	partner jumps?
—as if you were stuck in	zag or circular patterns?	
molasses?	—making various	
—as if you were on ice?	geometric shapes or	**Combinations**
	letters of the alphabet?	Numerous combinations of
Flow		effort, space and relationships
—with your arms and	*Range*	are possible.
legs held stiffly?	—as far as you can?	For example:
—Keeping your arms	—as near as you can?	—for distance and then for
out?	—landing with your feet	height?
—with your legs out?	wide apart?	—as short and as low as possible?
—in a relaxed manner?	—landing with your feet	—as fast and as far as possible?
—like a wooden soldier?	close together?	—as quietly and as far as you
		can?
		—and toss a ball?
		—and catch a ball?
		—to my rhythm?
		—to the music

VERTICAL JUMP

Can you jump up—

Effort	Space	Relationships
Force	*Level*	*Objects*
—and land lightly?	—as high as you can?	—and strike the hanging ball?
—and land heavily?	—as low as you can?	—with a weighted object?
—like an elephant?	—alternating high and	—with a ball?
—like a robot?	low jumps?	—on a trampoline?
	—and touch the same	—on a bounding board?
Time	spot five times?	—over a jump rope?
—as fast as you can?	—from a crouched	
—as slow as you can?	position?	*People*
—like a rocket?	—from an extended	—with a partner?
—like a growing flower?	position	—and alternate jumping up with a partner?
Flow	*Direction*	—while holding hands?
—without using your	—and land in the same	—and touch your partner's spot?
arms?	spot??	
—and use only one arm?	—and land in a different	
—and keep your head	spot?	**Combinations**
down?	—and land slightly	Numerous combinations of effort
—and remain stiff?	forward/backward/to the	space and relationships are
—as relaxed as you can?	side?	possible.
	—and turn?	For example:
		—jump up and toss a ball?
	Range	—jump up and shoot a basket?
	—and land in your own	—jump up and catch a ball?
	space?	—jump and hop over a jump
	—and land outside your	rope?
	space?	—jump and turn?
	—and land with your feet	—jump, turn, catch?
	wide apart?	—jump as lightly, high, and as
	—and land with your feet	fast as you can?
	close together?	

JUMPING FROM A HEIGHT

Can you jump—

Effort	Space	Relationships
Force —and land as lightly as you can? —and land as forcefully as you can? *Time* —and land as quickly as possible? —and stay in the air as long as possible? —in slow motion? *Flow* —with different arm actions? —without using your arms? —while holding one arm to your side?	*Level* —from a crouched position? —from a tucked position? —as high as you can? *Direction* —forward? —backward? —sideways? —and make a quarter turn? —and make a half turn? —and make a full turn *Range* —and land with your feet together? —and land with your feet apart? —and land in this spot? —and make yourself as big as you can?	*Objects* —over the wand? —through the hoop? —and catch the ball in the air? —and throw the ball in the air? —and catch a ball you toss while in the air? *People* —at the same time as a partner? —and land at the same time as your partner? —and do what your partner does? —and do the opposite of your partner? **Combinations** Numerous combinations of effort, space, and relationship activities involving exploration of jumping from a height are possible and should be used after the child has gained control of singular movements.

HOPPING

Can you hop—

Effort	Space	Relationships
Force —as quietly as you can? —as noisily as you can? —alternating hard and soft landings? —hard four times on your left, then softly four times on your right?	*Level* —in a small ball? —in a crouched position? —with little crouched hops? —as high as you can? —at a medium height? —staying lower than my hand? —staying at the same level as my hand?	*Objects* —over the rope? —on the carpet squares? —over the cones? —around the cones? —while bouncing a ball? —while catching a tossed ball? —while tossing and catching a self-tossed ball?

Effort	Space	Relationships
Time	*Direction*	*People*
—as fast as possible?	—in place?	—in rhythm with a partner?
—as slow as possible?	—forward?	—forward holding hands?
—starting slowly and getting slower?	—backward?	—facing each other and hopping in unison to the wall?
—in time to the music?	—sideways?	—imitating your partner's arm actions?
	—and turn in the air?	
Flow	—and make a quarter (half, three-quarter, full) turn?	
—without using your arms?		**Combinations**
—using only the arm opposite your hopping foot?	*Range*	Numerous combinations of effort, space, and relationships can be explored while hopping
—alternating feet every eight (four, two) beats?	—in your own space?	after control has been gained in single problem tasks. For
	—from spot to spot?	example: Can you hop as quietly
	—and land on a different carpet square each time?	as you can in a small ball, over the rope.
	—and land on the same spot?	
	—and land in as small a spot as possible?	
	—and land in as large a spot as possible?	

Guided Discovery Activities

Movement activities at this level should begin to focus on the proper mechanics involved in the various jumping and hopping patterns. A problem-solving approach that utilizes a variety of movement challenges is still used but the questions are more probing and limit the response possibilities by the child. Emphasis here is on moving the individual to the mature stage of jumping and hopping. The following is a sampling of some guided discovery activities appropriate for jumping and hopping:

Horizontal Jumping

1. First, explore several of the numerous variations of horizontal jumping found on page 113.
2. Now, begin to place limitations on the responses to the movement challenges you present. For example:

General—

a. Try to jump over the unfolded newspaper. Can you get over the short part without touching? How about the long part?

Arm action—

b. What happens when you jump and don't use your hands? Why don't you go as far? What *should* we do with our arms when we jump? Show me.

    c. What happens when you swing your arms forward very hard as you jump? Very softly? What happens when your arms swing all the way up to your head? Try it different ways and see which is best. Is it best to swing hard or soft, all the way up or only part way up when we jump as far as we can? Why? Show me.

Leg action—

    d. When you jump do you leave the ground with both feet at the same time or with one foot at a time? Try both. Why is it better to use both feet for a standing long jump? Try jumping as far as you can using both feet. Now put a beanbag on one foot and while trying to keep it there jump as far as you can. Which works better, one foot or both feet? Why?

Flight—

    e. What happens to your body when it is in the air? Can anyone show me what it looks like? Do you jump straight up? Do you just skim over the floor? Do you do something different?

Landing—

    f. How do you land? Should you land and sit back or fall forward? What happens to your knees when you land? Are they stiff or do you bend them. Why?

Total—

    a. Let's put it all together. Jump as far as you can. How does it feel? Can you get the legs and arms to work together? What happens when they do? Should you jump fast (explosively) or is it better to jump more slowly? Try both. Which works best? Why?

3. When the mature pattern has been reasonably mastered, combine it with other activities in order to reinforce the pattern and make it more automatic.

    a. Play jumping games

    b. Conduct cooperative jumping contests where partners try to jump the same distance. Two points are scored for jumping the same distance. One point deducted for jumping different distances.

    c. Jump from different surfaces. What happens to your distance when you jump from a very soft surface? Why?

Vertical Jumping

1. First, explore several of the numerous variations of vertical jumping found on page 114.

2. Now, begin to place limitations on the response possibilities to the movement challenges you present. For example:

Arm action—

    a. What happens when you jump without using your arms? Does one arm help? When you use both arms, which way is best? Try three ways then tell me which works best for you. Many of you thought that swinging your arms up as your legs uncoiled was best. Why is that so?

b. Try bending your knees at three different levels when you jump. Which is best? Why? Measure the height of your jumps from three different leg positions. Why is there a difference with each jump?

Trunk action—

c. Does your trunk stay bent forward when you jump or does it extend? Try both ways. Which is best? Why?

Head action—

d. Jump as high as you can with your head and eyes in three different positions. Which is best for you? Many thought looking up was best. You're right. Think of yourself as a puppet with a string attached to your nose. Every time you jump up you stretch your entire body out and reach to the sky with your nose.

Landing—

e. Try landing in different ways. Which do you think is best? Why do you bend your knees when you land? How much should you bend them? Why? Did you land in the same spot you took off from? See if you can. Some people are landing in front of their take off spot. Do you get more height or less height when that happens? Why?

3. When the mature pattern has been reasonably well mastered using these and other guided discovery challenges, you will want to combine vertical jumping with other activities in order to reinforce the pattern, and make it more automatic. For example:
   a. Try jumping on different surfaces.
      (1) bounding board
      (2) tires
      (3) trampoline
   b. Try jumping with other objects.
      (1) jump ropes
      (2) high jumping
      (3) stretch ropes
   c. Play jumping games.

Jumping from a Height

1. First, explore several of the variations of jumping from a height found on page 115.
2. Now, begin to place limitations on the response possibilities to the movement challenges you present. For example:

Take-off—

a. How do you take-off when you jump? Do you leave with one foot leading or do both feet leave at the same time? Try it both ways. Which way gives you more control or balance? Why? Try turning in the air after you take-off or try a two-footed take-off.

Flight—

b. What do you do while you are in the air? Try different things with your arms, your legs. To keep your balance best show me how you would use your arms. Several are doing this (demonstrate) with their arms, why? Oh, I see. It helps you keep your balance.

Landing—

    c. Can you show me several different ways to land? Try it now just doing different things with your feet. Now try landing with your feet way apart, close together, and in between. Which worked best for you? Why? What happens to your knees when you jump? Why? Would there be any difference if I jumped from a very high height or from a very low height?

Total—

    d. When you put the entire jump together what do you do with your head and eyes? Try three different things with your head (look up, down, straight ahead). Which works best? Now try jumping with your eyes closed. Scarey, isn't it? Why? What should we remember about the use of our head and eyes when we jump from a height?

    3. When the mature pattern has been reasonably well mastered you will want to combine jumping from a height with other activities in order to reinforce the pattern and make it more automatic. For example:

    a. Jump and assume different postures in the air

    b. Jump and perform turns in the air

    c. Jump, land, and roll

    d. Jump, turn, land, and roll

Hopping

    1. First explore several of the variations of hopping found on pages 115–116.

    2. Now, begin to place limitations and questions on the response possibilities you present. For example:

General—

    a. Hop in place on one foot. Can you do the same on the other foot? Can you hop to the wall on one foot and come back on the other?

Leg action—

    b. Try hopping and putting your free leg in different positions. Which is easiest when you are hopping in place? For distance? Why? Try the same experiment with the other leg. Why do some people hop better on one leg than on the other? Do you have a better leg?

Arm action—

    c. Try hopping as far as you can using three different helps with your arms. Try it without using your arms at all. Which works best for you? Several seem to lift and swing the arms forward when they hop for distance. Try it. How does that feel?

    d. Lets try that same arm action while hopping in place. What happened? Why? What do you want to do with your arms when hopping in place? Show me.

3. Once the mature hopping pattern has been reasonably well mastered for both the left and the right leg you will want to move on to activities that utilize hopping in combination with other skills. Incorporation of hopping with other skills will reinforce the pattern and make it more automatic. For example:
   a. Step-hops
   b. Various dance steps (schottische, step-hop, polka)
   c. Jump rope activities
   d. Track and field event activities

Skill Development Activities

After the patterns of jumping and hopping have been mastered and can be performed at the mature stage consistantly, it becomes appropriate to begin focusing on higher levels of skill development. The individual performing at the mature stage can cross the "proficiency barrier" and work for higher performance levels in terms of distance or height jumped or hoppped. Jumping and hopping can be combined effectively with other skills and applied to a variety of sports. Failure to achieve the mature stage prior to embarking on sport skill development in jumping and hopping, as well as any other fundamental locomotor or manipulative movement, will cause the learner definite problems. The immature actions of the fundamental movement will be carried over to the sport skill resulting in poor performance

In order to begin focusing at higher skill levels, skill combination, and refinement you may wish to:

1. Return to the exploratory activities found on pages 113–116 this time devising experiences that stress extensive combinations of effort, space, and relationships.
2. Incorporate additional problem-solving activities into the lesson.
3. Incorporate a variety of jumping and hopping games into the lesson such as those found in Chapter 9.
4. Begin focusing on the application of jumping and hopping skills into a variety of sport related activities such as:
   a. Standing long jump
   b. Running long jump
   c. High jumping
   d. Triple jump
   e. Rebounding

The use to which the mature jumping and hopping patterns are put will depend on the needs, interests, and developmental level of the children being served.

SUMMARY

During the course of implementing this skill theme you will want to evaluate the progress that is being made in jumping and hopping abilities. Observational assessment during a game of Crossing the Brook (p. 167) generally works quite well. If you are unable to answer "yes" to each of the following questions, in terms of individual class members as well as the entire group, you will need to make modifications in your lessons to more closely suit the specific needs of the group or particular individual:

Jumping/Hopping:	Yes	No	Comments
1. Can the children jump or hop in good control of their bodies?			
2. Can the children take off simultaneously with both feet and land on both feet at the same time in all three jumping patterns?			
3. Can the children take off on one or both feet and land on one foot when hopping?			
4. Can they hop equally well on either foot?			
5. Are the hopping and jumping actions smooth, fluid and rhythmical?			
6. Is their improved summation of focus used to produce a hop or jump?			
7. Is there an easy transition from one pattern to another?			
8. Is there observable improvement in their jumping and hopping abilities?			

The movement patterns of jumping and hopping are basic to numerous athletic, dance, and recreational activities. It is essential that the mature stage of each of these patterns is obtained at an early date. Once the mature stage has been achieved, the teacher and the child may begin to focus on improved performance scores and combining hopping and jumping with a variety of other locomotor and manipulative skills.

CHAPTER 7

Skipping, Sliding, and Galloping

Skipping, sliding, and galloping are fundamental movement abilities that begin developing during the preschool years and should be mastered by the first grade. Generally speaking, children are able to gallop prior to being able to skip. This may be explained by the fact that galloping as a unilateral activity requiring less differentiation and integration of neural mechanisms as the neurologically more complex bilateral action of skipping. It is recommended, therefore, that prior to introducing skipping, children be given opportunities to explore the many movement variations of galloping. Guided discovery activities should also be incorporated with galloping in order that this pattern may be at the mature stage prior to introducing a teaching progression for skipping. In other words, if the child is not yet at the mature stage of galloping (with either foot leading) it is unwise to develop lessons that focus on skipping.

Sliding is similar in many ways to galloping except that it is conducted in a sideward direction. Once again, it is generally more appropriate to introduce sliding after the child has experienced some success with galloping. The sliding pattern is utilized extensively in a variety of athletic and dance activities that require rapid lateral movement. Although separated here for other reasons, sliding and dodging are two patterns that may be incorporated together effectively when developing and presenting a skill theme.

In order to make the best use of your time when focusing on skipping, galloping, and sliding as a skill theme, it will be helpful to use the sequence of events that follow:

1. *Preplanning:* Determine when and approximately how long you wish to focus on skipping, galloping, and sliding as a skill theme.
2. *Observing and Assessing:* Study the verbal and visual descriptions provided for each stage of skipping and galloping that are found on the following pages. Then informally assess the skipping and galloping abilities of the class or of individual children. Determine if their actions are typically at the initial, elementary, or mature stages.
3. *Planning and Implementing:* Study the Teaching Tips and Concepts Children Should Know found on pages 125–126, and 128–131. Based on this and your assessment information, select activities from the Developmental Activity Teaching Progression Chart for skipping, galloping, and sliding located on page 131.
4. *Evaluation and Revision:* Regularly reassess skipping, galloping, and sliding in terms of improved mechanics. The questions found in the Summary on page 137 will be helpful. Based on this information modify your lessons to suit more closely individual and group needs.

SKIPPING

Developmental Sequence Checklist

Initial Stage:
- "One-footed skip"
- Deliberate step-hop action
- Double hop or step sometimes occurs
- Exaggerated stepping action
- Arms of little use
- Action appears segmented

Elementary Stage:
- Step and hop coordinated effectively
- Rhythmical use of arms to aid momentum
- Exaggerated vertical lift on the hop
- Flatfooted landing

Mature Stage:
- Rhythmical weight transfer throughout
- Rhythmical use of arms but reduced during time of weight transfer
- Low vertical lift on the hop
- Toe landing

Visual Description Checklist

Initial Stage:

Elementary Stage:

Mature Stage:

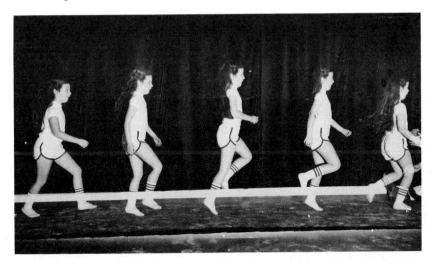

Teaching Tips

Common Problems

- Stepping on one foot and hopping on the other
- Poor rhythmical flow
- Failure to lift the forward leg sharply upward causing too much gain in distance
- Inability to use both sides of the body
- Heavy stepping or landing
- Extraneous movements of the arms
- Inability to move in a straight line
- Undue concentration on the pattern

Recommendations

- Child should be able to gallop with either leg leading before teaching skipping.
- Child should be able to hop well on either leg before attempting to skip.
- Introduce skipping when child is ready.
- You may need to provide a slow motion demonstration.
- Once the basic pattern is mastered, encourage exploration of variations of skipping.

− Utilize rhythmic activities that require skipping.

− Work for a rhythmical, flowing motion.

Concepts Children Should Know

Skill Concepts

− Step forward then hop *up* on the same foot.

− Do the same with the other foot.

− Lift your knees sharply upward.

− Swing your arms upward in time with your legs.

− The skipping pattern is used in many folk and square dances and is basic to good footwork in numerous sports.

Movement Concepts

− You can skip in different directions, pathways, and floor patterns.

− You can skip at different speeds.

− You can skip in a smooth and free manner or it can be jerky and bound.

− You can skip at different levels and land heavily or lightly.

− You can skip with a partner and while carrying objects.

− Skipping is a combination of two movements—stepping and hopping.

− Skipping requires you to use both sides of your body in a rhythmical fashion.

SLIDING AND GALLOPING

Developmental Sequence Checklist

Initial Stage:	− Arhythmical at a fast pace
	− Often reverts to a run
	− Trail leg fails to remain behind and often contacts in front of the lead leg
	− Forty-five percent flexion of trail leg during flight phase
	− Felt contact in a heel-toe combination
	− Contact is in a heel-toe combination
	− Arms of little use in balance or force production
Elementary Stage:	− Moderate tempo
	− Appears choppy and stiff
	− Trail leg may lead during flight but lands adjacent to or behind the lead leg upon contact
	− Exaggerated vertical lift
	− Feet contact in a heel-toe, or toe-toe combination
	− Arms slightly out to the side to aid balance

Mature Stage: — Moderate tempo
                          — Smooth rhythmical action
                          — Trail leg lands adjacent to or behind lead leg upon contact
                          — Both legs flexed at 45° angle during flight
                          — Low flight pattern
                          — Heel-toe contact combination
                          — Arms not needed for balance; may be used for other purposes

Visual Description Checklist

Initial Stage:

Elementary stage:

Mature Stage:

Teaching Tips

Common Problems

- −Keeping the legs too straight
- −Exaggerated lean of the body
- −Jerky movements
- −Overstepping of the trailing leg
- −Too much elevation
- −Inability to move in different directions

Recommendations

- −Work on sliding in both directions.
- −Stress not crossing the feet.
- −Begin with exploratory experiences then progress to skill drills and other activities involving sliding.
- −Stress keeping the knees slightly bent, trunk forward, and staying on the balls of the feet.
- −Rhythmical accompaniment aids sliding.
- −Work for ease of movement in both directions.

Concepts Children Should Know

Skill Concepts

- Step to the side and draw the other foot up to it quickly.
- Repeat the action, landing with the same foot.
- Use your arms only as needed for balance.
- Move on the balls of your feet.
- Keep your knees bent slightly.
- Lean forward at the waist slightly.
- Sliding is used in a variety of sports such as tennis, baseball, basketball, and fencing. It is also used often in dance.

Movement Concepts

- You can slide to the left or right.
- When you slide forward or backward it is called a gallop.
- Your movements can be fast or slow, smooth or jerky, free or bound.

Sliding is a important skill used in the sport of basketball.

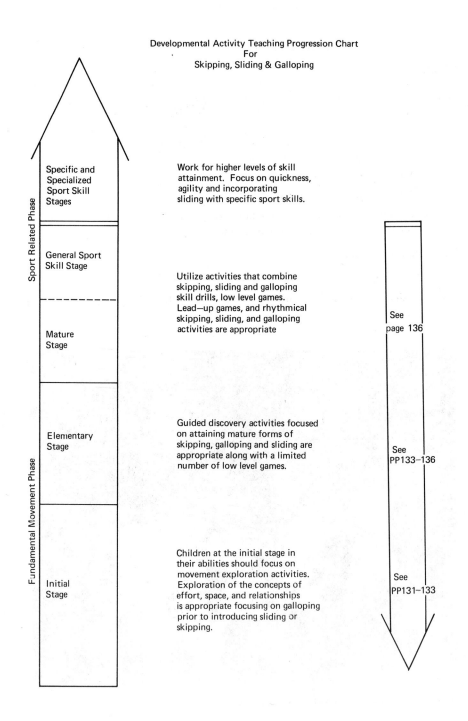

Developmental Activity Teaching Progression Chart
For
Skipping, Sliding & Galloping

Sport Related Phase

Specific and
Specialized
Sport Skill
Stages

Work for higher levels of skill
attainment. Focus on quickness,
agility and incorporating
sliding with specific sport skills.

General Sport
Skill Stage

Mature
Stage

Utilize activities that combine
skipping, sliding and galloping
skill drills, low level games.
Lead—up games, and rhythmical
skipping, sliding, and galloping
activities are appropriate

See
page 136

Fundamental Movement Phase

Elementary
Stage

Guided discovery activities focused
on attaining mature forms of
skipping, galloping and sliding are
appropriate along with a limited
number of low level games.

See
PP133—136

Initial
Stage

Children at the initial stage in
their abilities should focus on
movement exploration activities.
Exploration of the concepts of
effort, space, and relationships
is appropriate focusing on galloping
prior to introducing sliding or
skipping.

See
PP131—133

 —You can slide at different levels and for different distances.

 —You can slide with a partner.

 —You can dodge while sliding.

 —When sliding sideward remain on your feet and don't fall to your knees.

Exploratory Activities

A wide variety of exploratory activities can be easily incorporated into the movement skill themes of sliding, galloping, and skipping. The purpose of these exploratory activities should be to help the individual get the general idea of the numerous movement possibilities involved in these fundamental movements. Efforts should center around getting the gross general framework idea and *not* on focusing on skill development.

  Free exploration of the various aspects of effort, space, and relationships should be encouraged prior to combining movement concepts.

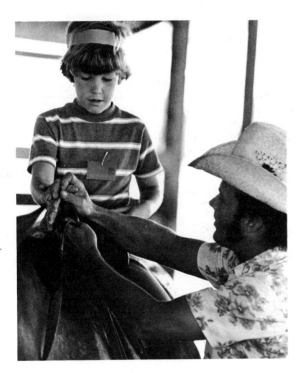

Children can learn to gallop like a horse.

Sliding and Galloping

Can you slide/gallop—

Effort	Space	Relationships
Force —landing flatfooted? —landing on your toes? —very quietly? —while pretending you are dragging an elephant? —while pretending that you are trying to escape a charging elephant? *Time* —in either direction? —as fast as you can? —as slow as you can? —to the beat of the drum? —in time to the music? *Flow* —keeping both legs stiff? —keeping one leg stiff? —keeping your trunk erect? —bending forward to your waist?	*Level* —sideways and get smaller? —sideways and get bigger? —somewhere in between big and small? —and change levels as I raise or lower my hand? *Direction* —sideways? —forward/backward (gallop)? —to the left/right? —to the left four steps then to the right four steps? —to the left two steps then to the right two steps? —alternating left and right? —in the direction I point? *Range* —to your right (or left) as far as you can until I say stop? —taking big steps? —taking small steps?	*Objects* —from one line to the other? —from one line to the other and return? —from one line to the other as many times as you can in thirty seconds? —in either direction while bouncing and catching a ball? —in either direction while dribbling a ball? —in either direction to catch a ball? *People* —facing a partner and travel in the same direction? —facing a partner and travel in an opposite direction? —facing a partner and travel four steps in the opposite direction, then four steps in the same direction? **Combinations** After exploring the many variations of sliding and/or galloping in isolation, you will want to combine various aspects of effort, space, and relationships. For example: Can you slide in either direction four steps and touch the line while bouncing and catching a ball?

Skipping

Can you skip—

Effort	Space	Relationships
Force —as quietly as you can? —as a giant would? —as loud as you can? —landing heavily on one foot and lightly on the other? —alternating loud/quiet, and hard/soft skips?	*Level* —while making yourself very small? —and gradually get smaller? —as tall as you can? —with a high knee lift? —barely raising your feet off the ground?	*Objects* —without touching any of the lines on the floor? —without touching any cracks in the cement? —and try to step on each line or crack? —while carrying a heavy object? *People* —with a partner?
Time —as fast as you can across the room? —as slow as you can? —as if you were on a sandy beach? —downhill? —uphill? —to the beat of the drum?	*Direction* —forward/backward? —sideways (left/right)? —in a straight line? —in a curved or zig zag pattern? —in a circle?	—going backward while your partner moves forward? —in unison with a partner? —while holding both of your partner's hands?
Flow —without using your arms? —swinging your arms outward/inward/diagonally? —like a toy soldier? —in a relaxed manner?	*Range* —and see how many complete skips it takes to cross the room? —and measure how much space you cover in one complete skip? —with your legs wide apart?	**Combinations** Numerous ingenious combinations of effort, space, and relationships can be explored. For example: Can you skip as quietly as you can while making yourself very small and without touching any of the lines on the floor?

Guided Discovery Activities

The purpose of the guided discovery activities that follow is to enable the child to experiment with a variety of movement challenges that will help lead her or him to the mature stage of galloping, sliding, and skipping. It will be best, in most instances, to begin first with the galloping activities that follow prior to the sliding and stepping experiences for reasons mentioned earlier.

Galloping

1. First explore several of the numerous variations of galloping found on page 132.
2. Then begin to place limitations on the response possibilities to the movement challenges you present. For example:

General—

    a. Put one foot forward and gallop around the room. Try it with the other foot leading. Which is easiest? Why?

Leg action—

    b. Try galloping with your legs stiff. Try with them very bent. Now, try different amounts of knee bend. What works best for you? Why do you think some knee bend is good?

Foot action—

    c. What happens to your back foot when you gallop forward? Does it come up to meet your front foot or does it overtake it and move in front? Which do you think is best? Try both. Why is it best not to overtake your front foot with the rear foot?

Arm action—

    d. Gallop across the room. What did you do with your arms? Now gallop back as fast as you can. Did your arms do anything that time?

    e. How can your arms help you when you gallop? Let's time our partner going across the room first using his or her arms and then without using them. Which was fastest? Which was most comfortable? Why?

3. After the mature pattern has been reasonably well mastered, combine it with other activities in order to reinforce the pattern and make it more automatic.

    a. Experiment with the wide variety of combinations of effort, space, and relationships that are possible.

    b. Conduct a story play or mimetic activities that utilizes imagery with "galloping horses."

    c. Practice galloping to the uneven beat of a drum or tamborine.

    d. Gallop to some form of musical accompaniment. Can you gallop to an even beat or an uneven beat?

Sliding

1. First, explore the numerous movement variations of sliding found on page 132.
2. Then begin to place limitations on the response possibilities to the movement challenges you present. For example:

Leg and trunk action—

    a. When you slide sideways try doing it with your legs stiff. How does it feel? How do you think you could slide better? What happens when your knees are slightly bent and your trunk is bent forward slightly? Which is best: legs straight and back straight, or knees bent slightly and trunk bent slightly? Try both ways.

Foot action—

b. Do you cross your feet when you slide? Have a partner watch you and check. Now watch my finger and slide in the direction I point changing direction as fast as you can when I point in the opposite direction.

c. It's best not to cross your feet, right? Why? When moving to your left which foot should move first? What about to the right?

3. After the mature pattern has been reasonably well mastered, combine it with other exploratory and guided discovery activities in order to reinforce the pattern and make it more automatic.

a. Watch my hand and slide in the direction I point.

b. Close your eyes and listen to my call of ''left'' or ''right'' then move in that direction.

c. Count for your partner and see how many times he or she can slide left and right between these two lines (indicate two parallel lines ten feet apart) in thirty seconds.

d. Slide left or right to catch the ball thrown to you in that direction. Why don't you cross your feet? What happens when you do?

Skipping

1. First, explore several of the movement variations of skipping found on page 133.

2. Then help the children discover how their body works when they skip. For example:

Leg action—

a. Try skipping around the room. Experiment with big steps, little steps, and in between steps. When would you want to use each?

b. Be a detective and see if you can find out what two movements with your legs the skip is made up of. Who knows the answer? Good! Show me. Let's all take it apart.

Arm action—

c. What do you do with your arms when you skip? Try four or five different things. How does it feel when your arms swing as you skip?

d. Watch your partner, do his or her arms swing with the same arm and leg leading alternately or with opposite arm and leg leading alternately?

e. What other locomotor skills do we do with alternating opposite arms and leg leading? Why do you think we do that? Try leading with the same arm as the leg that is leading. How does it feel? What do your friends look like? So you see it probably is best that we walk, run, and skip with leg and arm alteration because it is more comfortable and helps us move better.

3. When the mature pattern has been reasonably well mastered using the above and other guided discovery challenges, you will want to combine skipping with other activities to reinforce the pattern and make it more automatic. For example:

    a. Play skip tag
    b. Skip to a drum beat
    c. Skip to selected musical accompaniment
    d. Modify chasing and fleeing games to incorporate skipping rather than running
    e. Teach the children folk dances that incorporate skipping

Skill Development Activities

After galloping, sliding, and skipping have been mastered and are executed at the mature stage with ease and efficiency you will want to focus on further refinement of these mature patterns, especially the sliding pattern. Emphasis should now be placed on improving speed and agility of movement and being able to coordinate sliding with other sport skills found in activities such as fielding in baseball, guarding in basketball, or returning a ball in tennis or racketball.

In order to begin focusing on higher skill levels you may wish to:

1. Return to various combinations of the exploratory activities found on pages 132 and 133.
2. Incorporate additional problem-solving activities that stress sliding and skipping into the lesson.
3. Incorporate a variety of locomotor games that have been modified for galloping, sliding, and skipping. Several of the locomotor games found in Chapter 9 can easily be modified for this purpose.

The following is a list of some additional activities that are suitable for children who have attained the mature stage of sliding, skipping, and galloping.

1. Relays
2. Shuttle relays
3. Thirty second agility slide
4. Soccer goalie skill practice
5. One-on-one in basketball
6. Mirror image sliding agility drills

SUMMARY

At intervals during this skill theme you will want to informally evaluate the progress that is being made in sliding, skipping, and galloping. Observational assessment during a game of skip tag, galloping around the gymnasium, or sliding left and right in an informal partner drill should be adequate. You should be able to answer "yes" to each of the following questions, in terms of both individual class members as well as the group. If you are unable to do so, you will need to make modifications in your lessons in order that they more closely meet the specific needs of the group or particular individuals:

Galloping:	Yes	No	Comments
1. Can they gallop while leading with either the left or right foot?			
2. Does the toe trailing foot remain behind the heel of the leading foot?			
3. Is the action smooth and rhythmical?			
4. Is there observable improvement?			
Sliding:	Yes	No	Comments
1. Can the children slide equally well in both directions?			
2. Do they slide without crossing the feet?			
3. Is the action smooth and rhythmical?			
4. Is there observable improvement?			
Skipping:	Yes	No	Comments
1. Is the skipping action smooth and rhythmical?			
2. Is there rhythmical alteration of both sides of the body?			
3. Is there sufficient knee lift?			
4. Is the arm action appropriate for the purpose of the skip?			
5. Is there observable improvement?			

Sliding will be used as an integral part in many sport and dance activities. Lateral movement needs to be smooth with the ability to make rapid changes in direction. The teacher/coach should be sure to point out specific instances where sliding is used in a sport and be sure that this skill is mastered in relation to that activity.

CHAPTER 8

Leaping and Climbing

Leaping is a fundamental movement that may be viewed as an extension of the running pattern. The development of mature leaping is dependent somewhat on efficient running. The leap is similar to the run except that a longer flight phase is involved and it is generally performed as a discrete rather than a continuous skill. In other words, when one leaps, the act is either from a stationary position or proceeded by a run. The performance of consecutive leaps is possible but a momentary hesitation from one leap to the next is easily observable in all but the most skilled. The fundamental leaping action is used extensively in contemporary dance and ballet, gymnastics, and track and field. It is used in football, basketball, and baseball. Leaping is also used in the play and recreational activities of children and adults when playing hopscotch, hurdling a jump rope, or crossing a brook.

Climbing is a fundamental movement that begins developing around the time the infant learns how to creep. The mature climbing pattern is not unlike the creeping movements of the infant and toddler. The child's first climbing experiences usually center around ascending and descending stairs. The developmental stair-climbing behavior of the child generally proceeds in the following sequence:

1. Creeping using a homolateral pattern
2. Creeping using a contralateral pattern
3. Climbing with hands and feet using a single foot lead (common step) and a single hand lead

4. Climbing with feet only using a single foot lead
5. Climbing with feet only using an alternating foot lead

All five aspects of the above sequence may not be present. Some children will skip one or more parts depending upon the age of their exposure to stairs and their neuromuscular maturity.

The developmental sequence for descending stairs generally proceeds in the following manner:

1. Child backs down the stairs using either a homolateral or contralateral creeping pattern.
2. Child backs down the stairs using both hands and feet in either a homolateral or contralateral manner.
3. Child faces the stairs and walks down using a single foot lead and a handhold for support.
4. Child faces the stairs and walks down using an alternating foot lead and a handhold for support.
5. Child faces the stairs and walks down using an alternating foot lead and does not require a handhold for support.

The pattern of movement found in ascending or descending stairs is similar to climbing a ladder, playing on a jungle gym, or rock climbing. It is important that children be provided with opportunities to develop their climbing skills in order that they may be applied to their recreational, play, and work experiences.

In order to make the best use of your time when planning a skill theme on leaping and climbing, it will help to use the following sequence:

1. *Preplanning:* Determine when and for how long you wish to focus on leaping and climbing as a skill theme.
2. *Observing and Assessing:* Study the verbal and visual description provided for each stage of leaping and climbing that are found on the following pages. Then informally assess the leaping and climbing abilities of the class or of individual children. Determine if their performance is typical of the initial, elementary, or mature stage.
3. *Planning and Implementing:* Study the Teaching Tips and Concepts Children Should Know found on pages 142–143, and 145–146. Based on this and your assessment information, select activities from the Developmental Activity Teaching Progression Chart for leaping and climbing located on page 147.
4. Evaluation and Revision: Informally reassess leaping and climbing performance in terms of improved mechanics. The questions found in the Summary on pages 153–154 will be helpful. Based on this information, modify your lessons to more closely suit individual and group needs.

LEAPING

Developmental Sequence Checklist

Initial Stage:
- Child appears confused in attempts
- Inability to push off and gain a distance and elevation
- Each "attempt" looks nearly like another running step
- Inconsistant use of take-off leg
- Simultaneous landing on both feet
- Arms ineffective

Elementary Stage:
- Appears to be thinking through the action
- Looks like an elongated run
- Little elevation
- Little forward trunk lean
- Stiff appearance
- Incomplete extension of legs during flight
- Arms used for balance rather than aiding in force production

Mature Stage:
- Relaxed rhythmical action
- Forceful extension of take-off leg
- Good mimation of horizontal and vertical forces
- Definite forward trunk lean
- Definite arm opposition
- Full extension of legs during flight

Visual Description Checklist

Initial Stage:

Elementary stage:

Mature Stage:

Teaching Tips

Common Problems

- Failure to use the arms in opposition to the legs
- Restricted movement of the arms or legs
- Lack of spring and elevation in the push-off
- Landing flatfooted
- Failure to stretch and reach with the leading leg
- Inability to lead with either leg

Recommendations

- Provide definite objects or barriers to leap over
- Combine leaping with two or three running steps
- Leap over very low objects followed by higher objects up to mid-thigh level
- Encourage leading with either foot
- Young children enjoy imagery when leaping "over deep canyons," or across "raging rivers"
- Use Velcro straps or other devices that give-way if the child comes in contact with the object that is leaped

Concepts Children Should Know

Skill Concepts

- Push upward and forward with your rear foot.
- Stretch and reach with your forward foot.
- Keep your head up.
- Lean forward at the trunk as you leap.
- Alternate your arm action with your leg action.
- The leaping pattern is used in getting over obstacles and in track and field events.

Movement Concepts

- Your leap can be very forceful or it can be light.
- Your leap can be combined with running.
- Your leap can be high or low or in between.
- Your leap can only be in one direction—forward.
- Your leap can be long or short or in between.
- You can leap over objects or across objects or both.

—You can leap to rhythmical accompaniment.

—Your leap has a longer flight phase than the airborne part of your run and covers a greater distance.

CLIMBING

Developmental Sequence Checklist

Initial Stage:

—Leans body weight forward toward the climbing surface to insure balance
—Begins action with the feet
—Uses a follow step and a follow grip

Elementary Stage:

—Tends to lead with same foot and same hand
—Supports body weight with good balance
—Begins action with preferred foot
—Uses homolateral arm and leg action and appears in control

Mature Stage:

—Good balance and body control
—Can lead off with either hand or leg
—Smooth, fluid, rapid motion
—Utilizes a contralateral arm-leg action

Visual Description Checklist

Initial Stage:

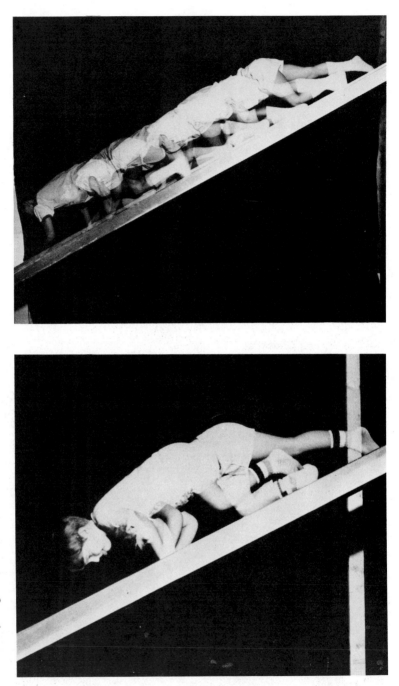

Mature Stage:

Elementary Stage:

144

Teaching Tips

Common Problems

- Failure to wrap the thumbs around the grasping object
- Improper sequencing of the movements of the limbs
- Uneven or irregular use of the two sides of the body
- Inability to transfer the basic elements to climbing other objects (for example: rope, pole, ladder)
- Inability to use alternating hand and/or foot placement

Recommendations

- Assess entry skill level
- Begin with exploratory activities
- Spot carefully
- When child is climbing with use of the hands, stress wrapping the thumbs around the object
- Place a mat under the climbing object
- Stress alternating hand and foot action

Concepts Children Should Know

Skill Concepts

- Place your thumbs around the bar
- Pull with your arms and push with your legs
- Move one hand and the opposite leg at the same time
- Use a follow grasp and/or a follow step
- The climbing movements that you make with your hands and feet are similar to the movements you made when creeping and crawling as a baby

Movement Concepts

- You climb using your legs only when you climb stairs
- You can climb using both your arms and legs as when climbing a ladder or pole
- You can climb using your hands only as when climbing an inclined ladder
- You use the same hand action when traveling forward on a horizontal ladder
- You can climb in different directions
- You can climb quickly or slowly

Children enjoy learning how to climb and swing from objects.

—The distance of your climb is limited by your strength and endurance
—You can climb many different objects and in many different ways

Exploratory Activities

The purpose of incorporating exploratory activities in the movement lessons focusing on leaping and climbing is to provide the individual with opportunities to get the gross general framework idea of these two fundamental movement patterns. Activities should be presented in such a way as to permit free exploration without an attempt to focus on skill development. The teacher will, however, have to be careful to structure challenges that do not go beyond the limits of the individual and to provide for the safety of the children. Activities that involve climbing are thrilling to young children, but at the same time involve an element of danger. Careful supervision is a must.

Developmental Activity Teaching Progression Chart
For
Leaping and Climbing

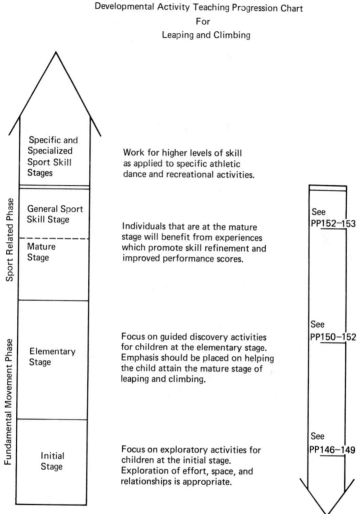

Specific and Specialized Sport Skill Stages

Work for higher levels of skill as applied to specific athletic dance and recreational activities.

General Sport Skill Stage

Mature Stage

Individuals that are at the mature stage will benefit from experiences which promote skill refinement and improved performance scores.

See PP152–153

Elementary Stage

Focus on guided discovery activities for children at the elementary stage. Emphasis should be placed on helping the child attain the mature stage of leaping and climbing.

See PP150–152

Initial Stage

Focus on exploratory activities for children at the initial stage. Exploration of effort, space, and relationships is appropriate.

See PP146–149

Sport Related Phase

Fundamental Movement Phase

LEAPING

Can you leap—

Effort	Space	Relationships
Force	*Level*	*Objects*
—and land lightly?	—as high as you can?	—over a rope?
—and land without a	—as low as you can?	—over a hurdle?
sound?	—at many different	—over a partner?
—and land forcefully?	levels?	—across two outstretched ropes?
—alternating hard and	—alternating low and	—over two outstretched ropes?
soft landings?	high leaps?	—from one carpet square to the
—and swing your arms		next?
forcefully?	*Direction*	—from one footprint to a
—and keep your arms at	—forward?	corresponding footprint?
your side?	—backward?	
—holding your arms in	—diagonally?	*People*
different positions?	—with your left foot	—the same distance as your
	leading?	partner?
Time	—with your right foot	—over your partner?
—and stay in the air as	leading?	—the length of your partners
long as you can?	—alternating left and	body?
—and land as quickly as	right foot lead?	—in unison with your partner?
you can?		
—and swing only one	*Range*	
arm?	—as far as you can?	**Combinations**
—in time to the accented	—and keep one leg bent?	After several variations of
beat of the drum?	—and bend both legs in	leaping have been explored
—in time to the accented	the air?	singularly, try combining various
beat of the music?	—and keep both legs	aspects of effort, space, and
	straight?	relationships. For example: Can
Flow	—and twist your trunk in	you leap lightly as high as you
—from a 3-step	the air?	can over a rope held by two
approach?	—and find different	partners?
—from a 2-step	things to do with your	
approach?	arms while in the air?	
—from a 1-step	—on different surfaces?	
approach?		
—from a stationary		
position?		

CLIMBING

Can you climb—

Effort	Space	Relationships
Force	*Level*	*Objects*
—very quietly?	—and keep your body as	—the stairs?
—very loudly?	small as you can?	—the ladder?
—quietly with your left	—and keep your body as	—the rope?
side and loudly with	stretched as you can?	—the pole?
your right?		—the jungle gym?
	Direction	—the hill?
Time	—vertically?	—the rocks?
—as fast as you can?	—diagonally?	—while carrying an object in one
—slowly?	—down?	hand?
Flow	—across?	—while carrying an object in
—like a monkey?	—over?	your arms?
—like a robot?	—through?	
—using a common grip	—under?	*People*
with your hands and	—behind?	—with a partner?
follow step with your	—underneath?	—while holding on to your
feet (ladder)?		partner?
—hand-over-hand (rope	*Range*	—while linked to your partner
or pole)?	—using big steps?	with a rope?
—with the same hand	—using tiny steps?	—in unison with your partner?
leading?	—one rung (stair) at a	—just the opposite as your
	time?	partner?
	—several rungs (stairs) at	
	a time?	
	—using different grips?	**Combinations**
	—using your feet in	Climbing variations may be
	different ways?	combined after they have first
		been explored singularly. For
		example: Can you climb like a
		monkey using different grips on
		the horizontal ladder?

Leaping is a difficult fundamental movement for the young child to master

Guided Discovery Activities

The guided discovery activities that follow are designed to give the individual an opportunity to experiment with various aspects of leaping and climbing while leading him or her to the mature stage. Questions and movement challenges should be presented in such a manner that they focus on mechanically correct execution of these fundamental movements.

Leaping

1. First, explore the movement variations of leaping found on page 148.
2. Then begin to place limitations on the response possibilities to the movement challenges you present. For example:

Leg action—

a. Try to leap as far as you can. What do you do when you want to go far? Can you show me? If you don't want to leap far what do you do? Show me. Try pushing off forcefully with your trailing foot and stretching out with your lead foot. Does it make a difference?

b. Try leaping and pushing off from different parts of your trailing foot. Try pushing off flat-footed and off the ball of your trailing foot. Which works best? See if there is any difference in the distance leaped trying both ways.

Trunk action—

c. Try leaping and bending your trunk at different angles. Now try keeping your trunk erect. Which ways feel the most comfortable? Do you bend your trunk differently for different purposes? Watch your partner and see if he/she bends at the waist differently when trying to leap different heights and various distances.

d. What do we know about bending at the waist? When is it best to bend far forward? When is it best to have very little bend at the waist? Experiment with a partner then let me know your answer.

Arm action—

e. Try leaping with your arms in many different positions. How does it feel? Which way helps you leap the furthest or the highest? Experiment and find out.

General

f. See if you can leap and coordinate the use of your arms, legs, and trunk. What are some important things we should remember when leaping?

g. Try leaping from a standing position. Now try it from a running approach. Which way helps you go further? Why?

h. Try leaping off one foot. Now try the other. Is there a difference? Why? Practice both ways.

3. After a mature leaping pattern has been reasonably well mastered, combine it with other exploratory and guided discovery activities in order to reinforce the pattern and make it more "automatic."

a. Listen to the beat of the drum and leap on every hard note.

b. Beginning at one end of the gym perform three leaps in combination with running.

c. Try to leap over the outstretched ropes I have placed on the floor.

d. Let's try to run across the gym alternating leaping off our left and right foot.

e. Can you leap and catch a tossed ball while in the air?

f. Try leaping across the outstretched ropes and touching the balloon overhead (ringing a suspended bell is a real challenge).

g. Using carpet squares or hoops, practice leaping from spaceship to spaceship being sure that no other astronaut is in a spaceship that you leap to.

Climbing

1. First explore the movement variations found on page 149.
2. Then, begin to place limitations on the response possibilities to the movement challenges you present and structure challenges in such a way that you encourage focusing on the process rather than the product. For example: (climbing a ladder)

Leg action—

   a. Find three different ways to use your feet when you climb the ladder. Show me. Which way is easiest? Hardest? Why? If you were a firefighter and needed to get to the top as quickly as possible, which type of step would you use? If you were at the top and had to carry someone over your shoulder to the bottom, which step would you use? Why?

Arm action—

   b. Find three different ways to use your hands when you climb the ladder. Show me the easiest. Show me the fastest.

Total—

   c. When your legs use a follow-step (alternate lead) what are your hands doing? What about when you use a common (single lead) step? Do your hands and feet work together?

   d. When using a follow step and your right leg is in the lead where is your right hand? What about when your left leg is leading? Try creeping on the floor. Is there anything similar between creeping and climbing? What?

   e. If you are leading with the same hand and leg, try leading with the opposite hand and leg. Did you notice how it is very much like creeping on the floor when you were a baby except that you are going up and down instead of forward and backward?

3. After the mature ladder-climbing pattern has been reasonably well-mastered, combine it with other exploratory and guided discovery activities in order to reinforce the pattern and make it more automatic.

   a. Climb an inclined ladder.

   b. Climb on the underneath side of an inclined ladder.

   c. Work for utility in the climbing pattern helping the individual to alter the pattern according to the demands of the activity.

     (1) Climb with a cup of water in your mouth trying not to spill a drop.

     (2) Climb with a "baby" (basket) in your hand.

     (3) Climb with a "person" (bag of balls) over your shoulder.

      (4)   Climb on the jungle gym using all of the different ways of climbing that you know.

Skill Development Activities

Leaping and climbing are used in many sport, recreational, and work situations. After each has been mastered and can be performed with ease and fluidity, you will want to focus on further refinement of these mature patterns. The leaping pattern, especially, is used in sport. Emphasis should now be placed on combining leaping with the demands of other sport skills found in hurdling in track, base running in baseball, open field running in football, or stretching for a ball in tennis.

Probably the most important aspect of climbing is the neurological maturity required for using an alternating leg and arm action. The actual pattern utilized in play, recreational, and work situations will vary according to the requirements of the task. The individual should, however, be able to make adjustments in the pattern with ease and be able to use the mature contralateral pattern at will. Climbing is used throughout life in work experiences, such as climbing a ladder. The climbing pattern is also related to stair climbing which is an almost daily activity for each of us. Climbing is an integral part of the recreational sport activities of rock climbing and mountain climbing.

In order to focus more fully on higher skill levels of leaping and climbing you will find it helpful to incorporate the following:

1. Return to the exploratory leaping and climbing activities found on pages 148 and 149 focusing now, however, on various combinations of effort, space, and relationships.
2. Incorporate additional problem-solving activities into the lesson.
3. Incorporate a variety of leaping and climbing games into the lesson such as those found in Chapter 9.

SUMMARY

During the implementation of a skill theme on leaping or climbing you will want to assess the progress of individuals or the group. Your assessment can be informal and conducted in a play situation. Observational assessment of leaping, the game of crossing the brook, or climbing on a jungle gym or cargo set should be adequate. You should be able to answer "yes" to each of the following questions both in terms of individual class members and the entire group. If you are unable to do so, you will need to make some modification in your lessons in order that they more closely meet the specific needs of individuals or the group.

Leaping:	Yes	No	Comments
1. Can they leap leading with either foot?			
2. Can they make adjustments in height and distance with ease?			
3. Is appropriate body lean used for the distance leaped?			
4. Are the arms used properly in conjunction with the legs?			
5. Is there observable improvement?			

Climbing:	Yes	No	Comments
1. Are they able to climb a vertical ladder without a display of fear or uncertainty?			
2. Are they able to climb using a rhythmic alteration of hands and feet?			
3. Are they able to alter their climbing pattern as the demands placed on them require?			
4. Is there observable improvement in the climbing pattern?			

Leaping and climbing are important fundamental movement patterns to be developed and refined by the child. These skills may be dealt with together in a common skill theme or they may be used effectively in conjunction with other skills. Jumping from a height and climbing can be combined nicely as can running and leaping.

9

Locomotor Game Activities

Games can play an important role in refining a wide variety of fundamental movement abilities *if* they are properly incorporated into the lesson. All too often teachers include active games in their program simply for the sake of having fun or reinforcing certain social skills. Although these are certainly worthwhile objectives, they should not be viewed as the primary objectives of game activities by the teacher responsible for the physical education period.

Games, if they are to be of any real value, must be viewed from a developmental perspective. They must be carefully selected and implemented with regard to the particular movement abilities that they reinforce. During the preschool and elementary years it is crucial that we assist children in learning how to move with greater efficiency and control. Therefore we must not take it for granted that they will develop and refine the movement abilities necessary for successful performance in active games on their own. Children must first be provided with a variety of individualized movement experiences designed to enhance their movement abilities before emphasis is placed on incorporating these skills into game activities.

It seems only logical that practice first be provided with specific movement patterns before they can be effectively incorporated into a game activity. We need only to look at football or basketball coaches and the emphasis that they place on "learning the fundamentals" through drill situations prior to the actual playing of the game of football or basketball. It is much the same with young children. That is, a wide variety of movement experiences that incorporate movement exploration, problem-solving, and skill drills should be practiced *prior* to the playing of games that utilize the particular movements practiced. In other words, games for children should be viewed as *tools* for further enhancing and implementing the particular movement skills dealt with during the individualized portion of the lesson. It is with this thought in mind that this chapter has been written.

Various locomotor games are presented in this chapter. Many have been used for generations and may be found in numerous textbooks. They have been selected

Hide-and-seek is still a favorite game of today's children.

for inclusion here because they: (1) provide for maximum activity of all children, (2) promote inclusion rather than exclusion, (3) are easily modified and varied, (4) aid in the development of a variety of movement abilities, and (5) are fun for children to play. A format is used in which each game is first viewed from the particular *movement skills* that it incorporates followed by the *desired outcomes, formation, equipment,* and *procedures* to be followed.

The general objectives of the movement experiences contained in this chapter are to: (1) enhance fundamental locomotor abilities, (2) contribute to the physical and motor fitness of children, (3) aid in developing and reinforcing a variety of social competencies, and (4) provide an avenue for implementing a variety of fundamental movement abilities.

GAMES FOR ENHANCING LOCOMOTOR ABILITIES

There is an almost endless variety of locomotor games that children enjoy playing. The vast majority of locomotor games, however, are designed around running as the primary mode of movement. The alert teacher will feel free to substitute other locomotor movements as they suit the nature of the lesson and the skills being stressed. *Each of the games that follow may be modified in a variety of ways in order to suit the particular needs and age level of the children.* Care should be taken to use these games *after* the children have had an opportunity to explore and experiment with the exploratory and guided discovery activities contained in the preceding chapters.

Objectives

1. To enhance fundamental locomotor abilities.
2. To enhance agility and general body coordination.
3. To enhance rhythmic performance of locomotor movements.
4. To enhance ability to participate in a team effort.
5. To develop listening skills.
6. To enhance the ability to follow directions and obey rules.

Movement Experiences

Brownies and Fairies

Movement skills	Running, dodging, pivoting, starting, and stopping.
Desired outcomes	1. To enhance a variety of fundamental movement abilities.
	2. To learn that sliding on one's knees is not a proper way to stop.
	3. To learn how to tag properly.
Formation	Two lines with the children facing each other.

Equipment	None.
Procedures	The class is divided into two groups. One group is called "brownies," the other "fairies." The groups line up at each end of the playing area facing each other. The "brownies" turn around and close their eyes and "fairies" quietly sneak up behind them. One of the brownies is designated to listen for the fairies and call "here come the fairies" when he feels they are too close. When she calls out, the fairies run to their goal and the brownies give chase. All persons tagged join the brownies. The game is repeated with the fairies being the chasers. Be sure to spend some time teaching proper tagging procedures and how to start and stop quickly and safely.

Crows and Cranes

Movement skills	Running, dodging, pivoting, starting, and stopping.
Desired outcomes	1. To enhance a variety of fundamental movement abilities.
	2. To enhance listening skills.
	3. To enhance auditory discrimination.

Formation	Two lines of children facing each other about 10 feet apart.
Equipment	None.
Procedures	The class is divided into two groups. One group is called the "crows" and the other, the "cranes." The groups line up at each end of the playing area facing each other. On a signal, they will advance toward one another. The instructor either calls crows or cranes. If she calls crows, they chase the cranes back to their goal and all persons caught join the crows. If she calls the cranes, they become the chasers. The instructor calls various names beginning with "cra . . . " before calling crows or cranes (e.g., cra . . . ckers, cra . . . yfish, cra . . . yons).

Squirrels in the Trees

Movement skills	Running and dodging.
Desired outcomes	1. To enhance fundamental movement abilities.

	2. To enhance dodging and agility.
	3. To enhance listening skills.
Formation	Groups of threes. Two children stand with hands joined, third is in between.
Equipment	None.
Procedures	One player is designated as a fox, the others as squirrels. The remaining players scatter around in groups of threes. Two of the players stand and hold hands above their head (tree): the others squat between them (squirrel).
	The game begins with the fox chasing the squirrel. To avoid being caught, the squirrel may run under a tree and the squirrel originally under the tree must flee from the fox. When tagged by the fox, the squirrel becomes the fox and the fox becomes a squirrel.

Frozen Tag

Movement skills	Running and dodging.
Desired outcomes	**1.** To enhance fundamental movement abilities.
	2. To enhance agility.
Formation	Scatter.
Equipment	None.
Procedures	One person is designated as "it" and chases the other players. If a player is tagged, he becomes "it." A player may "freeze" to avoid being tagged.
Variations	Have players squat, stand on a line, and so on rather than "freeze."

Red Light

Movement skills	Walking, stopping, and starting.
Desired outcomes	**1.** To enhance fundamental movement abilities.
	2. To enhance starting and stopping abilities.
	3. To enhance listening skills.
Formation	Players at one end of play area. "It" at the other end.
Equipment	None.
Procedures	The class lines up at the one end of the play area and one player, "it," stands in a line 50–60 feet away with his back to the group. The game begins with "it" calling "green light." When the other children hear their call, they begin to run toward the line where "it" is standing. "It" then calls "red light" and quickly turns to face the children. He calls the name of any children who have not completely stopped. These children must return to the starting line and the procedure is repeated. The first child to reach the line where "it" is standing becomes "it."

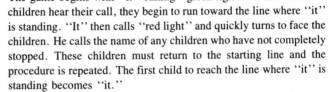

Colors

Movement skills	Running.
Desired outcomes	**1.** To enhance fundamental movement abilities. **2.** To enhance color naming and identification. **3.** To enhance listening skills.
Formation	Two lines of players facing one another.
Equipment	None.
Procedures	The groups stand on opposite goals with the teacher in the middle. Each group chooses a color and then moves toward the center of the playing area until the two groups are about 5–10 feet apart. The teacher calls out a color. When she calls the color selected by either side, the players on that side run to their goal and the other group chases them. Those tagged before they reach their goal must join the other side. The teacher may call several colors before he calls one of the colors selected. The side having the most players at the end of the playing time wins the game.

Magic Carpet

Movement skills	Skipping running, and walking.
Desired outcomes	**1.** To enhance fundamental movement abilities. **2.** To reinforce shape and color concepts.
Formation	Scatter formation with lines, circles, and spots on the floor.
Equipment	None.
Procedures	The entire play area is considered to be the "carpet." Spots, circles, and other markings on it represent the "magic spots." The class follows the leader in a simple file around the play area. When the leader stops, the children run to a "magic spot" and stand. Those that do not reach a spot are eliminated. The game ends when there are only as many "magic spots" as there are children.
Variations	Designate specific shapes or colors to go to.

Flowers and the Wind

Movement skills	Running and dodging.
Desired outcomes	**1.** To enhance fundamental movement abilities. **2.** To enhance agility. **3.** To reinforce the ability to name flowers.

Formation	Two lines of children facing each other.
Equipment	None.
Procedures	The class divides into two groups, facing each other about 60 feet apart. One group is designated as flowers and the other as wind. The group designated as flowers decide upon a particular flower and advance toward the wind. While they are advancing, the other groups tries to guess what kind of flower they have selected. When the right flower is named, they chase the group back to their goal. All persons tagged join their group. The game is continued in this manner until all persons are caught or the groups can alternate roles.

Midnight

Movement skills	Running and dodging.
Desired outcomes	1. To enhance fundamental movement abilities. 2. To enhance the concepts of time.
Formation	Single line of children facing the leader ("fox").
Equipment	None.
Procedures	One player is the fox and he stands at one end of the gym (his den). The other players are sheep and go to the other end of the play area (the barn). On a signal, they walk toward the player that is the fox and call out, "What time is it, Mr. Fox?" If the fox answers "10 o'clock," "4 o'clock," and so on, the sheep are safe. Should the fox answer "Midnight" the sheep run back to the barn and the fox chases them. The game is repeated and all persons caught by the fox join her and help catch the remaining sheep.

Stop and Go

Movement skills	Running, stopping, and starting.
Desired outcomes	1. To enhance fundamental movement abilities. 2. To enhance agility and coordination. 3. To enhance listening skills.

Formation	Single line of children facing the teacher.
Equipment	None.

Procedures	Players stand side by side facing a line 50−60 feet away. The teacher blows a whistle and the children start to run toward the line. The whistle is blown again and the players must run in the opposite direction. They continue this procedure (i.e., blowing the whistle at irregular intervals) until somebody reaches the goal line.

Red Rover

Movement skills	Running.
Desired outcomes	**1.** To enhance fundamental movement abilities. **2.** To enhance agility and coordination.
Formation	Two lines facing each other with hands joined.
Equipment	None.
Procedures	The group is divided into two teams. They hold hands and line up side by side at a distance of about 20 feet from each other. On a signal, one team chants ''Red Rover, Red Rover, we dare (call a name of a person on the other team) over.'' The person receiving the dare must try to run through the line of the other team. If she is successful, she may choose any member of that team to join his. If she does not break through, she must join the opposing team. This procedure is repeated with the other team uttering the chant.

Automobiles

Movement skills	Walking, stopping, and starting.
Desired outcomes	**1.** To enhance fundamental movement abilities. **2.** To be able to follow directions of starting, stopping, and using caution from given signal. **3.** To be able to manipulate a make-believe steering wheel.
Formation	Free formation according to manner in which the area is set up.
Equipment	Each child has a ''steering wheel.''
Procedures	Each child is to be a driver of an automobile and needs a ''steering wheel.'' This can be a hoop, deck tennis ring, or something the child has made out of cardboard. The teacher has three flash cards colored red, green, and yellow. These are the traffic-control colors. The children drive around the area, steering various paths responding as the teacher raises the cards one at a time. The children follow the traffic directions: red—stop, green—go, and yellow—caution.
Variations	An ambulance station and fire station can be established with appropriate ''cars.'' When one of these come forward with the characteristic siren noise (made by the driver), all other ''cars'' pull over to the side.

Back-to-Back

Movement skills	Running, skipping, hopping, jumping, and sliding.
Desired outcomes	1. To be able to move quickly on signal.
	2. To be able to perform correct directed movement.
	3. To work successfully with a partner.
	4. To enhance auditory perception.
Formation	Partners standing back-to-back with one extra child.
Equipment	None.
Procedures	The number of children should be uneven. On signal, each child stands back-to-back with another child. One child will be without a partner. This child can clap his hands for the next signal, such as face-to-face, side-to-side, and all children change partners with the extra player seeking a partner.
Variations	Other commands can be given such as "everybody run—or hop, skip, jump, slide" or "walk like an elephant." When the whistle is blown, they immediately find a partner and stand back-to-back.

Hunter

Movement skills	Running.
Desired outcomes	1. To enhance fundamental movement abilities.
	2. To maneuver caller's position between the goal and the group.
	3. To take off quickly on signal and run directly to the goal.
	4. To run swiftly without falling down or colliding with others.

Formation	Scatter.
Equipment	None.
Procedures	One child is "hunter" and says to the other children, "come with me to hunt tigers." The other children fall into line behind him and follow in his footsteps as he leads them away from the goal line. When the hunter says, "bang!" the other children run to the goal as the hunter tries to tag as many as possible. As each child is tagged, the hunter calls out the child's name. The hunter chooses a new hunter from the players who reached the base safely.

| Variations | Since the setting of this game is believed to be a jungle imitations of animal movements (e.g., bearwalk, kangaroo hop, elephant drag) could be used instead of running. |

Spaceship

| Movement skills | Running, starting, and stopping. |
| Desired outcomes | 1. To enhance fundamental movement abilities.
2. To run rapidly in a circle.
3. To start quickly.
4. To avoid collisions with other runners. |

Formation	Scatter.
Equipment	An object to represent the Earth (beanbag, tree, etc.).
Procedures	Children and teacher decide upon an object that will represent the Earth, such as a tree, beanbag, circle, base, and so on. Children are space ships, and on the countdown, "Five, four, three, two, ONE!" the rockets blast the spaceships off the ground; they quickly pick up speed and go into orbit around the earth. After one or more orbits, spaceships return and "splash down." The game may be repeated any number of times, with spaceships flying any number of orbits. To improve endurance, children try to run longer and faster each time.

Touch and Follow

| Movement skills | Walking, skipping, and galloping. |
| Desired outcomes | 1. To enhance fundamental movement abilities.
2. To be able to imitate another child's activity.
3. To be able to stand in a circle with arms stretched outward.
4. To be able to lead a new activity if chosen by the previous "it." |

Formation	Single circle facing in.
Equipment	None.
Procedures	The children stand in a large circle with their hands held out toward the center, palms upward. One child is chosen to be in the center of

the circle. He moves about and then lightly touches the outstretched hand of some child. The child who is touched must follow the first child around the circle, imitating any activity chosen by him. They may skip, gallop, trot, or perform any other appropriate activity. They go around the circle and then the follower becomes the one in the center.

Variations	The game could be played in which the entire circle could imitate "it" rather than involve just one other child.

Walk, Walk, Run

Movement skills	Running and walking.
Desired outcomes	1. To enhance fundamental movement abilities. 2. To move quickly to tag another and to avoid being tagged. 3. To assume responsibility for maintaining the vacant spot in the circle. 4. To accept defeat without argument.
Formation	Single circle facing in.
Equipment	None.
Procedures	Children stand in a circle, facing the center. One child is "it" and walks around outside the circle, chanting, "walk, walk, walk" touching each player gently on the shoulder as he passes them. When he touches a player and says "run!" the player touched chases him around the circle. If the chaser touches him before he can reach the chaser's place in the circle, he must go into the "mush pot," which is in the center of the circle, and stay there until another child enters the mush pot. If he is not tagged before reaching the chaser's place in the circle, he stays in the new circle position. In either instance, the chaser becomes the new "it," and the game continues.

Variations	May be used for other types of locomotor skills; "it" may say, "Walk, walk, walk, skip!" or "Hop, gallop, slide," and so on.

Where's My Partner?

Movement skills	Skipping, galloping, walking, running, and hopping.
Desired outcomes	1. To enhance fundamental movement abilities. 2. To move in the opposite direction than the facing circle. 3. To be able to "halt" when the command is given. 4. To know right from left.
Formation	Double circle of couples facing each other.
Equipment	None.

Procedures

The children are arranged in a double circle by couples, with partners facing each other. The inside circle has one more player than the outside. When the signal is given, the circles skip to the player's right. When the command "halt" is given, the circles face each other to find partners. The player left without a partner is in the "mush pot."

Variations

The game could be played with music. When the music stops, the players seek partners.

The game could also be altered to a gallop, run, walk, or hop, rather than a skip.

Whistle Stop

Movement skills

Running, stopping, and chasing.

Desired outcomes

1. To enhance fundamental movement abilities.
2. To improve speed and time in running.
3. To stop and start quickly on signal.
4. To avoid running into others.
5. To respond appropriately to the sound of a whistle.

Formation

Scatter formation.

Equipment

Whistle.

Procedures

Children are scattered around the playing area. On the signal "run!" the children run in any direction until the whistle blows, then they stop immediately. They start again on the signal, "run!" Children must be able to run and stop in appropriate signals, staying within the boundaries and avoiding other runners.

Variations

The game may be varied to explore directions, time, and movement:
1. Run in a circle and stop when whistle blows.
2. Walk like an elephant and stop when the whistle blows.
3. Run sideways.
4. Skip toward the teacher.
5. When whistle blows, stop and clap your hands.

Frog in the Sea

Movement skills

Running.

Desired outcomes

1. To move quickly to avoid being tagged.
2. To accept the challenge of the game.
3. To work together to tag others.

Equipment	None.
Procedures	One child is the frog and sits in the center of a circle. Other children dare the frog by running in close to him and saying, ''Frog in the sea, can't catch me!'' If a child is tagged by the frog, he also becomes a frog and sits in the circle beside the first frog. Frogs must tag from a sitting position. The game continues until four players are tagged. Then the first frog chooses a new frog from the players who were not tagged.
Variations	Jumping like a frog could be performed rather than running.

Crossing the Brook

Movement skills	Jumping and leaping.
Desired outcomes	1. To enhance fundamental movement abilities. 2. To promote agility.
Formation	File.
Equipment	Chalk or tape.
Procedures	Two lines are drawn to represent a brook. The children try to jump over. If they fall in they must return home and change shoes and socks. The width of the brook should vary from narrow to wide in order that all will find a degree of success.
Variations	Place an object in the brook to be jumped on as a stepping stone.

Jump the Shot

Movement skills	Jumping and hopping.
Desired outcomes	1. To enhance fundamental movement abilities. 2. To enhance eye-foot coordination. 3. To enhance temporal awareness.

Formation	Single circle facing in.
Equipment	Beanbag on the end of 10-foot line.
Procedures	The teacher squats down in the center of the circle and swings the rope around at 3–6 inches off the ground. The end of the rope should be beyond the outside of the circle. The children jump to

	avoid being hit. Be sure to warn the children of the dangers of tripping and do not turn the rope too fast.
Variations	Have the children gallop, side hop or perform tricks over rope.

Jack Be Nimble

Movement skills	Jumping
Desired outcomes	1. To enhance fundamental movement abilities.
	2. To be able to learn a simple rhyme.
Formation	Lines of four or more.
Equipment	Indian clubs to represent candles. One for each team.
Procedures	The following rhyme is recited by the children

Jack (Jane) be nimble,
Jack be quick,
And Jack jump over the candlestick.

As the rhyme is repeated, the first player in each line runs forward and jumps over the candle. The others follow. Anyone knocking down the candle must set it up again. Caution the children to wait for the signal to "jump over the candlestick."

Come Along

Movement skills	Skipping.
Desired outcomes	1. To enhance fundamental movement abilities.
	2. To reinforce concepts of working together.
	3. To enhance listening skills.
Formation	Single circle, facing counterclockwise.
Equipment	None.
Procedures	One child is selected to start the game. He or she begins skipping around the outside of the circle and takes one other child by the hand and says, "come along!" as they continue to skip. When the teacher calls, "go home!" the youngsters drop hands and run to their places. The first one to reach his home position will begin a new game. Be sure that each child has an opportunity to be selected at least once.

SECTION **Three**

FUNDAMENTAL MANIPULATIVE SKILL THEMES

CHAPTER 10

Throwing and Catching

Throwing and catching are two fundamental movements that fit especially well together in the presentation of a skill theme. Throwing may take many forms. It may be performed in an overhand, underhand, or sidearm pattern, and with either one or both hands depending on the purpose of the throw. The overhand throwing pattern is dealt with here. It is probably the throwing pattern most frequently used by both children and adults. Throwing abilities begin developing early in life and it is common to see individuals functioning at the elementary level in the overhand throw who have not received any formal instruction and have had only limited opportunity for practice. Most children progress to the elementary stage more as a function of maturation than experience. In most cases, however, they will continue to perform at this stage even as adolescents and adults unless there is sufficient practice and/or some form of instruction.

The situation is much the same with catching as with throwing. Individuals often fail to progress to the mature stage unless ample opportunities for practice and/or some form of instruction are provided. Practice in throwing and catching can be facilitated with the use of objects of varying sizes, shapes, colors, and firmness. The child at the initial stage, for example, generally experiences greater success with catching a soft, brightly colored beanbag rather than a ball of comparable size. The child is able to grip the beanbag more securely than the ball. There is little fear of injury if the child is hit in the face or a finger by the beanbag. The wise teacher provides opportunities for children to practice throwing and catching with a variety of objects. Care is taken to set up experiences that will not result in an avoidance reaction of the head or a closing of the eyes out of fear as the object approaches. During the early stages of learning we should not require the individual to adapt to the equipment; rather we should modify the equipment to the developmental needs of the child.

When planning a skill theme with throwing and catching, you will find it helpful to utilize the following sequence in order to make the most efficient use of the limited time that you may have:

1. *Preplanning:* Determine when and for about how long you will need to focus on throwing and catching as a skill theme.

2. *Observing and Assessing:* Study the verbal and visual description provided for each stage of throwing and catching. Informally assess the throwing and catching of the class or of individual children. Determine if their patterns are typically at the initial, elementary, or mature levels.

3. *Planning and Implementing:* Study the Teaching Tips and Concepts Children Should Know found on pages 174–175, and 177–180. Based on this and your assessment information, select appropriate activities from the Developmental Activity Teaching Progression Chart for throwing and catching located on page 179.

4. *Evaluation and Revision:* Periodically reassess throwing and catching abilities in terms of improved mechanics. You may wish to use the questions found in the Summary on page 186 as a guide. Modify your lessons to suit more closely specific individual and group needs.

THROWING

Developmental Sequence Checklist

Initial Stage:
—The action is mainly from the elbow
—Elbow of the throwing arm remains in front of the body; action resembles a push
—Fingers spread at release
—Follow through is forward and downward
—Trunk remains perpendicular to the target
—Little rotary action during throw
—Body weight shifts slightly rearward
—Feet remain stationary
—There is often purposeless shifting of feet during preparation of throw

Elementary Stage:
—In preparation, arm is swung upward, sideways, and backward to position of elbow flexion
—Ball is held behind head
—Arm is swung forward, high over the shoulder

—Trunk rotates toward the throwing side during preparatory action
—Shoulders rotate toward throwing side
—Trunk flexes forward with forward motion of arm
—Definite forward shift of body weight
—Steps forward with leg on same side as throwing arm

Mature Stage: —Arm is swung backward in preparation
—Opposite elbow is raised to balance preparatory action in the throwing arm
—Throwing elbow moves forward horizontally as it extends
—Forearm rotates and thumb ends up pointing downward
—Trunk markedly rotates to throwing side during preparatory action
—Throwing shoulder drops slightly
—A definite rotation through hips, legs, spine, and shoulders during throw
—Weight during preparatory movement is on the rear foot
—As weight is shifted, there is a step with the opposite foot

Visual Description Checklist

Initial Stage:

Elementary Stage:

Mature Stage:

Teaching Tips

Common Problems

- Forward movement of the foot on the same side as the throwing arm
- Inhibited back swing
- Failure to rotate the hips as the throwing arm is brought forward
- Failure to step out on the leg opposite the throwing arm
- Poor rhythmical coordination of arm movement with body movement
- Inability to release the ball at the desired trajectory
- Loss of balance while throwing

Recommendations

- Provide numerous opportunities for practice. One or two sessions will *not* be enough to develop a consistent mature pattern.
- Focus first on throwing for distance *not* accuracy.
- Work for speed of movement and good hip rotation.
- Use carpet squares, hoops, or tires as cues for stepping out on the opposite foot.
- Be sure to have an ample supply of balls or beanbags that can be easily gripped.
- Beanbags, newspaper balls, yarn balls, and stocking balls all work well.
- Use beanbags for wall drills in order to emphasize the throwing action and not for catching or retrieving.
- Speed, accuracy, and distance are the performance elements of throwing. Work first for distance, then speed, and finally accuracy.
- Follow a logical teaching progression using the above recommendations as a guide.
- There should be 100 percent participation.

Concepts Children Should Know

Skill Concepts

- Stand with the leg that is on the other side of the throwing arm leading.
- Turn your shoulder toward the target.
- Raise your free arm and point toward the target.
- Raise your throwing arm and hold the ball close to your ear.
- Lead with your elbow on the forward swing.

- Bring your rear foot forward and follow through.
- The overhand throwing pattern is used in the sports of baseball, softball, and on the fast break in basketball. It is also similar to the overhand serves in volleyball and tennis and the smash shot in badminton.

Movement Concepts

- The effort that you give to your throw will influence how fast the ball will travel and the smoothness with which your throwing motion is performed.
- When you throw a ball it can travel through space in a variety of directions and levels.
- A ball may be thrown using throwing patterns ranging from overhand and underhand patterns to a variety of sidearm patterns.
- You can throw many different types of objects. The size, shape, and weight of the object will affect the distance it travels as well as the pattern you use.
- The coordinated use of your arms, trunk, and legs will affect the speed and distance of your throw.

CATCHING

Developmental Sequence Checklist

Initial Stage:
- There is often a definite avoidance reaction of turning the face away or protecting the face with arms (the avoidance reaction is learned and therefore may not be present)
- Arms are extended and held in front of the body
- There is limited movement until contact
- The catch resembles a scooping action
- Uses the body to trap ball
- Palms are held upward
- Fingers are extended and held tense
- Hands are not utilized in the catching action

Elementary Stage:
- Avoidance reaction is limited to the child's eyes closing at contact with ball
- Elbows are held at sides with an approximately ninety degree bend
- Since initial contact made with the child's hands is often unsuccessful, the arms trap the ball
- Hands are held in opposition to each other: thumbs are held upward
- At contact, the hands attempt to squeeze the ball in a poorly timed and uneven motion

Mature Stage:
- Any avoidance reaction is completely suppressed
- Arms are held relaxed at sides and forearms are held in front of body

- Arms give upon contact to absorb the force of the ball
- Arms adjust to the flight of the ball
- Thumbs are held in opposition to each other
- Hands grasp the ball in a well-timed simultaneous motion
- Fingers make a more effective grasping motion

Visual Description Checklist

Initial Stage:

Elementary Stage:

Mature Stage:

Teaching Tips

Common Problems

- Failure to maintain control of the object
- Failure to "give" with the catch
- Keeping the fingers rigid and straight in the direction of the object causing jamming
- Failure to adjust the hand position to the height of the object
- Inability to vary the catching pattern for objects of different weight and force
- Taking the eyes off the object
- Improper stance (that is, a straddle rather than a stride position in the direction of the oncoming object) causing loss of balance when catching a fast moving ball
- Closing the hands either too early or too late
- Failure to keep the body in line with the ball (that is, reaching out to the side to catch)

Recommendations

- Use soft objects for initial catching experiences. Yarn balls and beanbags work best.

—Give the child verbal cues such as ''ready—catch'' in order to avoid surprises.

—Begin with large balls and progress to smaller sizes.

—Use brightly colored balls.

—Be aware of the background against which the ball is to be caught. Avoid figure-ground problems.

—Vary the speed, level, and trajectory of the ball as skill increases.

Concepts Children Should Know

Skill Concepts

—Get directly in the path of the ball.

—Place one foot ahead of the other.

Notice the positioning of the hands and arms in preparation for the catch.

Developmental Teaching Progression Chart
For
Throwing and Catching

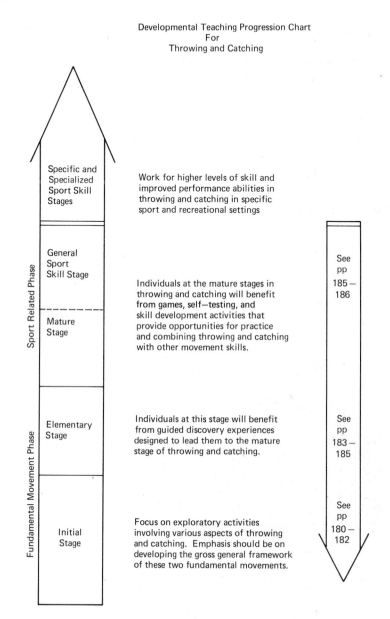

Specific and
Specialized
Sport Skill
Stages

Work for higher levels of skill and
improved performance abilities in
throwing and catching in specific
sport and recreational settings

General
Sport
Skill Stage

Sport Related Phase

Mature
Stage

Individuals at the mature stages in
throwing and catching will benefit
from games, self—testing, and
skill development activities that
provide opportunities for practice
and combining throwing and catching
with other movement skills.

See
pp
185 —
186

Elementary
Stage

Fundamental Movement Phase

Individuals at this stage will benefit
from guided discovery experiences
designed to lead them to the mature
stage of throwing and catching.

See
pp
183 —
185

Initial
Stage

Focus on exploratory activities
involving various aspects of throwing
and catching. Emphasis should be on
developing the gross general framework
of these two fundamental movements.

See
pp
180 —
182

— Adjust your hand position for the height of the ball.

a. Thumbs in—above the waist.

b. Thumbs out—below the waist.

— Curve your fingers and keep your eyes on the ball.

— Pull the ball in toward your body.

Movement Concepts

- −You can catch an object in many different ways.
- −You can catch with different body parts.
- −You can catch from a variety of positions.
- −The object you catch may vary in size, shape, color, or texture.
- −The object you catch can come toward you at different levels and with varying degrees of speed.
- −You can play a variety of games that involve catching.

Exploratory Activities

Exploration of a variety of movement challenges involving throwing and catching is an essential aspect of developing fluid, relaxed movements. Simple exploratory activities provide children with opportunities for experimenting with variations in effort, space, and relationships. When the child is at the mature stage in throwing and catching a return to exploratory activities but in a more complicated form is beneficial to higher skill development. Numerous challenges with a variety of combinations and variations of throwing and catching can be devised.

The overhand throwing pattern begins developing early but requires practice.

THROWING

Can you throw—

Effort	Space	Relationships
Force	*Level*	*Objects*
—as soft as you can?	—up high?	—a wiffle ball?
—as hard as you can?	—down low?	—a fluff ball?
—so that the ball makes a	—as low as you can?	—a softball?
loud noise when it hits	—at the wall as high as	—a baseball?
the wall?	you can?	—a football?
—alternating hard and	—at high, low, and	—a newspaper ball?
soft throws?	medium height targets?	—a playground ball?
—stepping forward with	—alternating high and	—at a target?
a loud noise?	low throws?	—into the bucket?
		—over the rope?
Time	*Direction*	—from inside a hoop or inner
—as slowly as you can?	—forward?	tube?
—as fast as you can?	—backward?	
—moving your throwing	—to the side?	*People*
arm as fast as you can?	—at an angle?	—to a partner?
—and twist your body		—as far as your partner?
(hips) as fast as possible?	*Range*	—as hard/soft as your partner?
	—as far as you can?	—the same way as your partner?
Flow	—as near as you can?	
—using as little	—with your right hand?	
movement as possible?	—with your left hand?	**Combinations**
—using as much of your	—with both hands?	Initial experiences should focus
body as possible?	—overhand?	on exploring the various aspects
—like a robot?	—underhand?	of effort, space, and relationships
—like plastic person?	—sidearm?	in isolation prior to structuring
—without using your	—with your arm going	experiences involving
legs?	through short and long	combinations such as: Can you
—without using your	ranges of motion?	and your partner find three
trunk?		different ways to throw at the
—using only one other		target from a far distance?
part of your body besides		
your throwing arm?		
—as smoothly as you		
can?		

CATCHING

Can you catch—

Effort	Space	Relationships
Force −with your arms in different positions? −without making a sound with your hands? −as loud as you can? −keeping your arms straight? −keeping your arms bent?	*Level* −a ball tossed at a low level? −a ball tossed at waist level? −a ball tossed at a high level? −at many different levels? −from a sitting position? −from a lying down position? −in many different positions?	*Objects* −a playground ball? −a small ball? −a large ball? −a beanbag? −five different objects? −five different types of balls? *People* −a ball while holding both hands with a partner? −while holding one hand with a partner?
Time −and go with the ball? −without going with the ball? −the ball as quickly as you can? −after waiting for the ball as long as you can?		
Flow −a ball as smoothly as you can? −with varying degrees of smoothness?	*Direction* −a ball tossed from in front of you? −a ball tossed from an angle? −a ball tossed from the side? −a ball coming down from above? −catch a tossed ball coming at you from different directions?	**Combinations** Exploratory experiences should begin with these and other activities first in isolation. Later, combinations of effort, space, and relationship should be added. For example: Can you catch a ball at waist level while jumping in the air?
	Range −using different body parts? −from different positions? −with one eye closed? −with both eyes closed?	

Guided Discovery Activities

The following guided discovery activities are intended to help the individual focus more closely on the overhand throwing and catching patterns. These progressions are designed to lead the child to the mature stages of throwing and catching utilizing an approach that initially permits exploration followed by questions and movement challenges that focus on mechanically correct execution.

Throwing

1. First, explore the movement variations of throwing found on page 181.
2. Now, begin to place limitations on the response possibilities to the movement challenges that you present. (You may want to use a beanbag rather than a ball for these activities in order to promote a minimum of confusion when retrieving the thrown objects.) For example:

General—

a. Stand about a body length from the wall and throw your beanbag at it. Now try the same thing from here (15−20 feet). Try it again from here (30−50 feet). Do you have to do anything different in order to hit the wall each time? Why?

Leg action—

b. Experiment with different ways of using your legs as you throw. Try throwing with your feet together (initial stage). Now try it by stepping out on the foot on the same side as your throwing arm (elementary). Try it this time by stepping out on the opposite foot (mature). Did you notice any difference in how far the ball went? Which way does a baseball player use? Why?

Trunk action—

c. Try throwing without twisting your trunk. Now try it with twisting. Experiment with different combinations of twisting your trunk and using your legs. Now, show me the best combination. Can you stand facing this wall but throw the ball at the wall to your left? Try it first without bringing your hips around. Now try it with bringing your hips around to the left (for right hand throw). Now try it with stepping out on your left foot and turning to your left.

Arm action—

d. Experiment with different ways of using your arms when you throw. Can you find hree different arm patterns you can use when throwing? Let's work on the overhand throw. Throw the ball overhand without rotating your hips. Try it while rotating your hips. Which way caused the ball to go the farthest? Throw the ball so that it hits high on the wall. Throw it now so that it hits the wall as hard as possible. See if you can throw the ball as far as you can. Now throw far but over the outstretched rope (6−8 feet high).

Total—

   e. Let's see if we can put it all together. Try throwing while stepping forward on the opposite foot and turning your trunk while your arm moves forward. Practice throwing with a partner. Now pretend that it is a hot potato that you must throw back as fast as you can. What happens when you try to get rid of the ball fast? Some of you went back to the elementary level instead of throwing at the mature level, why? Will it help to practice?

3. After the mature throwing pattern has been reasonably well mastered in practice sessions, begin to combine it with other activities. Apply it to numerous situations in order to make it more automatic.

   a. Introduce basic throwing and catching games that will provide plenty of opportunities for practice.

   b. Throw different objects.

   c. Throw distances that encourage mature use of the pattern.

   d. Throw for distance.

   e. Throw at a stationary target.

   f. Throw at a moving target.

   g. Combine distance and accuracy throwing.

Catching

1. First explore the movement variations of catching found on page 182.

2. Then, begin to place limitations on the response possibilities to the movement challenges you present. You may find it helpful to experiment with brightly colored balls and different backgrounds. Also, it will be helpful to catch non-threatening objects such as a fleece ball or beach ball. Practice with catching different sized objects is also important. The following are a few examples of movement challenges that will help lead children to the mature stage of catching:

General—

   a. Experiment with catching a lightly tossed ball. How many ways can you catch the ball? Try experimenting with different arm positions. Now try catching the ball without it touching your body. Can you catch the ball in your hands only?

Arm action—

   b. What should your arms do when they catch a ball? Do they stay straight? Do they stay bent as if you were making a basket or are they first straight and then do they bend as you catch the ball? Why do they give (bend) when you catch the ball? Try catching a softly thrown ball and a ball thrown hard. Is there any difference in how much your arms give as you catch? Why?

Hand action—
   c. Experiment with different ways of holding your hands when you catch. Is there a difference in how you place them for a high ball and for a low ball? Can you catch a low ball with your little fingers together side-by-side? Now try it with your hands facing each other. Are there times when you want to use one ball catching method and times when you use another? Let's try the same experiment while catching a ball that is above the waist.

Eyes—
   d. We all know it's best to catch a ball with our eyes open and looking at the ball but sometimes we close our eyes or turn our head away. Why do you think some people do that? What are some things we can do to help people look at the ball and not turn away? Let's play catch with a partner and see if we can find some ways to help our partner if he or she has this problem. Should we use a large ball or small ball? Why? Should we tell them we are going to toss the ball or not? Why? Let's try each and see what works best. Find what works best for your partner and practice until he/she feels comfortable. Then begin to try out different size balls, speeds, and heights.

  3. After the mature catching pattern has been mastered in a structured environment you will want to provide experiences that permit further practice and use of catching in various situations. The attempt now should be to help make the mature pattern more automatic and adaptable to a variety of backgrounds, ball sizes, colors, objects, speeds, and positions in relationship to the body.

   a. Introduce basic catching and throwing games.

   b. Stress variations in ball size and hardness.

   c. Try fielding grounders, fly balls, and balls not directly in line with the body.

Skill Development Activities

Throwing and catching are basic to the performance of games, sports, and recreational activities. After the patterns of throwing and catching have been mastered and can be performed consistantly at the mature stage you will want to introduce games and sport-related activities that focus on further refinement and utilization. Both throwing and catching are an integral aspect of baseball, basketball, and football activities common to the lives of most children.

In order to focus more fully on higher skill levels of throwing and catching you will find it helpful to:

1. Return to the exploratory activities found on pages 181 and 182. Attention now, however, should be on various combinations of effort, space, and relationships and higher level exploratory experiences.
2. Incorporate additional problem-solving activities into the lesson.
3. Incorporate a variety of throwing and catching game activities into the lesson such as those found in Chapter 14.

SUMMARY

Periodically during your throwing and catching skill theme lessons you will want to evaluate the progress of individuals and the group. Your assessment can be informal and conducted during a game of Teacher Ball (see page 242) or a partner practice activity. You should be able to answer "yes" to each of the following questions. If you are unable to do so, you will need to make modifications in your lessons in order that they more closely meet the specific needs of your students.

Throwing:	Yes	No	Comments
1. Does the child throw consistantly with a preferred hand?			
2. Is the child able to control the trajectory of the ball?			
3. Does the child utilize arm and leg opposition?			
4. Is there definite hip rotation?			
5. Is there efficient summation of forces in use of the arms, trunk, and legs?			
6. Is there noticeable improvement in throwing ability?			

Catching:	Yes	No	Comments
1. Does the child maintain eye contact with the ball throughout?			
2. Is the child able to adjust easily to a ball thrown at different levels?			
3. Is the child able to adjust easily to a ball thrown at different speeds?			
4. Are proper adjustments made in the arm and hand action for large and small balls?			
5. Is the catching action smooth, coordinated, and in good control?			
6. Is there observable improvement in catching abilities?			

Throwing and catching are a natural together as a skill theme. The teacher can, in many cases, utilize a partner approach and peer teaching techniques that simultaneously facilitate both throwing and catching. The importance of mastering these two fundamental abilities cannot be overemphasized. Mature performance in throwing and catching is basic to successful participation in many games, sports, and recreational activities.

CHAPTER 11

Kicking and Trapping

Kicking and trapping are two fundamental movement patterns that fit nicely together into a common skill theme. Basically, kicking involves imparting force to an object with use of the foot and leg. Kicking may take the form of kicking at a pebble, a can, or a ball. It may be part of a low level game, the sport of soccer, punting in football, or by the goalie in soccer. Emphasis in a skill theme focusing on developing the mature pattern of kicking should be on kicking for *distance*. Distance kicking (or kicking as forcefully as possible) will promote the mature pattern. More complete action of the kicking leg on the windup and follow-through is necessary for a long kick as well as the coordinated action of the trunk and arms in adding to the summation of forces. Kicking for accuracy should not be of concern until after the mature pattern has been mastered.

Trapping is a fundamental movement pattern that requires use of various parts of the body in stopping the forward momentum of an oncoming object. With young children, trapping a rolled ball should preceed trapping a tossed object. The focus of the lessons on trapping should be on gaining control of the ball and being able to make appropriate adjustments relative to the speed of the ball and level of contact.

When planning a kicking and trapping skill theme you will find it helpful to utilize the following suggested sequence in order to make the most efficient use of your limited time:

1. *Preplanning:* Determine when and for about how long you wish to focus on kicking and trapping as a skill theme. Locate an ample supply of balls so that there is one ball for every two children.

2. *Observing and Assessing:* Study the verbal and visual descriptions provided for each stage of kicking and trapping. Then informally assess the kicking and trapping abilities of the class or of individual children. Determine if they are at the initial, elementary, or mature level.

3. *Planning and Implementing:* Study the Teaching Tips and Concepts Children Should Know found on pages 191–193 and 195–196. Based on this information and your assessment information, select appropriate activities from the Developmental Activity Teaching Progression Chart for kicking and trapping located on page 197.

4. *Evaluation and Revision:* After implementing your program for several lessons, informally reassess kicking and trapping abilities in terms of improved mechanics. Use the questions found in the Summary on pages 203–204 as a guide. Modify your remaining lessons to more closely suit specific individual and group needs.

KICKING

Developmental Sequence Checklist

Initial Stage:
— Movements are restricted during the kicking action
— Trunk remains erect
— Arms are used to maintain balance
— Kicking leg is limited in backswing
— Forward swing is short: no follow-through
— Child kicks "at" ball rather than kicking it squarely and following through
— A pushing rather than a striking action is predominant

Elementary Stage:
— Preparatory backswing is centered at the knee
— Kicking leg tends to remain bent throughout the kick
— Follow-through is limited to forward movement of knee
— One or more deliberate steps are taken toward the ball

Mature Stage:
— Arms swing in opposition to each other during kicking action
— Trunk bends at waist during follow-through
— Movement of kicking leg is initiated at hip
— Support leg bends slightly at contact
— Length of leg swing increases
— Follow-through is high; support foot rises to its toes or leaves the surface entirely
— The approach to the ball is from a run or a leap

Visual Description Checklist

Initial Stage:

Elementary Stage:

Mature Stage:

Teaching Tips

Common Problems

- Restricted or absent backswing
- Failure to step forward with the non-kicking leg
- Tendency to lose balance
- Inability to kick with either foot
- Inability to alter the speed of kicked balls
- Jabbing at the ball without any follow through
- Poor opposition of the arms and legs
- Failure to use a summation of forces by the body to contribute to the force of the kick
- Failure to contact the ball squarely or missing it completely (eyes not focused on the ball)
- Failure to get adequate distance due to lack of follow through and forceful kicking

Recommendations

- Focus on kicking for distance rather than accuracy. Accuracy kicking will not promote use of the mature pattern.
- If possible, have a ball for every other child.
- Begin with a variety of exploratory experiences, but progress to guided discovery experiences without too much delay.

−Encourage kicking with the non-preferred foot after the mature level has been reached with the preferred foot.

−Work jointly with kicking and trapping using a peer teaching approach.

−Be sure to work for control of the height of the ball. This will make it necessary to teach the instep and inside-of-the foot kick as well as the ever popular toe kick.

−After the mature kicking pattern has been achieved, introduce accuracy kicking activities.

−Incorporate kicking into low level games and lead up games after the mature stage has been reached.

−Work for total body control when kicking.

−Practice kicking using playground balls as well as soccer balls.

−Practice kicking a stationary ball prior to a moving ball.

−Be sure to use balls about the same size as a standard soccer ball.

Concepts Children Should Know

Skill Concepts

−Stand behind the ball and slightly to one side.

−Step forward on the non-kicking foot.

−Keep your eyes on the ball.

−Swing your kicking leg back and then forcefully forward from the hip.

−The snap down from the knee gives the ball its speed.

−Contact the ball with the top portion of your foot (low ball) your toe (high ball) or with the inside portion of your foot (ground ball).

−Follow through in the direction that the ball is to go.

−Use your arms for balance, and force production.

−The kicking pattern is basic to the sport of soccer and is used in kicking games such as kickball.

Movement Concepts

−You can kick a ball at different levels (high, medium, low) by contacting it with different parts of your feet.

−You can kick for distance or for accuracy but the process will look different.

−The manner in which you coordinate the use of your entire body will influence the direction, distance, level, and pathway that the ball takes.

−You can kick the ball at objects and to people. Great precision is needed when kicking at or to something.

- It is important for you to keep your eyes on the ball when it is about to be kicked.
- Your kicks can be long or short, fast or slow, hard or soft and may travel in a variety of directions and at different levels.

TRAPPING

Developmental Sequence Checklist

Initial Stage:
- Trunk remains rigid
- No "give" with the ball as it makes contact
- Inability to absorb the force of the ball
- Difficulty getting in line with the object

Elementary Stage:
- Poor visual tracking
- "Gives" with the ball but movements are poorly timed and sequenced
- Can trap a rolled ball with relative ease but cannot trap a tossed ball
- Appears uncertain as to what body part to use
- Movements lack fluidity

Mature Stage:
- Tracks ball throughout
- "Gives" with the body upon contact
- Can trap both rolled and tossed balls
- Can trap balls approaching at a high velocity
- Movements are refined, fluid, and under control
- Moves to intercept ball with base of the foot

Visual Description Checklist

Initial Stage:

Elementary Stage:

Mature Stage:

Teaching Tips

Common Problems

- Failure to position the body directly in the path of the ball
- Failure to keep the eyes fixed on the ball
- Failure to "give" as the ball contacts the body
- Failure to let the ball meet the body but causing the body to meet the ball
- Inability to maintain body balance when trapping in unusual or awkward positions

Recommendations

- Begin with trapping activities involving the feet and legs (foot trap, single, and double knee trap).
- Learn how to trap a rolled ball prior to an elevated ball.
- Stress eye contact with the ball throughout.
- Introduce trapping a tossed ball only after the concepts involved in trapping a ground ball are mastered.
- Use a yarn ball, beachball or partially inflated ball in the beginning.
- Beanbags work nicely for the introduction of trapping an elevated object.
- Work for control with the stomach and chest traps trying to deflect the ball downward.
- Emphasize the importance of getting in the path of the ball, giving with it, and absorbing its force over as much surface area as possible.
- Do not introduce kicking and trapping games until both patterns are at the mature stage.
- During partner practice, prohibit the use of toe kick unless foam rubber balls are used. If soccer balls are used, they will travel too high and may hit the partner in the face.
- Work for control and a feel for the ball.
- Use a soccer ball only after the principles of trapping are understood.

Concepts Children Should Know

Skill Concepts

- Get directly in the path of the ball.
- Keep your eyes on the ball.
- "Give" with the ball as it touches the body part.

—Deflect an elevated ball downward.

—Let the ball meet your body.

—The trapping pattern is basic to the sport of soccer and any other activity in which the feet, legs, or trunk is used to stop an object.

Movement Concepts

—You can use any part of your body to trap a ball except your hands and arms.

—You can trap a ball at different levels.

—You can trap objects other than balls.

—You and your partner can practice trapping and kicking together.

—Your control of the ball will influence the success of your trapping.

Children at the initial stage of trapping have great difficulty stopping a ball without using their hands.

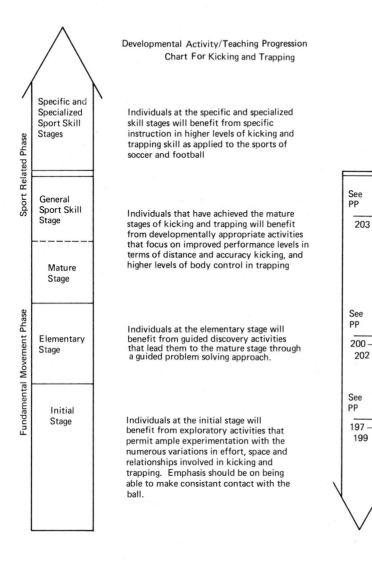

Developmental Activity/Teaching Progression
Chart For Kicking and Trapping

Sport Related Phase

Specific and Specialized Sport Skill Stages

Individuals at the specific and specialized skill stages will benefit from specific instruction in higher levels of kicking and trapping skill as applied to the sports of soccer and football

General Sport Skill Stage

Individuals that have achieved the mature stages of kicking and trapping will benefit from developmentally appropriate activities that focus on improved performance levels in terms of distance and accuracy kicking, and higher levels of body control in trapping

See PP 203

Mature Stage

Fundamental Movement Phase

Elementary Stage

Individuals at the elementary stage will benefit from guided discovery activities that lead them to the mature stage through a guided problem solving approach.

See PP 200 – 202

Initial Stage

Individuals at the initial stage will benefit from exploratory activities that permit ample experimentation with the numerous variations in effort, space and relationships involved in kicking and trapping. Emphasis should be on being able to make consistant contact with the ball.

See PP 197 – 199

Exploratory Activities

A variety of activities can be explored with both kicking and trapping. Activities at this stage should focus on experimenting with the numerous variations in effort, space, and relationships that are possible. Care should be taken to use partially deflated balls for initial trapping experiences and to avoid combinations of movement concepts until reasonable skill levels are obtained.

KICKING

Can you kick the ball—

Effort	Space	Relationships
Force	*Level*	*Objects*
—as hard as you can?	—high?	—and hit the wall?
—as soft as you can?	—low?	—and hit a big target?
—with a forceful leg	—as high as you can?	—and hit a small target?
swing but light hit?	—so it stays on the	—over the goal?
—with a lazy leg swing	ground?	—into the goal?
but a forceful hit?	—so it doesn't go higher	—under the stretched rope?
	than your waist?	—through the chair legs?
Time		—around the cones using several
—so it goes fast?	*Direction*	controlled kicks?
—so it goes very slowly?	—forward?	
—from here so it hits the	—backward?	*People*
wall in five seconds?	—sideways?	—to a partner?
—from here so it hits the	—diagonally?	—to a partner while walking
wall in two seconds?	—alternating left and	(passing)?
—from here and turn	right feet (dribbling)?	—at different levels to a partner?
around before it hits the		—in different directions to a
wall?	*Range*	partner?
—and touch the floor	—as far as you can?	—with different amounts of force
before it hits the wall?	—as near as you can?	to a partner?
	—with your feet wide	—at different speeds to a partner?
Flow	apart?	
—with a big leg swing?	—with your body in	**Combinations**
—with no knee bend?	different positions?	Numerous exploratory activities
—without using your	—with your opposite	that combine elements of effort,
arms?	foot?	space, and relationship can be
—while swinging *both*		explored after first trying them in
arms back?		isolation. For example: Can you
—while swinging both		find ways to kick the ball with
arms forward?		different amounts of force, at
—with no follow		different levels, with your
through?		partner?
—with no backswing?		

TRAPPING

Can you trap—

Effort	Space	Relationships
Force	*Level*	*Objects*
—a ball that is rolled slowly toward you?	—a ball that is rolling toward you?	—a beanbag?
—a ball that is tossed lightly at you?	—a ball that is rolling off to one side?	—a beachball?
—a ball that is rolled rapidly toward you?	—a ball at waist level?	—a fleeceball?
—a ball that is tossed forcefully at you (use a fleeceball)?	—a ball at stomach level?	—a playground ball?
	—a ball at chest level?	—different size balls?
Time		—a soccer ball?
—in slow motion?	*Direction*	
—a fast moving ball?	—a ball moving toward you?	*People*
—a slow moving ball?	—a ball moving away from you?	—a ball and kick it back to your partner?
	—a ball moving in front of you?	—a ball and have your partner count the number of different ways you can do it?
Flow	—a ball moving to one side?	
—a ball and "give" with the ball?		
—a ball without "giving" with the ball?	*Range*	**Combinations**
	—a ball wtih your foot?	Combinations of effort, space, and relationships can be devised and explored after a variety of isolated activities are explored. For example: Experiment with how much you must "give" with your body when trapping five different types of balls.
	—a ball with your shin?	
	—a ball with your stomach?	
	—a ball with your chest?	
	—a ball with either foot?	
	—a ball with either shin?	
	—a ball with a large body part?	
	—a ball with a small body part?	

Guided Discovery Activities

The following activities are intended to provide the learner with a variety of interesting and challenging kicking and trapping activities that lead to the mature patterns of movement. Emphasis should be placed on structuring and sequencing meaningful movement challenges that help the child discover the mechanically correct and most efficient ways in which to kick or trap a ball.

Notice the arm and leg opposition

Kicking

1. First, explore the movement variations of kicking found on page 198.

2. Then begin to place limitations on the response possibilities to the movement challenges you present. For example:

Leg action—

a. Try kicking the ball without bending your leg. Now, bend first at your kicking knee then kick the ball. Which way caused the ball to go farther? Which felt best?

b. Try kicking the ball as far as you can using different amounts of knee bend but no follow through (that is, stopping your leg as soon as you contact the ball). Now try the same thing but follow all the way through. Which amount of knee bend works best? Does a follow through on your kick help the ball go farther?

c. Try different ways of approaching the ball before you kick it using a full bend at the knee of your kicking leg and extending at the hip. Does the ball go farther after a kick from standing still, or does it help to take a step or two?

Why? Let's practice kicking as far as we can using a step to the ball.

Trunk action—   **d.** Do you think it will help if you move your trunk backward when you kick the ball? Try it. Now keep your body straight and then try leaning far forward. Do you notice any differences? Let's try to kick the ball as far as we can and practice leaning back a little as we make contact with the ball.

Arm action—   **e.** What do you do with your arms when you kick the ball? Watch your partner. What does she/he do? Experiment with different arm positions as you kick. Which way works best? Let's practice kicking as hard as we can and swing our arms so the arm opposite our kicking leg is swung forward while the other moves backward.

Total—   **f.** Try kicking the ball as far as you can and as hard as you can. Now try kicking at the target (a suspended hula hoop works fine). Did you notice any changes in how you kick when you kick for accuracy rather than distance?

g. Try kicking a rolling ball. Try kicking while on the run. Experiment with kicking the ball but first tell your partner if it will be a high, medium, low, or ground kick. Can you control the level of your kick? What must you do to control the level? Show me. Try using different parts of your foot when you kick. Use your toe, your instep, the inside of your foot. What differences do you notice in level, in speed, in accuracy, in distance?

3. After a mature kicking pattern has been reasonably well mastered, it is important to combine it with other exploratory and guided discovery activities in order to reinforce the pattern and make it more automoatic.

a. Make quick kicks
b. Kick at a stationary target
c. Kick at a moving target
d. Kick at a target from a run
e. Kick for control in high, low, and ground level kicks
f. Kick back and forth to a partner while moving in the same direction (passing)
g. Maneuver and kick at a target against a defense
h. Play kicking relays
i. Play kicking games

Trapping

1. First, explore several of the movement variations of trapping found on page 199. Remember that a primary purpose of these exploratory activities is to lead the child to a better understanding of the movement concepts of effort, space, and relationships as applied to trapping an object.

2. Then, begin to place limitations on the response possibilities to the movement challenges that you present. Remember that your reason for doing this is so that you may lead the individual to the mature pattern of movement through his or her own discovery of the solution to the movement problems that you structure. Trapping, for example, may be performed in a variety of ways. There is the foot trap, knee trap, stomach trap, and chest trap. Although each utilizes a different part of the body to intercept and stop the oncoming object, all incorporate the same principles of movement. Namely: (1) absorbing the force of the ball over the greatest surface area as possible, and (2) absorbing the force of the ball over the greatest distance required for successful trapping. The following are examples of several movement challenges to present that help bring out these movement principles.

   a. Try to stop a rolling ball with your feet. What happens to the ball when you let it hit your feet without "giving" when it hits? Why does this happen? How can you cause the ball to stop right after it hits your feet? What do you have to do?

   b. Let's try the same thing with the ball being tossed at your legs (stomach, chest, etc.). What must you do each time in order to get the ball to drop and stop in front of you? Try different ideas then show me the one that works best for you. Did you notice how you had to "give" with the ball to get it to stop?

   c. Do you have to give with the ball as much if the ball is traveling slowly as when it is traveling fast? Why? Show me how you give with the ball when it is coming fast and then when it is coming slowly.

   d. Is it best to try trapping the ball with a small body part or a large body part? Try both ways. Which works best? Why?

   e. If a ball is traveling fast would you want to give with the ball over a longer distance or a shorter distance? How about over a large part of your body or over a small part? Experiment with the different ways of trapping and let me know which is best.

3. After trapping has been reasonably well mastered in controlled guided discovery lessons, you will find it helpful to structure experiences that demand greater control and rapid decision making. For example:

   a. Trap a ball kicked by a partner then kick it back.

   b. Trap a ball coming from different directions and levels and at different speeds.

   c. Play games and take part in relay races involving kicking and trapping.

Skill Development Activities

Kicking and trapping are fundamental movements basic to the sport of soccer. After the individual has had an opportunity to explore and discover the many facets of these two movement patterns, you will want to introduce low level games and lead-up games that focus on further refinement and utilization. A wide variety of kicking games can be played as well as numerous soccer lead-up games.

In order to focus more fully on skill development, you will find it helpful to:

1. Return to the exploratory ideas found on pages 198 and 199. Structure more complex experiences emphasizing various combinations of effort, space, and relationships.
2. Include additional problem-solving activities into the lesson.
3. Introduce a variety of games that incorporate kicking and trapping such as those found in Chapter 14.

SUMMARY

During the time that you are implementing the kicking and trapping skill theme you will want to make periodic observations of the progress that is being made by the class. Your observational assessments can be conducted informally during a game of kick ball (p. 249), circle soccer (p. 250), or pin guard (p. 249). You should be able to answer "yes" to each of the following questions. If you cannot, you will need to make modification in your lessons to more closely meet the needs of your students.

Kicking:	Yes	No	Comments
1. Does the child make consistent contact with a stationary ball?			
2. Can the child make good contact with the ball from an approach?			
3. Can the child control the direction, level, and distance of his/her kick?			
4. Is there an acute bend at the knee and backward extension at the hip when the child is kicking for distance?			
5. Is the entire trunk and arms brought into play for a forceful kick?			
6. Can the child consistently kick a moving ball?			
7. Is there noticeable improvement in the kicking pattern?			

Trapping:			
1. Can the child trap a rolled ball?			
2. Can the child trap a tossed ball?			

	Yes	No	Comments
3. Does the child make easy adjustments for trapping balls traveling at different speeds?			
4. Does the child make adjustments for the surface area used to trap the ball based on the speed of the ball?			
5. Are the movements of the child fluid and in control?			
6. Is there observable improvement in trapping abilities?			

Kicking and trapping go well together as a developmental skill theme. Like throwing and catching they are natural companions in a skill theme lesson. Care should be taken, however, to be certain that you adjust the tasks that you present according to the skill level of the children. It is often wise to use fluff balls, beach balls, and playground balls prior to the use of soccer balls. They not only provide experiences with different mediums but are safer. Care must be taken to remember that in the early stages of learning the objective is to help the child gain control over his or her movements and progress to the mature stage in these fundamental skills. After the mature pattern has been mastered we can then go to the use of soccer balls and focus on the skilled aspects of kicking and trapping.

CHAPTER 12

Dribbling and Volleying

The fundamental movement patterns of ball bouncing (dribbling) and volleying are applied primarily to the sport activities of basketball, soccer, speedball, and volleyball. They are unique in that they are of only limited direct value to most recreational and daily living skills. Volleying and dribbling do, however, provide the individual with important experience in interrupting an object and require the sophisticated interaction of sensory and motor processes at a precise moment in time. Therefore, when we view dribbling and volleying as fundamental movements we may also view them as ideal tasks for helping the individual learn how to coordinate the use of the eyes with the hands.

Dribbling is a fundamental movement that involves receiving force from an object and immediately imparting force from that object in a downward (hand dribble) or ground level horizontal direction without the use of an implement (foot dribble). The developmental sequence for hand dribbling appears to be: (1) bouncing and catching, (2) bouncing and ineffective slapping at the ball, (3) basic dribbling with the ball in control of the child (4) basic dribbling with the child in control of the ball, and (5) controlled dribbling with advanced abilities.

Volleying is a fundamental skill that involves receiving force from an object and *immediately* imparting force to that object in a roughly vertical direction as with volleyball, or heading and juggling in soccer. The developmental sequence for effective volleying is much like dribbling beginning with ineffective, uncontrolled efforts followed by gradual control and increased proficiency. Volleying also involves the complex interaction of visual and motor processes.

It will be helpful to initiate skill theme activities with the use of balloons, beach balls, or other light objects that enable the individual to have a longer visual tracking period. The size and color of the ball may also influence volleying and dribbling activities. Care should be taken to be sensitive to these possible influencing factors. The teacher should be ready to make adjustments in ball type, size, or color in order to maximize the child's success potential.

When planning a skill theme involving dribbling or volleying or both, you may want to use the following sequence:

1. *Preplanning:* Determine approximately how many lessons you will need to focus on dribbling and/or volleying. Locate a sufficient number and variety of balls so that there is one for every other child.

2. *Observing:* Study the verbal and visual description of each of the three stages of dribbling and volleying. Based on this information informally assess the group or individual children on their dribbling and volleying abilities. Determine if they are at the initial, elementary, or mature level.

3. *Planning and Implementing:* Study the Teaching Tips and Concepts Children Should Know found on pages 208−209, and 212−213. Based on this information and the results of your observations, consult the Developmental Activity Teaching Progression Chart found on page 214.

4. *Evaluation and Revision:* Informally reassess dribbling and volleying abilities in terms of improved mechanics. The questions found in the Summary on pages 220−221 will prove helpful. Modify your remaining lessons to more closely suit specific individual and group needs.

DRIBBLING

Developmental Sequence Checklist

Initial Stage:
- Ball held with both hands
- Hands placed on sides of the ball with palms facing each other
- Downward thrusting action with both arms
- Ball contacts surface close to body, may contact the foot
- Great variation in height of the bounce
- Repeated bounce and catch pattern

Elementary Stage:
- Ball held with both hands one on top and the other near the bottom
- Slight forward lean with the ball brought to chest level
- Downward thrust with top hand and arm
- Force of downward thrust inconsistent
- Hand slaps at ball for subsequent bounces
- Wrist flexes and extends and palm of hand contacts ball on each bounce
- Visually monitors ball
- Limited control of the ball while dribbling

Mature Stage:
- Feet placed in narrow stride position with foot opposite dribbling hand forward

—Slight forward trunk lean
—Ball held waist high
—Ball pushed toward ground with follow through of arm, wrist, and fingers
—Controlled force of downward thrust
—Repeated contact and pushing action initiated from the finger ti[
—Visual monitoring not necessary
—Controlled directional dribbling

Visual Description Checklist

Initial Stage:

Elementary Stage:

Mature Stage:

Teaching Tips

Common Problems

- Slapping at the ball rather than pushing the ball
- Ball controlling the child rather than child controlling the ball
- Inability to remain in one place while dribbling
- Inability to move about under control while dribbling
- Inability to dribble with either hand
- Poor visual monitoring of the ball
- Insufficient follow through on the push causing the ball to fail to return to desired height
- Inconsistent or inappropriate force applied to the ball

Recommendations

- Utilize a playground ball or other ball that does not require as much force in dribbling as a basketball.

— Use different colors or striped balls in order to avoid blending of figure and ground.

— Work first for controlled bouncing and catching.

— Provide plenty of opportunities for practice in an atmosphere of exploration and experimentation.

— As skill develops, challenge the children with a variety of guided discovery activities that focus on being more aware of the process.

— Do not introduce low level games, relays, or lead-up games until the mature stage of dribbling has been reasonably well achieved.

— Practice dribbling with either hand.

— Stress eye contact at the initial and elementary stage but work for kinesthetic control at the mature stage.

— Structure experiences that require making modification in the dribbling pattern congruent with the situation.

— As a last resort, physically manipulate the occasional child who is unable to coordinate the bounce of the ball with the push of the hand. Do this only as long as needed to get a "feel" for the timing of the ball.

Concepts Children Should Know

Skill Concepts

— Push the ball down.

— Your wrist controls the bounce.

— Use your fingertips.

— Follow through.

— Push the ball slightly forward.

— Keep the ball below your waist.

Movement Concepts

— You can bounce the ball at different levels.

— You can bounce the ball with different amounts of force.

— You can control the amount of time between bounces by using different amounts of force and bouncing at different levels.

— The rhythmical flow of the bounced ball is important for controlled dribbling.

— You can bounce many kinds and sizes of balls.

— The density of the ball will influence its bouncing capabilities.

VOLLEYING

Developmental Sequence Checklist

Initial Stage:
- Inability to accurately judge the path of the ball or balloon
- Inability to get under the ball
- Inability to contact the ball simultaneously with both hands

Elementary Stage:
- Failure to visually track the ball
- Gets under the ball
- Slaps at ball
- Action mainly from the hands and arms
- Little lift with the legs or follow through
- Unable to control the direction or intended flight of the ball
- Wrists relax and ball often travels backward

Mature Stage:
- Gets under the ball
- Good contact with both hands
- Contact with fingertips
- Wrists are stiff upon contact but extend as the arms follow through
- Good summation of forces and utilization of the arms and legs
- Able to control the direction and intended flight of the ball

Visual Description Checklist

Initial Stage:

Mature Stage:

Elementary Stage:

Teaching Tips

Common Problems

- Failure to keep the eyes on the ball
- Inability to accurately judge the flight of the ball and to time the movements of the body properly
- Failure to keep the fingers and wrists stiff
- Failure to extend all of the joints upon contacting the ball (lack of follow through)
- Inability to contact the ball simultaneously with both hands
- Slapping at the ball
- Poor positioning of the body under the ball

Recommendations

- Work for good positioning under the ball.
- Begin using balloons, progress to beachballs or plastic balls prior to using a regulation volleyball.
- When using a volleyball, allow an intermediate bounce prior to contact if necessary.
- Teach the children to make a "window" with the thumbs and index fingers nearly touching.
- Emphasize looking through the window when contacting the ball.
- Work for good force production by stressing the importance of extending at the ankles, knees, hips and shoulders upon contact.

Concepts Children Should Know

Skill Concepts

- Get into position directly beneath the ball.
- Watch the flight of the ball between the opening formed by your two hands.
- Extend the arms and legs as the ball touches your fingertips.
- Keep the fingers and wrist stiff throughout.
- Follow through in the direction that the ball is to go.
- Keep your eyes on the ball.
- Volleying is a striking pattern that is used in many games and in the sport of volleyball.

Movement Concepts

- You can vary your body position when you control the ball.
- You can alter the level of your body.
- You can make changes in the force that you apply to the ball.
- The coordinated contact of the ball will be influenced by how well all of your body works together.
- You can give direction to the ball.
- You can control the distance that the ball travels.
- You can volley many different objects.
- You can play volleying games with other people.

Notice the full extension of the entire body upon contact with the ball.

Developmental Activity Teaching Progression Chart
For Dribbling And Volleying

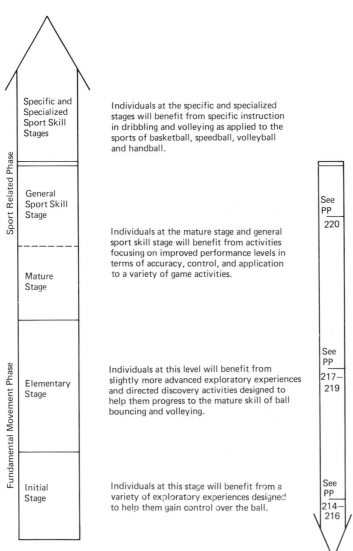

Exploratory Activities

The primary purpose for incorporating exploratory activities into the movement lessons on dribbling and volleying is to help the child get the gross general framework idea of these two fundamental patterns. Initial experiences should be presented in such a way that they permit free exploration without attempting to focus on skill development. The teacher will have to be careful not to structure activities that go beyond the skill level of the children. The use of balloons and beachballs works especially well for initial volleying activities as do fully inflated, brightly colored, playground balls for dribbling. Once the child has mastered the mature pattern you will want to return to exploration of more complex combinations of effort, space, and relationships.

DRIBBLING

Can you bounce (or dribble) the ball—

Effort	Space	Relationships
Force	*Level*	*Objects*
—as hard as you can?	—at knee level?	—around the chairs?
—as soft as you can?	—at waist level?	—under the outstretched rope?
—changing from hard to	—at leg level?	—over the outstretched rope?
soft?	—higher than your head?	—while walking close to the
	—lower than your knees?	wall?
Flow	—and change levels with	—if it is a basketball?
—and catch it?	each bounce?	—if it is a playground ball?
—repeatedly after		—and notice any difference with
catching it repeatedly?		different types of balls?
—without catching it	*Direction*	
(dribbling)?	—in front of you?	
	—to one side?	
Time	—behind you?	*People*
—as fast as you can?	—in different pathways?	—to your partner?
—as slow as you can?	—in a straight line?	—alternating with a partner?
—alternating fast and	—in a circle?	—in time to your partner's
slow?	—in a curved line?	bounce?
—and allow as much	—in a zig zag line?	—and each move away and back
time as you can between		together with the same number of
bounces?	*Range*	bounces?
—as many times as you	—in your space?	
can until I say "stop"?	—hitting the same spot	
	each time?	**Combinations**
	—while moving around	As the individual gradually gains
	the room?	control of the ball rather than the
	—as far away from you	ball controlling him/her, add
	as you can?	various combinations of effort,
	—as close to you as you	space, and/or relationships. For
	can?	example: Can you dribble the
	—with other body parts?	ball at waist level but to one side
	—with your other hand?	of your body as you go around
		the court?

VOLLEYING

Can you volley the ball—

Effort	Space	Relationships
Force	*Level*	*Objects*
—very hard?	—when you are in	—if it is a beach ball?
—very softly?	different positions?	—if it is a balloon?
—high?	—from a seated position?	—if it is a large ball?
—low?	—from a kneeling	—if it is a small ball?
	position?	—if it is a volleyball?
Flow	—without it going above	—over the rope?
—alternating hard and	your head?	—over the net?
soft volleys?	—with it going as high as	—with different body parts?
—but relax your fingers?	possible?	—with your head (heading)?
—but tense your fingers?		—with your knees (juggling)?
—and give with the ball?	*Directions*	
—without giving with	—forward?	*People*
the ball?	—backward?	—to a partner?
	—to the side?	—tossed by a partner?
	—in a circle?	—back and forth to a partner?
Time		
—as many times as you	*Range*	
can until I say "stop"?	—and have it drop in	
—as few times as you	your personal space?	**Combinations**
can in 30 seconds?	—and have it drop	Simple exploratory activities
	outside your space?	with light objects (balloons and
	—from a position	beach balls) are essential prior to
	directly under it?	using volleyballs. Combine
	—from a position off to	activities only after reasonable
	one side?	control has developed. For
		example: Can you find different
		ways to volley the ball to your
		partner so that he or she can
		volley it back at different levels?

Guided Discovery Activities

The activities that follow are intended to provide the learner with a variety of activities that are interesting, challenging, fun, and lead to the mature patterns of dribbling and volleying. It is important that these movement challenges be presented in a manner that helps the child focus on the correct mechanics of dribbling and volleying and provides ample opportunity for practice.

The hand dribble is used in the sport of basketball.

Dribbling

1. First, explore several of the movement variations of dribbling found on page 215.

2. Then begin to place limitations on the response possibilities to the movement challenges you present. For example:

General—   **a.** Try dribbling your ball in your own space with your feet together, legs straight, and standing straight. How does it feel? Now try it several different ways. Which way feels best? Why?

Trunk action—   **b.** When you dribble the ball in place, what do you do with your feet? Your trunk? Is it easier to control the ball in one place standing straight or bent slightly forward at the waist? Try both. Which was best? Why?

Leg action—   **c.** Experiment with different foot positions when you dribble in place. Are there any differences? Why?

                     d. Try moving about the room while dribbling the ball. Is it easier or harder than when standing in your space? Why is it harder?

              e.   Listen to my commands and move only in the direction I call out. Can you do it? Why is this hard for some people and easier for others? All those who are "experts" try the same thing but use your opposite hand to dribble the ball. Did you "experts" notice any difference in how well you did? Why?

Arm and hand action—   **f.**   Experiment with using your hand and arm in different ways as you dribble the ball. What do we do with our fingers, our wrist, and our arms when we dribble the ball? Show me. Why do we push the ball down rather than slapping at it? Can you keep your wrist stiff and dribble the ball off your fingertips? Try it.

              g.   Try to stay in your own space dribbling the ball off your fingertips, with a stiff wrist and good follow through. Now try it with slapping at the ball. Which ways gives you the most control? Show me. Why?

Eyes—   **h.**   Look at the ball as you dribble. Now try the same thing looking up here at me. Try it now with your eyes closed. Which was easiest? Which was hardest? When you are playing basketball is it best to look at the ball as you dribble or is it better to be looking where you are going? Let's try to dribble without looking at the ball.

General—   **i.**   Let's practice dribbling with the opposite hand. Now let's alternate dribbling first with one hand then the other. Is it harder with one hand then the other? Why?

              j.   See if you can dribble around an object changing hands each time around. Now change hands each time you change direction.

   3.   After the mature dribbling pattern has been fairly well mastered it should be combined with other exploratory and guided discovery activities in order to reinforce the pattern and make it more automatic.

      a.   Dribble around obstacles.

      b.   Dribble the ball while touching and changing hands, level, and/or the direction of the dribble.

      c.   Keep the ball away from an opponent while dribbling.

Volleying

   1.   First, explore several of the movement variations of volleying found on page 216 taking care to use an object appropriate to the abilities of the individual.

   2.   Then begin to place limitations on the response possibilities to the questions you ask. Focus on eliciting the mature volleying pattern first using a balloon, then a beachball, and finally a volleyball. In order to aid children with tracking and accurately interrupting the ball, you may permit an intermediate bounce of the ball before it is actually volleyed in the following activities:

General—

a. Can you hit the balloon, beach ball, etc. into the air so that it comes right back to you? Try hitting it several times in a row staying in your own space. What must you do to be sure that the ball comes back to you? What about your hands? Do you have more control with one or both hands?

Hand and arm action—

b. Try volleying your balloon with both hands, as many times as you can. What must you do to keep the ball up over your head? Show me. What do you do with your hands and fingers and wrists when you volley the ball?

c. Try volleying a beach ball or volleyball. Is it easier or harder than the balloon? Why?

d. Use your volleyball to volley with but let it bounce once before you try hitting it again. Is that easier than before? Why?

e. Let's try volleying different sized balls. Is there any difference? Can you use two hands as easily with a small ball?

Feet and leg action—

f. Experiment with different foot positions as you volley. Now try it with your knees locked, with them apart, with them bent slightly. Which works best?

3. Considerable time will need to be spent with discovery activities in order to help the children focus on control of the object. Intercepting a ball and volleying or striking it is an extremely complicated task requiring sophisticated interaction of visual and motor processes and exact timing. Be patient in your approach and be sure to utilize objects and activities that permit the beginner ample opportunity to track the ball visually prior to intercepting it. Once the volleying pattern has been mastered to a reasonable degree and the individual is exhibiting mature control of the ball it will be wise to focus on a combination of activities that reinforce the correct pattern and make it more automatic.

a. Volley the ball to different heights
b. Volley from different body levels
c. Volley continuously without an intermediate bounce
d. Volley against a wall
e. Volley with a partner
f. Volley with a group
g. Volley the ball in a direction different than that from which it came

Skill Development Activities

Dribbling and volleying are fundamental manipulative movements that are used almost exclusively in athletic activities. Dribbling with the hands is an integral aspect of basketball. Foot dribbling is crucial to the sport of soccer. Volleying is an important element of volleyball, and heading and juggling are important in soccer. After the individual has had opportunities to explore and discover the many facets of these two patterns of movement and after they have achieved the mature stage, you will want to introduce a variety of low level games, lead up games, and self-testing activities. Practice in these activities will provide opportunities for further refinement and practical utilization of these skills in play and game situations.

In order to focus more fully on higher skill levels of dribbling and volleying you will find it helpful to:

1. Return to the exploratory activities found on pages 215–216. However, attention should now be given to more complex combinations of effort, space, and relationships.
2. Incorporate additional problem-solving activities into the lesson.
3. Incorporate a variety of dribbling and volleying games into the lesson such as those found in Chapter 14.

SUMMARY

You will want to make periodic checks on the progress of your students during this skill theme. Assessment of progress can be easily done through observation of the class during a dribbling relay or a wall volley drill. You should be able to answer "yes" to each of the following questions. If you are unable to do so, you will have to make modifications in your lessons to meet more closely the needs of the group or individuals within the group.

Dribbling:	Yes	No	Comments
1. Is the child in control of the ball?			
2. Is the child able to dribble in her or his own space?			
3. Can the child dribble while moving about the room?			
4. Can the child dribble the ball without stopping to catch it?			
5. Does the child exhibit proper use of the fingers, wrist, and arm while dribbling?			
6. Is the trunk bent forward slightly while dribbling?			
7. Is the action smooth and rhythmical?			

	Yes	No	Comments
8. Can the child vary the height and direction of the ball at will?			
9. Can the child dribble with either hand?			
10. Is there observable improvement in the ability to dribble with control?			

Volleying:

	Yes	No	Comments
1. Can the child volley a balloon repeatedly with good control?			
2. Can the child volley a beach ball with good control?			
3. Can the child volley and remain in his/her own space?			
4. Can the child control the direction of the volley?			
5. Can the child volley a ball that has been permitted to bounce one time?			
6. Does the child exhibit controlled use of the fingers, hands, and arms?			
7. Does the child utilize an efficient summation of forces upon contact?			
8. Does the child maintain eye contact throughout?			
9. Is there observable improvement in volleying ability?			

CHAPTER 13

Striking and Ball Rolling

Striking is a fundamental movement pattern that may be performed in several different planes with or without the use of an implement. Striking may also involve contact with a stationary or moving object. However, even though the plane, implement, and nature of the object to be struck may differ in a number of ways, they are all governed by the same mechanical principles of movement. First, the amount of momentum generated depends on the length of the backswing, the number of muscles involved, and the proper sequential use of the muscles. Second, the object to be struck must be contacted at the precise moment that maximum speed of the swing has been reached. The striking implement must follow through toward the intended target. Fourth, the striking implement should make contact at a right angle to the object. Fifth, the implement should be held out and away from the body in order to achieve maximum momentum.

The forms that striking takes are many and its application to sports is varied. The horizontal striking pattern is found in baseball. The vertical striking pattern is found in tennis, golf, volleyball, badminton, handball, and racquetball. For our purposes we will describe the horizontal striking pattern with an implement in the pages that follow. You should, however, be quick to recognize that the Description, Teaching Tips, and Concepts Children Should Know apply equally well to striking an object in a vertical plane or without an implement.

The movement pattern of ball rolling has had very limited scientific study. Little is known, through controlled experimentation, about the emergence of ball

222

rolling abilities. Ball rolling is, however, a fundamental movement pattern that is often applied to the sport and recreational activities of bowling, curling, boccie, and shuffleboard. The basic ball rolling pattern may also be observed in underhand tossing, softball pitching, and lifesaving rope tossing techniques.

Both striking and rolling involve imparting force to an object. Therefore they may, if one wishes, be grouped together and presented as two skill themes within the same lesson or, you may wish to include them with the skill theme of throwing. Both striking and rolling have elements which are similar to the overhand and underhand throwing patterns respectively. In order to make the best use of the limited time you may have in presenting and developing this skill theme it is suggested that you utilize the following sequence for planning and implementing:

1. *Preplanning:* Determine approximately how much time you will need to be spent on this skill theme. Locate appropraite equipment being sure to have an ample number of balls and striking implements so that there will be plenty of opportunities for all.

2. *Observing and Assessing:* Study the verbal and visual description for striking and rolling and informally assess the striking and rolling abilities of the group. Determine if they are typically at the initial, elementary, or mature level.

3. *Planning and Implementing:* Study the Teaching Tips and Concepts Children Should Know found on pages 226−227, and 230−231. Based on this information and your informal observational assessment, select appropriate activities from the Developmental Activity Teaching Progression Chart for striking and rolling found on page 232.

4. *Evaluation and Revision:* Informally reassess striking and rolling abilities in terms of body mechanics. Use the questions found in the Summary on page 238 as your guide. Modify your remaining lessons to more closely suit specific individual and group needs.

HORIZONTAL STRIKING

Developmental Sequence Checklist

Initial Stage:	−Motion is from back to front
	−Feet are stationary
	−Trunk faces direction of tossed ball
	−Elbow(s) fully flexed
	−No trunk rotation
	−Force comes from extension of flexed joints in a downward plane
Elementary Stage:	−Trunk turned to side in anticipation of the tossed ball
	−Weight shifts to forward foot prior to ball contact
	−Combined trunk and hip rotation

— Elbow(s) flexed at less acute angle
— Force comes from extension of flexed joints. Trunk rotation and forward movement is in an oblique plane

Mature Stage: — Trunk turned to side in anticipation of the tossed ball
                       — Weight shifts to back foot
                       — Hips rotate
                       — Transfer of weight is in a contralateral pattern
                       — Weight shift to the forward foot occurs while the implement is still moving backward
                       — Striking occurs in a long full arch in a horizontal pattern
                       — Weight shifts to forward foot at contact

Visual Description Checklist

Initial Stage:

Mature Stage:

 Elementary Stage:

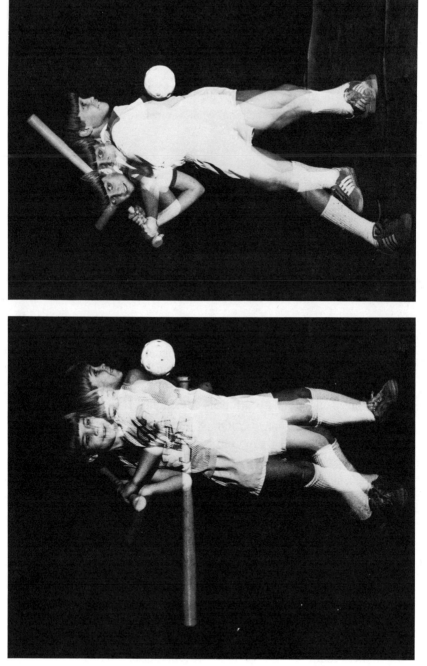

Teaching Tips

Common Problems

- Failure to keep the eyes on the ball
- Improper grip of the striking implement
- Failure to adjust properly for the intended flight of the ball
- Inability to sequence the required movements together in rapid succession in a coordinated manner
- Poor backswing
- "Chopping" swing
- Restricted body rotation
- Keeping the elbow too close to the body
- "Topping" the ball
- Failure to get in line with a moving ball prior to contact

Recommendations

- Follow a sequence of teaching that progresses from striking with the hand and other body parts to using short-handled implements and then using long-handled implements.
- Utilize balloons and beach balls at the initial stages.
- Practice hitting stationary objects prior to moving objects.
- Work with striking large objects and then progress gradually to striking smaller objects.
- Remember that the color of the ball and the background against which it is being struck may have an influence on the figure–ground perception of the object.
- Develop an efficient horizontal striking pattern before concentrating on the vertical plane.
- Check frequently to see that the proper grip is maintained and the eyes are on the ball.
- Work for effective weight shifting, summation of forces, and a level swing.
- Stress making a "big swing." Be sure that the ball is contacted with the elbows extended and at the maximum velocity of the swing.
- Stress following through in the direction of the target.

Concepts Children Should Know

Skill Concepts

- Be sure that your hands are touching when you grip a baseball bat and that your right hand is on top of your left (right hand pattern).
- Keep your eyes on the ball at all times.
- Always contact the ball at the point of complete arm extension.
- Shift your weight back then forward as you swing.
- Swing in a level fashion.
- Follow through.
- The striking pattern is used in many sport activities. Some sports use striking with the hand as the implement such as handball and volleyball. Others such as baseball, hockey, golf, tennis, and racquetball use an implement.

Movement Concepts

- You can strike a ball with different amounts of force.
- You can make the ball go fast or slow.
- The sequential and rhythmical use of your muscles will affect the force of your swing and the speed of the ball.
- The ball can be struck at many different levels.
- The ball may be contacted in a horizontal or vertical plane.
- You can hit a ball in many different directions.
- Objects other than balls can be struck.
- You don't always need to use an implement to strike something. You can use your hand, your head, or your feet effectively.
- Striking a moving object is a complex task requiring very precise coordination of your eyes and muscles.
- The success of your striking will be influenced by many factors including the size, shape, and color of the ball as well as the size and shape of the implement and the speed of the object.

BALL ROLLING

Developmental Sequence Checklist

Initial Stage:
- Straddle stance
- Ball held with hands on the sides of the ball with palms facing each other

-Acute bend at the waist with backward pendulum motion of the arms
-Eyes monitor the ball
-Forward arm swing and trunk lift with release of the ball

Elementary Stage: -Stride stance
-Ball held with one hand on bottom, other on top
-Backward arm swing without weight transfer to rear
-Limited knee bend
-Forward swing with limited follow through
-Ball release between knee and waist level
-Eyes alternately monitor target and ball

Mature Stage: -Stride stance
-Ball held in hand corresponding to trailing leg
-Slight hip rotation and trunk lean forward
-Pronounced knee bend
-Forward swing with weight transference from rear to forward foot
-Release at knee level or below
-Eyes on target throughout

Visual Description Checklist

Initial Stage:

Elementary Stage:

Mature Stage:

Teaching Tips

Common Problems

- Failure to transfer the body weight to the rear foot prior to moving it to the front foot
- Placing the hands improperly on the ball
- Releasing the ball too high causing it to bounce
- Releasing the ball at the wrong angle causing it to veer to one side
- Failure to execute a perfectly vertical swing of the arm
- Poor follow through resulting in a weak roll
- Failure to keep the eyes on the target
- Failure to step forward with the appropriate foot

Recommendations

- Begin practice with a large ball prior to using a small ball.
- Do not stress accuracy during the initial experiences.
- Focus on proper body mechanics. Have the children roll the ball at the wall from greater and greater distances.
- After the basic pattern has been mastered, begin working for greater accuracy. Begin with large targets in order to promote success.
- Gradually increase both distance and accuracy requirements.
- Do not use a bowling ball or other heavy object when working on the correct body mechanics.
- Practice rolling from a stationary position prior to adding an approach.

Concepts Children Should Know

Skill Concepts

- Stand with one foot leading.
- Swing your arm straight back as you rock back on your rear foot.
- Let go of the ball when it is six to twelve inches in front of your leading foot.
- Follow through with your swing in the direction of the target.
- Keep your eyes on the ball.
- The rolling pattern is basic to the sports of bowling, curling, and boccie. It is also used in games such as Pin Guard and Guard the Castle.

Developmental Activity Teaching Progression Chart
For
Striking and Ball Rolling

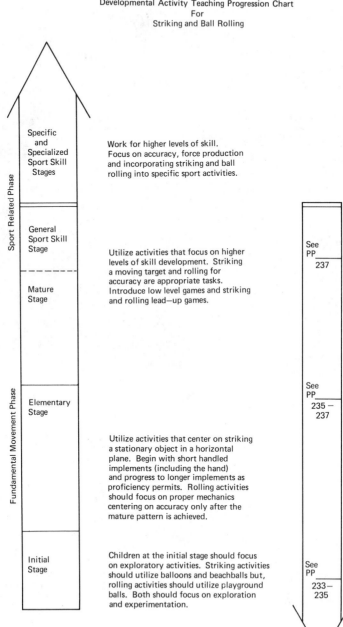

Sport Related Phase

Specific
and
Specialized
Sport Skill
Stages

Work for higher levels of skill.
Focus on accuracy, force production
and incorporating striking and ball
rolling into specific sport activities.

General
Sport Skill
Stage

Utilize activities that focus on higher
levels of skill development. Striking
a moving target and rolling for
accuracy are appropriate tasks.
Introduce low level games and striking
and rolling lead—up games.

Mature
Stage

See
PP_____
237

Fundamental Movement Phase

Elementary
Stage

See
PP_____
235 —
237

Utilize activities that center on striking
a stationary object in a horizontal
plane. Begin with short handled
implements (including the hand)
and progress to longer implements as
proficiency permits. Rolling activities
should focus on proper mechanics
centering on accuracy only after the
mature pattern is achieved.

Initial
Stage

Children at the initial stage should focus
on exploratory activities. Striking activities
should utilize balloons and beachballs but,
rolling activities should utilize playground
balls. Both should focus on exploration
and experimentation.

See
PP_____
233 —
235

Rolling a ball with precision takes practice.

Movement Concepts

-You can roll a ball at different speeds.

- The force you apply to the ball will control its speed.

- The coordinated use of your muscles as you roll the ball will influence the force of the ball and its speed.

-You can place your body in many different positions when rolling an object.

-You can roll a ball in many different directions and cause it to travel in different pathways.

-You can roll different size balls.

-You can devise many challenging game activities that use ball rolling.

Exploratory Activities

A wide variety of exploratory activities can be incorporated into a skill theme of either striking or rolling. The purpose of the exploratory activities that follow is to provide the individual with an opportunity to get the general idea of the numerous movement possibilities involved in these fundamental movements. Effort, therefore, should be focused on getting the gross general framework idea of striking and rolling and not on skill development. You will find it helpful to provide numerous exploration experiences prior to combining movement concepts. It will also be helpful to center activities around the use of balloons and beach balls for striking and playground balls for rolling.

STRIKING

Can you hit the ball (balloon, beach ball)—

Effort	Space	Relationships
Force —as hard as you can? —as soft as you can? —so it makes a loud noise? —like a strong monster? —squarely? *Flow* —limply? —with jerky movements? —with smooth movements? *Time* —slowly? —quickly? —firmly?	*Level* —so it travels at different levels? —with your body at different levels? —from a high level to a low level? —from a low level to a high level? *Direction* —in a straight line? —with a level swing? —up? —down? —forward? —backward? —in different pathways? *Range* —using different body parts? —and keep it in your space? —with your other hand? —from the other side? —with a wide base? —with a narrow base?	*Objects* —over the rope? —under the rope? —through the chairs? —around the chair? —into the bucket? —using different sized objects? —using objects with different shapes? —with different implements? *People* —to a partner? —as your partner does? **Combinations** After exploring the many variations of striking in isolation, it will be helpful to combine various aspects of effort, space, and relationships. For example: Can you hit the balloon as hard as you can so that it travels at a low level to a partner?

BALL ROLLING

Can you roll the ball—

Effort	Space	Relationships
Force —softly? —as hard as you can?	*Level* —while lying on the floor?	*Object* —no matter what size it is? —on the balance beam?

Effort	Space	Relationships
	−from your knees?	−on a line?
Time	−from a sitting position?	−between the boxes?
−as slow as possible?		−into the can?
−as fast as you can?	*Direction*	−through the tube?
	−in a straight line?	−under a wicket?
Flow	−so that it curves?	−at the pins?
−using your arms only?		
−using only one side of	*Range*	*People*
your body?	−around yourself?	−to a partner?
−smoothly?	−with your other hand?	−with a partner?
−like a robot?	−as far as you can?	−alternating back and forth?
−like a champion	−as accurately as you	−mirroring your partner?
bowler?	can?	−shadowing your partner?
	−without moving off the	
	line?	
	−with an approach?	**Combinations**
		Numerous combinations of effort, space, and relationship related to rolling are possible as well as combinations with other fundamental movements. For example: Can you roll the ball with different amounts of force? Can you roll the ball at a low level with a partner?

Guided Discovery Activities

The purpose of the following guided discovery activities is to enable the child to experiment with a variety of movement challenges that will help lead him or her to the mature stages of horizontal striking and ball rolling. The intent is to lead the child through a series of carefully structured tasks to higher levels of ability and a more complete understanding of the many factors involved in these two fundamental movements.

Striking

1. First, explore several of the numerous variations of striking found on page 234. Emphasis here should be on getting used to the idea of striking in terms of effort, space, and the ball's relationship to objects and people.

2. Then begin to place limitations on the response possibilities to the movement challenges you present. For example:

General—

a. Try hitting the balloon with your hand, a ping pong paddle, a wiffle ball bat. Which was easiest? Hardest? Why?

b. Now try to hit the beach ball the same way. First with your hand, then a ping pong paddle, then a bat. Which was easiest? Hardest? Why?

Arm action—

c. Try hitting the ball off the tee using your hand, a paddle, a bat. Which way caused the ball to go the farthest? Why?

d. Now try using a bat but keep your arms bent. Then try it with your arms straight when the bat hits the ball. Did you notice a difference? Which works best and why?

e. See if you can find different ways to swing your bat. Experiment with different ways of holding the bat. Can anyone tell me the best way to hold the bat and the best way to swing it if I want what I'm hitting to go as far as possible?

f. Now we want to have our right hand on top (right-handed batter) and our left on the bottom, and we want our swing to be level. Let's try it.

Leg action—

g. Let's try standing in different ways when we strike the ball. Try to find five ways to stand as you hit the ball off the tee. Which helps the ball go the farthest? Show me.

h. Now let's see what we can do with our feet when we hit the ball. Try standing with your feet together, wide apart, and less apart. Which feels best?

i. Will it help to step out as we swing at the ball? Try it. Why do you think that it helps?

General—

j. Let's practice hitting a suspended ball. Can you hit it as it is swung to you? Can you tell me what you need to do with your arms, your trunk, and your legs when you strike the ball? Do we do each separately or do we try to put them together smoothly? Why?

3. After a mature striking pattern has been reasonably well mastered you will want to begin practicing hitting a tossed ball. In order to maximize skill development you may want to:

a. Use a large ball then gradually work down to a small ball.

b. Use an oversized bat prior to using a regulation bat.

c. Use a bat that is slightly shorter or have the child "choke-up" on the bat.

d. Toss the ball slowly then gradually increase its speed.

e. Experiment with different pitching distances.

f. Experiment with different ball colors and backgrounds.

g. Incorporate the striking pattern into a variety of low level and lead-up games.

Ball Rolling

1. First, explore several of the numerous variations of rolling that are found on page 235.
2. Then begin to place limitations on the responsibilities to the movement challenges you present. Focus on how the body should move and why when rolling an object. For example:

General—

    a. Let's experiment with different ways of rolling the ball. How many ways can you find? Show me.

    b. What should we do if we want the ball to go as fast as possible? Show me. Why?

    c. What can you do to make the ball go as straight as possible?

    d. If you want the ball to go both fast and straight how would you roll it? Why?

Arm action—

    e. Try rolling the ball from between your legs. Now try placing it by your side and rolling. Which way allows the ball to go the fastest? Which is the most accurate? Why?

    f. What happens when I use a small ball and then a large ball? Which ball will go fastest? Which ball travels more accurately? Try both then tell me.

Leg action—

    g. Why do you think bowlers bowl like this (demonstrate)? Try doing different things with your legs as you roll the ball. Try standing with your feet together and your knees locked. Does it work well? What happened to the ball? Why did it bounce before it began to roll?

    h. See what you can do to prevent the ball from bouncing as it is rolled. Can you do anything with your trunk? Can you do anything with your legs that will help? Show me. Why does it help to bend forward and step out on the leg opposite the ball? Let's all try it and see how straight we can roll our ball.

3. After a mature ball rolling pattern has been reasonable well mastered it is time to begin focusing on accuracy and increasing the distance to the target. A variety of low level games and lead-up activities to bowling can be incorporated at this point. You will also want, however, to combine rolling with a variety of other movements in order to reinforce the proper pattern and make it more automatic. For example:

    a. Roll different sized balls

    b. Roll the balls on different surfaces

    c. Try to control the direction of a rolled ball

Skill Development Activities

After the striking and/or ball rolling patterns have been mastered and are performed acceptably at the mature level it is time to begin focusing on further refinement of these patterns and approaching them as sport skills. Emphasis should now begin to be placed on speed, accuracy, and implementation of these skills into a variety of low level games, lead-up, games and skill drill activities.

SUMMARY

Periodically during this skill theme you will find it helpful to informally evaluate the progress that is being made by an individual or the group as a whole. Observational assessment of ball rolling during a game of Guard the Castle (page 251) and of striking during a game of Long Base should be adequate. You should be able to answer yes to each of the following questions. If you are unable to do so, you will need to make modifications in your lessons in order to more closely meet specific individual or group needs.

Striking:	Yes	No	Comments
a. Can the child strike a balloon with good control (does the child control the balloon or does the balloon control the child)?			
2. Can the child strike a ball off a batting tee?			
3. Does the child use a level horizontal swing?			
4. Does the child grip the implement properly?			
5. Is the stance appropriate for the task?			
6. Does the child show evidence of proper summation of forces?			
7. Is there observable improvement?			

Ball Rolling:	Yes	No	Comments
1. Does the child use a rolling pattern to one side of the body?			
2. Can the child make adjustments for different size balls?			
3. Does the child adjust to the distance and accuracy required?			
4. Does the child exhibit a good backswing?			
5. Is there sufficient follow through?			
6. Can the child control the pathway of the ball?			
7. Is there observable improvement?			

Striking is an extremely complex movement pattern requiring high degrees of sensory-motor integration and the precise coordination of body parts with an implement. Striking a moving object is probably one of the most difficult single movement tasks. Therefore, the instructor will need to be very sensitive to individual readiness levels. Extreme care will have to be taken to insure that a developmentally sound orderly sequence of progression is followed.

14

Manipulative Game Activities

There are several game activities that may be used to reinforce the development and refinement of fundamental manipulative abilities. It is suggested, however, that practice with individualized activities precede the games portion of the lesson.

Manipulative games can serve as an effective reinforcer of the particular skills being stressed. The teacher must keep in mind the desired outcomes of the game and feel free to modify it whenever necessary to ensure maximum participation and practice of the skills being stressed.

Games For Enhancing Manipulative Abilities

The following games are appropriate for use with primary grade children and may in some instances be modified to include preschool children if different types of balls are used.

Objectives

1. To enhance fundamental manipulative abilities in throwing, catching, kicking, trapping, volleying, striking, bouncing, and rolling.
2. To enhance eye—hand and eye—foot coordination.
3. To be able to work together in a group effort.
4. To enhance listening abilities.
5. To be able to follow directions and obey rules.

Movement Experiences

Poison Ball

Movement skills   Tossing and catching.

Desired outcomes
1. To enhance fundamental manipulative abilities.
2. To enhance ability to grasp objects.
3. To enhance ability to follow directions.
4. To enhance fine motor coordination.

Formation   Single circle facing in.

Equipment   Two yarn balls or beanbags.

Procedures   The balls are passed around the circle to either the left or to the right. The balls are handed rapidly to the next person and not thrown. A signal is give to stop and the children left holding the ball are "poisoned." They drop out of the circle and the game continues until only two players remain.

Hot Potato

Movement skills   Tossing and catching.

Desired outcomes
1. To enhance fundamental manipulative abilities.
2. To be able to follow direction.
3. To enhance fine motor coordination.

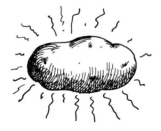

Formation   Single circle facing in.

Equipment   One 8-inch playground ball.

Procedures   The children sit in the circle an arm's length apart. On the command "go" the ball is passed around the circle until the signal to "stop" is given. The child left holding the ball drops out of the circle. The game continues until only two players remain.

Variations   To avoid the exclusion element of this and many other circle games, set up a point system. If a person gets three points against himself, for example, he has to sit in the "mush pot" in the center of the circle for one turn or perform a stunt for the class.

Fine motor activities need to be incorporated into the motor development program.

Teacher Ball

Movement skills	Tossing and catching.
Desired outcomes	1. To enhance fundamental manipulative abilities. 2. To enhance eye—hand coordination.
Formation	Several circles containing six to eight children each with the "teacher" in the center.
Equipment	One 8-inch playground ball for each group.
Procedures	One child stands in the center of the circle ("the teacher") and tosses the ball to each member of the circle. A new "teacher" then goes into the center. This game may be used as a practice drill or developed into a race between circles as the children's skill level increases.

Variations	Various sizes and types of balls may be used. Also various throwing, catching, kicking, trapping, and volleying skills may be developed this way.

Guess Who

Movement skills	Tossing and catching.
Desired outcomes	1. To enhance fundamental manipulative abilities. 2. To enhance listening skills.
Formation	Single line of six to eight children per group, one child 10—20 feet away.
Equipment	Playground ball.
Procedures	The players line up about 10—20 feet from a player chosen to be "it," who turns his back as the ball is passed along the line of players. At a signal from a chosen leader, the player who is holding the ball throws the ball at "it" and tries to hit him below the waist. If the player who throws the ball misses, he has to change places with "it." If "it" is hit by the ball, she turns around and gets one guess as to who hit her. If she guesses correctly, she changes places with the player who threw the ball.

Moon Shot

Movement skills	Throwing and catching.
Desired outcomes	1. To enhance fundamental manipulative abilities.
	2. To enhance ability to keep score.
	3. To enhance ability to follow rules.
Formation	Single circle facing in with an outer circle also drawn on the floor, one child in the center.
Equipment	Beanbags.
Procedures	Each child stands on the inner circle and in turn tries to "shoot the moon" with the beanbag. "Moon" is a small circle inside two larger circles. If the child is successful he moves to the outer circle and shoots from there when his turn comes again. When a child makes a successful throw, he moves to, or remains on, the outer circle. When he is unsuccessful he remains on or returns to the inner circle. Each successful throw from the inner circle counts one point, and from the outer circle, two points. The center player is retriever and throws the beanbag to each player in turn, or each player may retrieve his own beanbag and pass it to the next player. After the beanbag has gone around the circle once, the retriever (if one is used) chooses a player from the outer circle to be the new retriever and exchanges places with him.

Call Ball

Movement skills	Vertical tossing and catching.
Desired outcomes	1. To enhance fundamental manipulative abilities.
	2. To enhance eye—hand coordination.
	3. To enhance ability to follow directions.
Formation	Single circle facing inward with a leader in the center.
Equipment	One playground ball for each circle of eight to ten players.
Procedures	The leader stands in the center of the circle and tosses the ball into the air while calling another player's name. The player called runs forward and attempts to catch the ball before it hits the ground or after one bounce. She becomes the new leader if she succeeds. Otherwise the original leader tosses the ball into the air again.

Spud

Movement skills	Vertical tossing, throwing, and catching.
Desired outcomes	1. To enhance fundamental manipulative abilities.
	2. To enhance eye—hand coordination.
	3. To be able to follow directions.

Formation	Single circle facing in with the leader in the center.
Equipment	One playground ball for each circle of 8 to 10 players.
Procedures	The leader stands in the center of the circle and tosses the ball into the air and calls another player's name. The player called runs to the center of the circle and tries to catch the ball. At the same time the remaining players scatter. "It" catches the ball and says "stop" as soon as she gains control of it. The fleeing players freeze. "It" is permitted to take three "giant" steps in any direction. She then throws the ball at one of the players. If she hits that person, who is not permitted to move, he then becomes "it." If she misses, she remains "it" and begins the game again with a toss from the center of the circle.

Circle Dodge Ball

Movement skills	Throwing, catching, and dodging.
Desired outcomes	1. To enhance fundamental manipulative abilities. 2. To enhance agility and coordination.
Formation	Single circle of 10—12 participants facing in, one child in center.
Equipment	Playground ball.
Procedures	The children form a circle and one child is placed in the center. The children in the circle attempt to throw the ball and hit the child in the center. If the child is hit, the thrower takes his place. (Do not permit throwing at the head.)
Variation	Use more than one ball. Divide the class in half. Place one team inside the circle while all others attempt to hit them. Reverse the procedures after a given amount of time or after all are hit.

Keep Away

Movement skills	Throwing and catching.
Desired outcomes	1. To enhance fundamental manipulative abilities. 2. To enhance ability for teamwork. 3. To enhance eye—hand coordination. 4. To enhance agility.
Formation	Single circle of 10—15 participants facing in, one child in center.
Equipment	Playground balls.

Procedures   The children form a circle and one child is placed in the center. The remaining children attempt to pass the ball, keeping it away from the child in the center. If the child in the center catches the ball, the child who threw it takes her place in the center.

Tunnel Ball

Movement skills   Rolling.

Desired outcomes
1. To enhance fundamental manipulative abilities.
2. To enhance eye—hand coordination.

Formation   Single circle of eight to ten players facing in, one child in center.

Equipment   Playground balls.

Procedures   Ten players form a circle with one player in the center of the circle. The players in the circle spread their feet apart and the player in the center tries to roll the ball through their legs or between the players. If he is successful in his attempt, he takes the place of the player in the circle. The player in the circle can block the ball with his hands but he can't move his feet.

Roll and Catch

Movement skills   Rolling and catching.

Desired outcomes
1. To enhance fundamental manipulative abilities.
2. To enhance ability to identify balls of different sizes.
3. To enhance ability to tell why different balls roll at different speeds.

Formation   Double line, partners facing.

Equipment   Balls of various sizes.

Procedures   Give one ball to every couple. Players form double lines about 6 feet or more apart, partners facing each other. Partners roll the ball back and forth. If one of them misses the ball, have the pair sit. The couple remaining at the end of the game is the winner. Also have contests to see which pair can roll the ball the most times in a row without a miss.

Roll It Out

Movement skills   Rolling

Desired outcomes
1. To enhance fundamental manipulative abilities.
2. To enhance eye—hand coordination.

Formation   Single circle facing in, either seated or kneeling.

Equipment   One playground ball per circle.

Procedures

A ball is rolled into the circle. When it comes near a child, she tries to roll it between two of the circle players by batting it with her hand. She may stop it first and then roll it. If she succeeds, she changes place with the circle player on whose right side the ball goes out.

I'll Roll It To . . .

Movement skills	Rolling.
Desired outcomes	**1.** To enhance fundamental manipulative abilities. **2.** To enhance ability to follow directions. **3.** To enhance eye—hand coordination.
Formation	Single circle facing in, seated on the floor.
Equipment	Playground balls of different sizes.
Procedures	Teacher and children sit on floor in circle. Teacher has a utility ball. He says, for example, ''I'll roll the ball to Mary,'' and rolls the ball to her. Child stops the ball with both hands, then rolls it with both hands to another child, saying first, ''I'll roll the ball to . . .'' Game continues until all have received the ball several times. Then teacher takes a different-sized ball and starts a new game, using only one hand to roll the ball. Children stop the ball with one hand, using the same hand to roll it.

Kick-Away

Movement skills	Kicking and trapping
Desired outcomes	**1.** To enhance fundamental manipulative abilities. **2.** To enhance eye—foot coordination. **3.** To enhance agility. **4.** To enhance ability to follow directions.
Formation	Several circles with eight to twelve children per group.
Equipment	One 8-inch playground ball per group of 10—12 children.
Procedures	One player has ball on ground in front of him and his foot is resting on it. He kicks the ball across the circle, using the inside of his foot to avoid lofting it. The child receiving the ball traps it and kicks it quickly away from himself to another child. Children continue to kick ball until it goes outside of circle. The player who retrieves the ball brings it back to the circle and starts it again.

Free Ball

Movement skills	Kicking and trapping
Desired outcomes	1. To enhance fundamental manipulative abilities. 2. To enhance eye—foot coordination. 3. To enhance ability to follow directions.
Formation	Two parallel lines (30 feet apart) with four to six players per group.
Equipment	One 8-inch playground ball per group
Procedures	Child who is "it" stands behind one line facing the other players, who stand behind the opposite line. "It" calls a player's name and kicks the ball toward the opposite line. Player whose name is called tries to trap the ball and kicks it back to "it." This continues until "it" has kicked it once to each player. Then "it" calls "free ball" and kicks toward the opposite line. Player who stops the ball is the new "it."

Cross The Line

Movement skills	Kicking and trapping.
Desired outcomes	1. To enhance fundamental manipulative abilities. 2. To enhance eye-foot coordination. 3. To enhance ability to function as a team.
Formation	Five to eight players per group.
Equipment	One 8-inch playground ball per group.
Procedures	The "line" is a 25-foot line drawn a distance of 20—40 feet from the kicking circle. Other players scatter in playing field in front of the wall. Kicker places the ball on the ground inside the kicking circle. He calls, "Cross the line" and kicks toward the line. Any fielder who can trap the ball before it goes over the line is the new kicker. If the ball crosses the line, the original kicker kicks again. If no one stops the ball after he has kicked three times, he chooses a new kicker.

Balloon Volleying

Movement skills	Striking and volleying.
Desired outcomes	1. To enhance fundamental manipulative abilities. 2. To enhance eye—hand coordination. 3. To enhance temporal awareness.
Formation	Scatter.
Equipment	Enough round balloons and string for each child.

Procedures	Tie balloons around the children's wrist (left wrist if right-handed) an appropriate length to allow the child to volley it. The player who can keep it up the longest is the winner.

Bounce and Catch

Movement skills	Bouncing and catching.
Desired outcomes	**1.** To enhance fundamental manipulative abilities. **2.** To enhance eye—hand coordination. **3.** To be able to work with a partner.
Formation	Scatter.
Equipment	One playground ball per player.
Procedures	Each child has a rubber ball. They bounce it and catch it, using both hands, repeating the sequence several times. Then they try to bounce his ball to a partner and catch the partner's return bounce. Children bounce a ball against a wall and catch it as it bounces back. Teacher places several children in a line and bounces to each in turn.

Teacher's Choice

Movement skills	Bouncing and catching.
Desired outcomes	**1.** To enhance fundamental manipulative abilities. **2.** To enhance ability to toss and catch balls of various sizes. **3.** To enhance recognition of the functions of balls of different types.

Formation	Circle or line with six to eight players per group.
Equipment	Balls of different sizes.
Procedures	Children stand on a line facing the child who is "teacher." The "teacher" chooses any ball she wishes to use and throws or bounces

it to each child in turn. When each child has received the ball the "teacher" goes to the end of the line and the child who is at the head of the line becomes the new "teacher", choosing the ball to be used. The game continues until each child has been "teacher."

Kick the Can (or Pin Ball Soccer)

Movement skills	Kicking and trapping.
Desired outcomes	1. To enhance fundamental manipulative abilities. 2. To enhance eye-foot coordination. 3. To enhance the ability to function as a team.
Formation	Two parallel lines 30 feet apart with eight to ten players per group.
Equipment	Soccer ball, five large cans, Indian clubs or cartons.
Procedures	Divide players into two teams, each team standing on its own kicking line. Kicking lines are 30 to 60 feet from center line, depending upon skill of players. Give soccer ball to player on one team who kicks the ball at a can from her own kicking line. Opponents trap ball with their feet as it rolls to them, and kick from their line. Game continues until all the cans are down. A team makes one point for each can it knocks down. When all cans are down the team with highest score is the winner. A player may block the ball with his/her body but may not touch it with the hands unless it goes out-of-bounds, in which case it is carried to kicking line and started again. If the ball is touched with the hands, it is a foul, and opponents win one point.

Corner Kick Ball

Movement skills	Kicking, passing, deflecting, trapping, and dribbling.
Desired outcomes	1. To enhance fundamental manipulative abilities. 2. To enhance eye-foot coordination. 3. To enhance the ability to function as a team.
Formation	Two parallel lines 30 feet apart with 8 to 10 players per group.
Equipment	Soccer ball.
Procedures	Players divide into two teams, each team standing behind its own restraining line. The ball is placed in circle in center of field. On the signal "Go!" the two end players from each team run to the center and try to kick the ball to a teammate behind them or to the side. (The ball may *not* be kicked forward on the initial kick). Teammates try to pass the ball to the center person on their team who now attempts to kick the ball to the opponents' goal line. The successful team wins two points. After a score the kicking players all return to center positions in their own line, and four new ends run out. Line players try to block ball from going over the goal line, and kick or

throw it back to their centers. Line players may not cross their own restraining line. Center players may not use hands, but line players may use hands or body to block the ball. Out-of-bounds balls are played in from the point where they went out.

Circle Soccer

Movement skills	Kicking, trapping, and passing.
Desired outcomes	1. To enhance fundamental manipulative abilities.
	2. To enhance eye-foot coordination.
	3. To enhance the ability to function as a team.
Formation	Eight to 10 per team in a circle formation.
Equipment	Soccer ball. (A foam rubber ball is safest for beginners).
Procedures	Each team forms a semicircle; two opposing teams, or two semicircles, then join to form one circle. The object is to kick the ball *below* waist level between members of the other team. After each score, the players rotate one place to the right. If a ball comes to rest inside the circle, a player from that half of the circle may get the ball and take it to the circle and start again. One point is scored each time the ball goes through the opponent's team below the shoulder level. One point is also scored against a team that uses hands to stop the ball.
Variations	a. Play in a line or square formation.
	b. Players hold hands.

Teacher Kick Ball

Movement skills	Passing and trapping.
Desired outcomes	1. To enhance fundamental manipulative abilities.
	2. To enhance eye-foot coordination.
	3. To enhance the ability to function as a team.
Formation	Eight to 10 per team in a circle formation.
Equipment	Soccer balls.
Procedures	The object is for each team to perform the designated skill in the quickest possible time. Each team member, in turn, serves as leader for each skill by taking the center position. He then performs the skill with each team member, one by one. When finished, a new leader takes over. One point is scored for each team successfully completing the skill in the shortest time.
Variations	a. Perform only one skill. Do it several times around.
	b. See which team can head or volley the ball the longest without allowing the ball to hit the ground (use a beach ball).

Guard the Castle

Movement skills	Throwing, kicking, or trapping.
Desired outcomes	1. To enhance fundamental manipulative abilities. 2. To enhance fundamental stability abilities.
Formation	Circle with an empty milk carton in the center. Eight to 10 players per group.
Equipment	Utility ball.
Procedures	The circle players throw the ball at the carton attempting to knock it down. The guard tries to prevent it from being knocked down, stopping the ball in any manner. Who ever knocks the carton down becomes the new guard. If the guard accidently knocks down the carton, the circle player who last threw becomes the new guard. Don't allow circle players to move within the designated area and don't allow the guard to stand over the carton.

Target Bombardment

Movement skills	Throwing.
Desired outcomes	1. To enhance fundamental manipulative abilities. 2. To enhance fundamental stability abilities.
Formation	Two teams of 8—10 spread out on their respective sides of a half court line.
Equipment	Ten to 15 empty milk cartons lined up on the two ends of the playing area and two utility balls.
Procedures	Each team tries to knock down the cartons of the other team with thrown balls. The team knocking down all the other team's cartons is the winner. Players may not cross the center line. If a carton is knocked down, it must stay down; this includes cartons knocked down by players on the defending team. Players may not stand over the cartons in order to guard them.
Variations	Limit the time and see which team can knock down the most cartons in the allotted time.

SUMMARY

The preceeding games are representative of manipulation oriented games. These games as well as others may be modified to incorporate developmentally suitable manipulative skills. The game of circle soccer, for example, calls for a circle of standing children to kick a ball by or between the children on the opposing half of the circle. If these children have had little kicking experience, it might be advisable to have the children sit in the circle formation first and kick a large soft ball from this more stable base of support. If their kicking performances are more advanced, the base of support for kicking might become a one leg balanced position, or different types of kicks using the inside and outside of the foot may be done. The game objectives can remain the same but rolling or throwing skills might be used instead of kicking. Manipulative relays are task oriented in nature and can be used in isolation or in relay situations. The teacher must be aware of the children's abilities to understand the team concept that is essential in relay activities prior to incorporating them into the curriculum.

Four

FUNDAMENTAL STABILITY SKILL THEMES

15

Static and Dynamic Balance

Balance is generally defined as the ability to maintain one's equilibrium in relation to the force of gravity whether in a static posture or when performing a dynamic activity. In order for a person to be in balance, the line of gravity which passes through the individual's center of gravity must also lie within the base of support. If the line of gravity falls outside the base of support one cannot remain inbalance and will fall unless compensating movements are made. A static balance activity may be defined as any stationary posture, upright or inverted, in which the center of gravity remains stationary and the line of gravity falls within the base of support. Standing in place, balancing on a board, or performing a front scale are all examples of static balance from an upright posture. Examples of inverted postures include performing a tripod, tip-up, headstand, or handstand. The essential factor in any static balance activity is that the body is maintained in a stationary position for a specified period of time.

Dynamic balance involves controlled movement while moving through space. In a dynamic balance activity the center of gravity is constantly shifting. Most locomotor and manipulative movements involve an element of dynamic balance. Virtually all movement involves an element of static or dynamic balance, or both. Therefore, we may look upon it as the basis from which all controlled locomotor, stability, and manipulative movement emanates. As a result, the balance experiences engaged in by children play an important role in the development of total body control. Because of the unique relationship of dynamic and static balance to the movement pattern development of the individual in both locomotor and manipulative movements, the format of this chapter has been altered somewhat to focus on those activities which clearly place a premium on the gaining and maintaining of one's equilibrium. The one foot balance and beam walk have been selected as representative fundamental static and dynamic balance movement patterns, respectively. A wide variety of movement experiences are presented in Chapter 18 that are designed to enhance the gross general framework idea of the components of static and dynamic balance. These activities are *not* designed solely around balancing on one foot and walking on the balance beam. They go beyond this and include the use of ropes, hoops, benches, barrels, wands, and other forms of equipment.

When preparing a skill theme that focuses on static and dynamic balance, you may find the suggested sequence of events that follows helpfull:

1. *Preplanning:* Determine the approximate number of lessons you will devote to this skill theme (several short units throughout the year starting at the beginning is advised). Study the verbal and visual descriptions for the one foot balance and beam walk on the following page.
2. *Observing and Assessing:* Based on the above information informally assess the group or individual children on their static and dynamic balance abilities using the one foot balance and beam walk as you measure. Determine if the children are at the initial, elementary, or mature stage or beyond.
3. *Planning and Implementing:* Study the Teaching Tips and Concepts Children Should Know found on pages 261–262. Based on this information and the results of your observations, consult the Developmental Activity Teaching Progression Chart found on page 263. Involve the children in a variety of experiences that utilize different forms of equipment, contact surfaces, and environmental situations.
4. *Evaluation and Revision:* Informally reassess dynamic and static balance abilities on the beam, on one foot, or in other situations. The questions found in the Summary on page 264 should guide your evaluation. Modify your remaining lessons to more closely suit specific induvidual and group needs.

BEAM WALKING

Developmental Sequence Checklist

Initial Stage: −Balances with support
                          −Walks with lead
                          −Uses follow-step with dominate foot leading
                          −Focus on feet

                                    —Body rigid
                                    —No compensation movements

Elementary Stage: —Can walk a two-inch beam but not a one-inch beam
                                    —Uses follow-step with dominate foot leading
                                    —Focus is on beam
                                    —May "tie" one arm to the side of the body
                                    —Loses balance easily
                                    —Limited compensating movements
                                    —Forward movement only

Mature Stage: —Can walk a one-inch beam
                                    —Uses alternate stepping action
                                    —Focus beyond the beam
                                    —Both arms used at will to aid balance
                                    —Can move forward, backward, and sideways
                                    —Movements are fluid, relaxed, and in control
                                    —May lose balance occasionally

Visual Description Checklist

Initial Stage:

Elementary Stage:

Mature Stage:

One Foot Balance

Developmental Sequence Checklist

Initial Stage: — Raises non-support leg several inches so that thigh is nearly parallel with contact surface
— Either in or out of balance (no in between)
— Over compensates ("windmill" arms)
— Inconsistent leg preference
— Balances with outside support
— Only momentary balance without support
— Eyes directed at feet

Elementary Stage: — May lift non-support leg to a "tied-in" position on support leg
— Cannot balance with eyes closed
— Uses arms for balance but may "tie" one arm to the side of the body
— Performs better on dominate leg to a free position by bending at the knee

Mature Stage: — Can balance with the arms or trunk as needad to maintain balance
— Uses both arms or the trunk as needed to maintain balance
— Lifts non-support leg
— Focuses on external object while balancing
— Changes to nondominant leg without loss of balance

Visual Description Checklist

Initial Stage:

Elementary Stage:

Mature Stage:

Concepts Children Should Know (Static and Dynamic Balance)

Skill Concepts

- Holding your arms out to the side will help you balance.
- Focusing on an object will help you balance.
- When walking on the beam, you should try to use an alternate stepping pattern.
- Be sure to have a spotter at your side.
- Do not overdepend on your spotter.

Movement Concepts

- If your line of gravity falls outside your base of support you will loose balance.
- You can balance in control on many types of equipment.
- You can balance while moving with others.
- You can widen your base when you balance for greater stability.
- You can lower your body when you balance for greater stability.

Teaching Tips (Static and Dynamic Balance)

Common Problems

- Inability to maintain balance
- Inability to balance unaided
- Leading with one foot only
- "Tying" one arm to the side while balancing with the other
- Failure to use the arms to compensate for changes in balance
- Looking down at the feet
- Inability to alter level or direction

Recommendations

- Spot activities carefully but only as needed
- Offer your hand for assistance encouraging the child to grasp it less securely as balance is gained.
- Use a six-foot pole to aid in balancing with the use of both sides of the body.
- To encourage the child to focus properly have him or her identify numbers that are held up.
- Work for good body control in different directions and at different levels.

- Try picking up objects while balancing in order to alter the balance problem and change level.
- Provide plenty of variety and opportunity for experimentation remembering that your primary objective is to enhance balance and not just to enable the child to walk a balance beam or balance on a board.
- Provide numerous balance experiences utilizing various forms of equipment and relationships of the body.
- Begin with low level activities prior to introducing high level activities.
- Practice on a low bench and low balance beam is helpful prior to using a regulation beam.

It takes practice to be able to balance ones body with control in unusual positions.

SUMMARY

You will find it helpful to periodically assess the progress of your students as you implement this skill theme. Assessment of static and dynamic balance abilities can be easily done in an informal manner using the one foot balance and beam walk as your criterion. You should be able to answer "yes" to each of the following

Developmental Activity Teaching Progression Chart
For
Static and Dynamic Balance

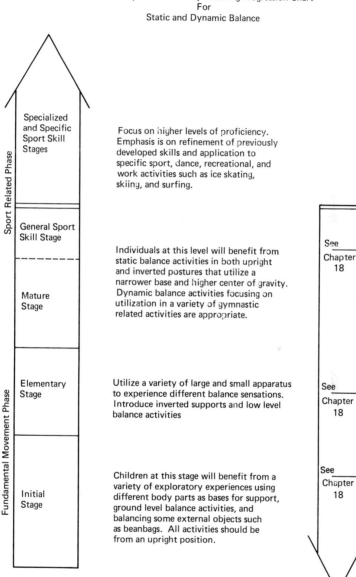

Specialized and Specific Sport Skill Stages

Focus on higher levels of proficiency. Emphasis is on refinement of previously developed skills and application to specific sport, dance, recreational, and work activities such as ice skating, skiing, and surfing.

General Sport Skill Stage

Mature Stage

Individuals at this level will benefit from static balance activities in both upright and inverted postures that utilize a narrower base and higher center of gravity. Dynamic balance activities focusing on utilization in a variety of gymnastic related activities are appropriate.

See Chapter 18

Elementary Stage

Utilize a variety of large and small apparatus to experience different balance sensations. Introduce inverted supports and low level balance activities

See Chapter 18

Initial Stage

Children at this stage will benefit from a variety of exploratory experiences using different body parts as bases for support, ground level balance activities, and balancing some external objects such as beanbags. All activities should be from an upright position.

See Chapter 18

Sport Related Phase

Fundamental Movement Phase

questions. If you cannot, you will need to make modification in your lessons to more closely meet the needs of your students.

One Foot Balance:	Yes	No	Comments
1. Can the child balance for 30 seconds on one foot?			
2. Does the child make adjustments with the arms as needed to maintain balance?			
3. Can the child balance for 10 seconds with both eyes closed?			
4. Does the child keep the non-support leg free?			
5. Does the child focus forward rather than downward?			
6. Can the child balance on either foot?			
7. Is there observable improvement?			

Beam Walk	Yes	No	Comments
1. Can the child walk a 10 foot long beam, 4 inches wide, unaided?			
2. Does the child use an alternating step?			
3. Can the child travel backward and sideways as well as forward?			
4. Does the child focus forward rather than downward?			
5. Can the child use both arms to compensate for changes in balance?			
6. Can the child change levels and direction with ease?			
7. Can the child walk independent of a spotter?			
8. Is there observable improvement?			

The development of efficient balance abilities is essential to the normal growth and development of children. Children that are at a low level in their static and dynamic balance proficiency will encounter difficulty with numerous locomotor, manipulative, and stability tasks. It is believed that several short but intensive balance themes throughout the year will be of greater benefit than only one or two longer units. The potential for including static and dynamic balance experience is almost unlimited and it is unlikely that you will run out of challenging activities.

CHAPTER 16

Body Rolling

Body rolling is a fundamental movement that requires the individual's body to move through space around its own axis while momentarily inverted. Rolling may be either forward, sideways, or backward. Children love to roll. The thrill of being up-side down along with the uncertainty of knowing where they are in space and dizziness all combine to make rolling an enjoyable activity for most children. Body rolling is a fundamental movement pattern that is integral to the sports of gymnastics and diving. It is also found in various forms in the martial arts, wrestling, and acrobatic skiing. The body awareness and spatial awareness demanded of the individual in any activity that involves rotating the body around its own axis is tremendous. Therefore, it is important that children have many and varied opportunities to develop their body rolling abilities.

The developmental sequence for rolling found on the following pages is limited to the forward roll. At the present time there is not ample experimental or observational information available to establish a developmental sequence for the sideways roll or the backward roll. When planning a skill theme around body rolling you may find it helpful to utilize the following sequence of progression:

1. *Preplanning:* Determine the approximate amount of time you wish to focus on rolling as a skill theme. Locate a sufficient number of tumbling mats for the class. Study the verbal and visual description for the forward roll on the following page.
2. *Observing and Assessing:* Based on the above information, informally

assess the group or individual children on their body rolling abilities. Determine if they are at the initial, elementary, or mature levels or beyond.

3. *Planning and Implementing:* Study the Teaching Tips and Concepts Children Should Know found on pages 268–270. Based on the information and the results of your observations consult the Developmental Activity Teaching Progression Chart found on page 271.

4. *Evaluation and Revision:* Informally reassess rolling in terms of improved mechanics. The questions found in the Summary on page 275 should guide your evaluation. Modify your remaining lessons to more closely suit specific individual and group needs.

FORWARD ROLL

Developmental Sequence Checklist

Initial Stage:
- Head definitely contacts surface
- Body curled in loose "C" position
- Inability to coordinate use of the arms
- Cannot get over backward or sideways
- Uncurls to "L" position after rolling forward

Elementary Stage:
- After rolling forward, actions appear segmented
- Head leads action rather than inhibiting it
- Head still touches surface
- Body curled in tight "C" position at onset of roll
- Uncurls at completion of roll
- Hands and arms aid rolling action somewhat but supply little push-off
- Can perform only one roll at a time
- Back of head lightly touches surface

Mature Stage:
- Head leads the action
- The head only *lightly* touches the surface
- Body remains in tight "C" throughout
- Arms aid in force production
- Momentum returns child to starting position
- Performs consecutive rolls in control

Visual Discription Checklist

Initial Stage:

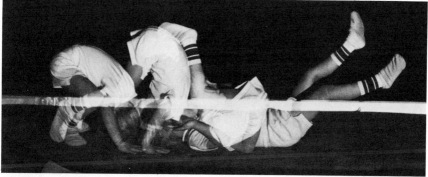

Elementary Stage:

Mature Stage:

Teaching Tips

Common Problems

- Failure to move in a straight line
- Failure to keep tucked in a small "ball"
- Failure to keep the limbs close to the body
- Failure to use the hands to absorb body weight and to aid in pushing the body over
- Placing the front or top of the head on the mat
- Uneven push-off with the hands or legs causing a "lopsided" roll
- Inability to utilize the forces of the body in a coordinated manner
- Inability to perform consecutive rolls
- Dizziness

Recommendations

- Use mats whenever possible.
- A grassy area or carpet will be adequate if mats are not available.
- Provide careful spotting wherever *needed*.
- It is not necessary to spot every child individually. If individual spotting is desired instruct the children in how it is done.
- Insist on good spotting when it is used.
- Work crossways on the mats to permit maximum practice.
- Use a block of wood and a tennis ball to demonstrate the difference between a round object (our curled body) and a nonrounded object (our uncurled body) when rolling.
- Set up four or five mat stations (forward roll mat, backward roll mat, combination mat, advanced mat, and trouble mat) stationing yourself wherever children need specific instruction.
- Begin with an exploratory approach but be sure that the movement challenges you present are within the ability level of your children.
- Use a directed discovery approach to facilitate an understanding of why the body moves as it does and how it moves when rolling.
- Children will often be at diverse levels of ability within a class. Be sure to provide experiences that meet the individual needs of each child. This will require diversity and creativity in teaching.

Concepts Children Should Know

Skill Concepts

 —Stay tucked in a small ball throughout your roll.
 —Use your hands to push-off so as little of your head touches the floor as possible.
 —Keep your chin against your chest.
 —Push off evenly with both hands.
 —If you stay tucked during your roll you will come all the way back to your starting position.
 —Focus your eyes on an object in front or behind you to help you roll in a straight line.
 —Rolling is basic to the sports of gymnastics and diving and plays an important part in wrestling and the martial arts.

Movement Concepts

 —You can roll in many directions.
 —You can roll from different levels.

A wide variety of body rolling variations need to be explored.

—You can roll using a variety of body positions.

—You can roll with objects and with people.

—You can roll at different speeds and with different amounts of force.

—Your roll can be smooth and coordinated or it can be disjointed and jerky.

—You can combine rolling with a variety of other activities.

Exploratory Activities

The use of movement exploration with rolling is intended to give children an opportunity to get the feel of being in a momentarily inverted position. Care should be taken, however, to be sure that these activities are geared to the ability level of the individual. Exploration for children at the initial stage should be different than that at the elementary stage. At the initial stage, exploration should be limited to movement variations of rocking, rolling along the long axis, and the forward roll. Exploration at the elementary stage may include the use of objects, combinations, and the sideward and backward rolls.

The same principles involved in rolling a tire are used in rolling the body.

Developmental Activity Teaching Progression Chart
For
Body Rolling

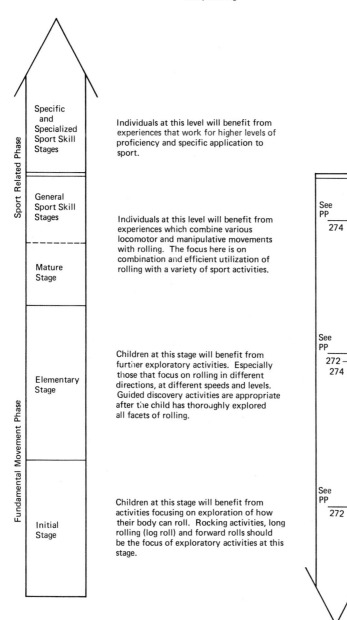

Sport Related Phase

Specific and Specialized Sport Skill Stages

Individuals at this level will benefit from experiences that work for higher levels of proficiency and specific application to sport.

General Sport Skill Stages

Mature Stage

Individuals at this level will benefit from experiences which combine various locomotor and manipulative movements with rolling. The focus here is on combination and efficient utilization of rolling with a variety of sport activities.

Fundamental Movement Phase

Elementary Stage

Children at this stage will benefit from further exploratory activities. Especially those that focus on rolling in different directions, at different speeds and levels. Guided discovery activities are appropriate after the child has thoroughly explored all facets of rolling.

Initial Stage

Children at this stage will benefit from activities focusing on exploration of how their body can roll. Rocking activities, long rolling (log roll) and forward rolls should be the focus of exploratory activities at this stage.

See PP 274

See PP 272 – 274

See PP 272

BODY ROLLING

Can you roll—

Effort	Space	Relationships
Force	*Level*	*Objects*
—as quietly as you can?	—from as low as you can go?	—on the mat?
—as loudly as you can?	—from as high as you can go?	—between the blue panels?
—so I cannot hear you?	—in a medium position?	—through the hoop?
—(rock) back and forth very hard?		—down the mat?
—(rock) very softly?	*Direction*	—over the rolled mat?
	—forward?	—on the bench?
Time	—sideways?	—while holding onto a ball?
—very fast?	—backward?	
—very slowly?	—in a straight line?	*People*
—in slow motion?		—with a partner?
—at your regular speed?	*Range*	—at the same time as your partner?
—(rock) fast?	—from a wide base?	—together?
—(rock) slowly?	—from a narrow base?	—and move apart?
	—in your own space?	—like twins?
Flow	—with your head touching the ground?	
—in a tight ball?	—without your head touching the mat?	**Combinations**
—in four separate steps?		After ample opportunity has been provided for free exploration of the various elements of rolling you may want to combine them. For example: Can you roll forward with a wide base from a high level?
—in one smooth motion?		
—in a jerky motion?		
—(rock) to my beat?		

Guided Discovery Activities

The activities that follow are intended to lead the child from the elementary to the mature levels. The movement challenges you present should be fun, challenging and help the child focus on the proper mechanics for the body rolling.

1. First, explore several of the movement variations and combinations of rolling found on page 272.
2. Then, begin to place limitations on the response possibilities to the movement challenges you present. For example:

General—

a. Try rocking back and forth from many different positions. How many ways can you find? Did you notice anything special when you were rocking on your front, or your back, or your side? Did you keep your body straight or did you curve your body? Why?

Trunk—
    b. Does your head do anything special when you rock? Why do you think you tuck your chin in when you rock on your back or from side to side? Try it with your head up. Does it work as well? Why not?

    c. When we do a forward roll do we keep our body curved or straight? Can anyone show me how curved they make their body when getting ready for a forward roll?

Head—
    d. What do you do with your head? Do you keep it up or curve it way down to your chest? Show me how your body and your head looks when you do your forward roll. Practice rolling.

Arms—
    e. What do we do with our hands and arms when we roll forward? Try it, then tell me. So our hands help us? How? See if you can use your hands more as you roll. Try it.

Feet—
    f. Can our feet help us when we roll? What can they do? Why does a good push off help? Show me.

Combination—
    g. Let's put it all together. Make a good tight ball with your body and head, push off with your feet, use your hands to catch your weight as you come over.

Finish—
    h. If we want to come right back to our feet what should we do? Try it. Can you get to your feet without using your hands to push you off?

3. After the mature rolling pattern comes under the child's control you will want to provide numerous opportunities for varying the pattern and combining it with other activities. For example:
    a. Consecutive forward rolls
    b. Wide base forward rolls
    c. One-handed rolls
    d. No-handed rolls
    e. Rolls along a bench
    f. Partner rolls (Eskimo Rolls)

You will also find it helpful to introduce the sideways and backward rolls using many of the same guided discovery activities used for the forward roll. Variations and combinations of these body rolling patterns can be elaborated upon also once the mature stage has been obtained. For example:
    a. backward roll to a squat
    b. backward roll to a stand
    c. backward straddle roll
    d. backward roll to a momentary handstand
    e. combination forward and backward rolls

Learning about balance begins early in life.

Skill Development Activities

The major focus for the child who has obtained the mature patterns of body rolling is on fluidity, versatility, and adaptability. If this is kept in mind you will be able to develop a multitude of ideas that are both challenging and fun. More importantly, however, you will contribute directly to the child's ability to apply the movement skills and movement concepts of body rolling to a variety of sport-related activities.

In order to focus more fully on higher skill levels of body rolling you will find it helpful to:

1. Return to the exploratory activities found on page 272. Attention should now, however, be given to more complex combinations of effort, space, and relationships.
2. Incorporate additional problem-solving activities into the lesson such as these found in Chapter 18.
3. Incorporate a variety of stunts and tumbling activities into the lesson.

SUMMARY

Throughout presentation of the body rolling skill theme you will want to make periodic checks on the progress of individuals or the group. Assessment of progress can be done both easily and informally as you observe small groups of four or five at one time. You should be able to answer "yes" to each of the following questions. If you are unable to do so you will need to make modification in your lessons to more closely meet the needs of the group or individuals within the group.

Body Rolling

(forward, backward, and/or sideways):	Yes	No	Comments
1. Does the child curve the body adequately?			
2. Does the child tuck the head?			
3. Does the child push off evenly with both feet?			
4. Does the child take the body weight on the hands and arms?			
5. Does the head and body stay tucked in throughout the roll?			
6. Is the child able to keep the front and top of the head from touching the mat?			
7. Can the child come to his/her feet unaided immediatly after the roll?			
8. Is the child able to travel in a straight line?			
9. Can the child perform consecutive rolls?			
10. Is there observable improvement?			

Body rolling movements are transitional postures in which the individual is required to maintain stability while the center of gravity is constantly shifting. Some may classify these fundamental movements as locomotor movements in nature because of the obvious change in body location from the start to the finish of a roll. They have, however, been viewed as stability movements here because of the *premium* which is placed on maintaining one's equilibrium during performance. Rolling is in essence the controlled loss and regaining of one's balance while moving through space in a momentarily inverted posture. Its importance can not be overemphasized nor can the necessity for including it as a fundamental movement skill theme.

CHAPTER 17

Dodging

Dodging is a fundamental movement ability common to the game, sport, and play activities of children and adults. Dodging is often accompanied with running and involves quick, deceptive changes in direction. In the running dodge the knees bend, the center of gravity moves lower, and the body weight is shifted rapidly in a sideways direction. Dodging may also occur from a stationary position and may involve a number of axial movements including bending, twisting, stretching, or falling.

Dodging is an important element in chasing and fleeing games and the dodgeball game of childhood. It is also an important element in the sports of football, hockey, soccer, baseball, rugby, and lacrosse. Because of the natural combination of running with dodging you may wish to group these two movement patterns into a common skill theme. The following planning sequence may be helpful:

1. *Preplanning:* determine when and for how long you wish to focus on dodging as a skill theme. Be sure that you have ample space free from obstructions

2. *Observing and Assessing:* study the verbal and visual description provided below for each stage of dodging. Then informally assess the dodging abilities of the class or group. Determine if they are at the initial, elementary, or mature stage.

3. *Planning and Implementing:* study the Teaching Tips and Concepts Children Should Know found on pages 279–280. Based on this information and your assessment information, select appropriate activities using

the Developmental Activity Teaching Progression Chart located on page 281 as your guide.

4. *Evaluation and Revision:* periodically reassess dodging in terms of improved mechanics. Use the questions found in the Summary on page 285 as a guide. Modify your lessons to more closely suit specific individual and group needs.

DODGING

Developmental Sequence Checklist

Initial Stage:
- −Definite segmented movements
- −Body appears stiff
- −Little knee bend
- −Weight is on total foot
- −Feet generally cross
- −No deception

Elementary Stage:
- −Movements coordinated but little deception
- −Performs better to one side than the other
- −Too much vertical lift
- −Feet may occasionally cross
- −Little spring in movement
- −Sometimes "outsmarts" self and becomes confused

Mature Stage:
- −Knees bent, slight trunk lean forward (ready position)
- −Fluid directional changes
- −Performs equally well in all directions
- −Head and shoulder fake
- −Good lateral movement

Visual Description Checklist

Initial Stage:

Elementary Stage:

Mature Stage:

Teaching Tips

Common Problems:

- Inability to fluidly shift the body weight in the intended direction of movement
- Slow to react
- Lack of deceptive movement
- Failure to bend at the knees
- Failure to shift the body weight back over the base of support during the initial change in direction
- Failure to bend at the knees in preparation for changing direction

Recommendations

- Stress bending at the knees in anticipation of dodging.
- Begin with activities that require changing direction on a cue or verbal command.
- Explore various aspects of dodging in conjunction with effort, space, and relationships.
- *Avoid* dodgeball activities as a central focus of the dodging skill theme.
- Utilize a limited amount of dodgeball-type activities only after the child has reached the mature level.
- Stress the necessity for quickness and deception.
- Work on dodging in all directions. Avoid activities in which only one direction is stressed.

Concepts Children Should Know

Skill Concepts

- Stop your movement suddenly and shift your body weight rapidly to one side.
- Keep your center of gravity low for better balance.
- You keep your center of gravity over your base of support for balance, but you must put your body weight outside your base momentarily in order to dodge with quickness and deception.
- Use your head, shoulders, eyes, or trunk to fake the new direction of your intended movement.
- Dodging is an important element in tagging and dodgeball games as well as sports such as football, basketball, lacrosse, soccer, and hockey.

Movement Concepts

- You can alter the effort that you use in your dodging to fit the demands of the situation.
- Your dodge can be altered in the amount of force applied, speed of performance, and flow.
- You can alter the space component in which you dodge.
- You can dodge in different directions and at different levels.

Dodging is one of the most exciting elements in sport.

Exploratory Activities

Exploratory activities at the initial and elementary stages of dodging enable the child to get the general idea of how dodging is performed. More importantly, however, these activities insure that the child begins to recognize the utility of dodging and its many movement variations. For children at the initial and elementary stage it is recommended that the dodging of objects not be included in the lesson unless a very light and harmless ball is used.

Developmental Activity Teaching Progression Chart
For Dodging

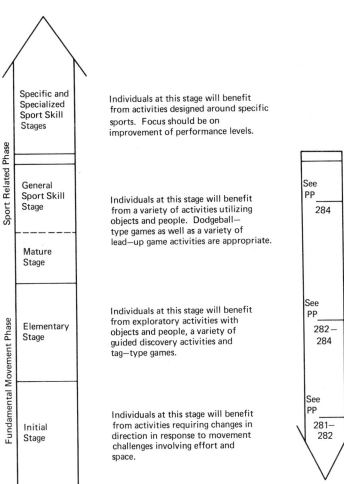

Specific and
Specialized
Sport Skill
Stages

Individuals at this stage will benefit
from activities designed around specific
sports. Focus should be on
improvement of performance levels.

Sport Related Phase

General
Sport Skill
Stage

Individuals at this stage will benefit
from a variety of activities utilizing
objects and people. Dodgeball—
type games as well as a variety of
lead—up game activities are appropriate.

See
PP
284

Mature
Stage

Fundamental Movement Phase

Elementary
Stage

Individuals at this stage will benefit
from exploratory activities with
objects and people, a variety of
guided discovery activities and
tag—type games.

See
PP
282—
284

Initial
Stage

Individuals at this stage will benefit
from activities requiring changes in
direction in response to movement
challenges involving effort and
space.

See
PP
281—
282

DODGING

Can you dodge—

Effort	Space	Relationships
Force	*Level*	*Objects*
—with great force?	—from a high level?	—a fleece ball?
—with no force?	—from a low level?	—a playground ball?
—with some force?	—from a high to a low level?	—a tossed ball?
	—from a low to a high level?	—a rolled ball?
Time	—keeping yourself at a medium level?	
—as fast as you can?		*People*
—as slow as you can?		—a person chasing you from behind?
—alternating fast and slow dodges?	*Direction*	—a person in front of you?
—at a medium speed?	—in different directions?	—in the same direction as your partner?
—with a burst of energy?	—sideways?	—in the opposite direction as your partner?
	—to your left?	
Flow	—to your right?	
—smoothly?	—backward?	**Combinations**
—roughly?	—forward?	After ample opportunities have been provided for free exploration of the various elements of dodging you may want to combine them, for example: can you dodge a rolled ball as fast as you can from a low level to a high level?
	Range	
	—and concentrate on making different body shapes?	
	—while staying in your own space?	
	—assessing all the space you need?	
	—while on one foot?	
	—without using your arms?	

Guided Discovery Activities

The following sampling of guided discovery activities are intended to help the child focus on the process of dodging itself. Initial experiences will focus on exploration but the final objective is to lead the child to the mature skill of dodging in which the proper mechanics are used. You may find the following guided discovery activities helpful.

1. First, have the children explore several of the variations of dodging found on the previous page.

Dodging is an integral aspect of chasing and fleeing games.

2. Then begin to place limitations on the response possibilities to the movement challenges you present. For example:

General—

a. Can you run forward and change direction quickly? Try it while running backward and sideways. What do you do when you change directions quickly? Do you do the same thing when moving in different directions? Why?

Leg action—

b. Try to tag your partner who is facing you. What does your partner do to try to avoid your touch? What does she/he do with her/his feet and legs? Why are her/his knees bent and the feet apart? Now, you try it, but try dodging your partner's touch from a position with your legs straight and starting with your feet together. Which way do you think works best? Try both ways. You're right, but, why is it better to dodge from a standing position with your feet apart and your knees bent?

Faking—

c. From a position facing your partner, try to avoid his/her tags while using deceptive (sneaking) movements of your head, eyes, or trunk. Does it work? What do you do with these body parts when you want to fake out your partner? Look at your starting position. Are your feet apart and your knees slightly bent? Don't forget to use that as your ready position and then use other body parts to give the impression that you are going one way but actually go the other.

Leg action—

d. Now try dodging your partner while being chased. What do you do to avoid being tagged? When you dodge to the right what do you do with your legs? Why does your right leg step out to one side as you pivot? Show me how you can do it to the opposite side.

e. Do you find it easier to dodge from a run in one direction than the other? Why? Let's practice dodging to our weak side.

3. When the mature dodging action has been reasonably well mastered you will want to combine dodging with other activities. Often children can dodge satisfactorally in an isolated experience. However, when placed in a situation requiring dodging an oncoming object or a complicated game that utilizes dodging as only one of many elements of the game, children often become confused and unable to dodge with proficiency. Activities such as those that follow will help develop more integrated utilization of dodging.

a. Dodge one or more persons while running across the playfield.

b. Dodge oncoming objects.

c. Use dodging manuevers to advance a ball downfield or down court. You can run, dribble, or kick a ball while dodging.

Skill Development Activities

After dodging has been mastered and can be performed consistently at the mature stage in a variety of play and game situations, it is appropriate to begin focusing on higher levels of skill development. Improved performance in terms of speed of movement, deception, fluidity, and control are the primary goals of movement experiences at this level. Dodging is an essential element of numerous sports amd must be executed with a high degree of skill in order to maximize success. Failure to reach the mature stage of dodging will hamper the individual attempting to combine this skill in football, soccer, basketball, wrestling, lacrosse, field hockey and numerous other activities. In order to avoid this you will find it helpful to:

1. Return to the exploratory activities found on page 282. Focus now on activities that utilize more extensive combinations of effort, space, and relationships.

2. Incorporate additional problem-solving activities in the lesson such as those found in Chapter 18.
3. Incorporate a variety of chasing and fleeing games into the lesson such as those found in Chapter 9.
4. Begin focusing on the application of dodging in a variety of activities such as:
   a. Soccer skills
   b. Football skills
   c. Basketball skills
   d. Wrestling skills
   e. Hockey skills

SUMMARY

Periodically during the course of implementing the dodging skill theme you will want to informally assess the progress of the group as individuals. Observational assessment during a game of tag or Steal the Bacon, should be adequate. If you are not able to answer "yes" to each of the following questions you will need to make modifications in your lessons to suit the specific needs of your students:

Dodging:	Yes	No	Comments
1. Can the child dodge a partner from a facing position?			
2. Can the child effectively dodge a partner from a fleeing position?			
3. Does the child dodge well in all directions?			
4. Is the child able to combine dodging with other game skills?			
5. Does the child use deceptive movements when dodging?			
6. Is the action quick, fluid, and in control?			
7. Is there observable improvement?			

Dodging is a developmental skill theme that may be incorporated with running, chasing, and fleeing. It is an important stability ability that makes many demands on the body's balance apparatus and is used in a variety of sport activities. Dodging abilities tend to improve as a function of both age and experience. Reaction time decreases as children mature but practice in dodging has also been shown to further enhance this important fundamental movement ability.

18

Individualized Stability Activities

The development and refinement of fundamental stability abilities is the most basic aspect of learning to move. Without the ability to maintain one's equilibrium, purposeful locomotor and manipulative movements are impossible. Children who are exposed to a variety of movement situations generally develop stability abilities with little difficulty. On the other hand, children who do not have a varied background of movement experiences often lag behind in the development of their stability abilities.

When we use the term "stability," it goes beyond the notion of static and dynamic balance. Stability requires the ability to sense a shift in the relationship of the body parts which alter one's balance along with the ability to compensate rapidly and accurately for these changes with appropriate compersate rapidly and accurately for these changes with appropriate compensating movements. Therefore stability encompasses nonlocomotor or axial movements as they are often called, as well as static, dynamic, and transitional body positions in which a *premium* is placed on the maintenance of equilibrium.

PROBLEM-SOLVING ACTIVITIES

Although the rudimentary stability abilities of infancy (control of the head, neck, and trunk; sitting and standing) are primarily maturationally determined, it would be a mistake to assume that the same is true with the development of fundamental stability abilities. Children need exposure to a variety of movement situations in which they have ample opportunity to explore and experiment with the movement dimension of stability. The activities contained in the following pages are dedicated to that end.

Objectives

1. To enhance nonlocomotor movement abilities.
2. To enhance dynamic balance.
3. To enhance static balance.
4. To develop increased abilities to gain and maintain one's equilibrium.

Movement Experiences

Bending Bending involves bringing one body part to another with a curling action produced by the body's parts. The following is a sampling of problem-solving activities involving bending:

1. How many ways can you bend?
2. How many parts of your body can you bend down?
3. Bend up the parts of your body that you can.

Can you touch the ground with three body parts?

4. Can you bend parts of your body when you are: (1) sitting down, (2) lying on your front, (3) lying on your back, (4) lying on your side, (5) kneeling, and (6) walking?

5. How many ways can you bend your head? What parts of your body can you touch by bending your head?

6. How many different ways can you bend your arms, wrist, fingers, legs, knees, ankles, and toes?

7. Can you bend up and down at the same time?

8. Can you bend to one side; to the other?

9. Can you connect parts of your body by hooking them together at the bends? Can you do that with a partner?

10. Can you make yourself smaller by bending?

Stretching Stretching is an unfolding motion at the joints. Stretching involves moving the joints in such a manner that there is a marked upward, outward, or downward movement of the body parts (extension). Stretching is the opposite of bending.

The body can stretch in many different ways.

1. How many parts of your body can you stretch?
2. Can you stretch your arms up, down, and to the sides?
3. How far can you stretch? (How tall can you make yourself?)
4. How wide can you make your arms, hands, and legs? (for example, how big can you make your arms?)
5. How many different ways (directions) can your body stretch at the same time?
6. How much of the floor can you cover by stretching?
7. Can you make two parts of your body touch by stretching
8. Can you combine stretching and bending movements to show how they differ?

Twisting Twisting involves rotation of one body part in relation to another. The body parts are turned in opposite directions or partially rotated while the remainder of the body remains in a fixed position.

1. Can you twist your head without using anything else?
2. Can you twist your shoulders without moving your waist?
3. Can you twist the whole top part of your body and then the whole bottom part of the body?
4. Can you twist your arms, wrists, leg, ankles, fingers, and toes?
5. Can you twist your arms around each other? Can you twist your legs around each other? Can you twist your arms and legs around each other?
6. Can you twist like a screwdriver?
7. Can you twist while standing on one foot? Can you twist while lying on your back, side, and front?
8. Can you twist the same body parts as a partner that is facing you?
9. Can you do the twist to music (fast or slow)?

Turning Turning is a movement in which the entire body revolves around its vertical or horizontal axis while in an extended or flexed position. The head serves as the controlling factor for the body.

1. Can you turn your body to make a circle?
2. Can you turn and make half a circle?
3. Can you turn quickly? Can you turn slowly? If you change the position of your arms what happens to your turn?
4. Can you turn without moving your head? Can you turn your head without moving your body?
5. Lying on the floor, how many different ways can you turn?
6. Kneeling on the floor, how many ways can you turn? Can your hands help?
7. Bend and turn your body to the right; to the left? Is one way easier?

Swinging Swinging is a pendular motion in which one end of the body remains fixed while the other parts move freely back and forth, forming an arc.

1. How many parts of your body can you swing? Can you swing them in different directions?
2. Can you swing quickly? Can you swing slowly?
3. Swing one arm and one leg. Can you swing them in different directions?
4. Can you swing your body at different levels, standing up, and bending over?
5. Can you swing from a bar? How do your legs help?
6. Can you swing from a bar and drop off at the end of the arc?
7. Can you travel on a horizontal ladder while hanging and swinging?
8. Can you swing from a bar and drop off at the front part of your swing?

Dodging Dodging is a movement in which the body is moved quickly in a direction other than the original line of movement.

1. How can you get out of the way of a ball that is coming right at you? Can you do it by stretching, bending, or jumping?
2. Can you dodge (change direction) with feet close together, wide apart, or on one foot? Which is easier?

Innovative playground equipment offers numerous opportunities to develop locomotor and stability abilities.

3. Can you dodge as high as you can, then as low as you can?
4. Can you run and change directions when I clap?
5. Can you dodge around an obstacle (chair, cones, other students, etc.)?
6. Look into a large mirror and practice dodging.
7. Can you face a partner and move laterally or forward and backward in the direction she/he points?
8. Can you dodge a partner who is trying to tag you?

Landing Landing is a movement that requires the individual to regain balance after a brief flight in the air. The force is taken on the balls of the feet, and ankles, knees, and hip joint bend upon impact.

1. How many ways can you land after jumping?
2. Can you land all the time without falling down?
3. Can you land with your feet together; apart? Which is easier?
4. Can you land without bending? Is it easier to bend?
5. Can you land and regain your balance with your arms at your sides, out straight, or up in the air? Which is easier?
6. Can you land on one foot and regain your balance?
7. Can you land on your feet and hands?
8. Can you make a turn in the air before landing?

Stopping Stopping involves coming to a halt with the feet in a stride position and the knees slightly bent.

1. Run and then "freeze" with your arms, legs, and other body parts in various positions.
2. Run and stop when I clap.
3. How many positions can your feet be in when you stop? Which is the easiest?
4. Stop on your whole foot, on the toes, and on the heels.
5. Run with a partner and stop on command.
6. Play a game of red light–green light.

Rolling Rolling involves moving through space in either a forward, backward, or sideways direction while the body is momentarily inverted. Rolling is considered to be a stability movement because of the premium placed on maintaining one's equilibrium.

1. How many ways can you roll (forward, backward, or sideways)?
2. Can you make yourself small and roll, or big and roll?
3. Can you roll with straight legs, bent legs, and legs apart?
4. Can you change your arm, leg, head, or body position when you finish your roll?

5. Can you stand up after your roll? Can you stand up and turn around after your roll?
6. Can you roll with a playground ball in your hand?
7. Can you perform consecutive rolls?
8. Can you roll in unison with a partner?
9. Can you combine forward, backward, and sideways rolls into a routine?

Upright Supports Upright supports are static balance activities in which the body is required to balance in a variety of positions while the center of gravity remains stationary.

1. Can you balance on different body parts (feet, knees, seat, back, and front)?
2. Can you balance on different objects (see following section)?
3. Can you balance at different levels? Which is easiest or hardest? Why?
4. Can you balance with your eyes closed?
5. Can you balance with a partner?
6. Can you balance with various objects (see following section)?

Inverted Supports Inverted supports involve supporting the body in an upside-down position for at least 3 seconds. An inverted support is generally considered to be one in which the shoulders are above the base of support and the feet and legs above the shoulders.

1. Can you find ways to balance with your feet above your shoulders?
2. Can you perform a tripod (head and hands form a tripod and balance the body in a tucked position)?
3. Can you perform a tip-up (from a squat position, the elbows push out on the knees as the body tips forward and balances)?
4. Can you balance on your head and hands (headstand)?
5. Can you find different ways to do a headstand?
6. How many different ways can you balance in an inverted position?

ACTIVITIES WITH SMALL EQUIPMENT

There are a variety of pieces of small equipment that may be used to enhance stability abilities. Although some of this equipment (for example, beanbags and ropes) is generally associated with manipulative and locomotor activities, it is possible to design numerous activities that place a great deal of emphasis on stability. The activity ideas that follow are a mere sampling of the almost endless variety possible. Keep in mind that it is important to first identify the specific movement abilities you desire to enhance and then to select appropriate activities, rather than proceeding in the reverse order.

Objectives

1. To enhance fundamental stability abilities.
2. To enhance static balance abilities.
3. To enhance dynamic balance abilities.

Movement Experiences

Balance Boards Balance boards are easily constructed and offer a variety of challenging activities. For young children a mat should be placed under the balance board to avoid slipping.

The balance board is an excellent piece of equipment for enhancing static balance.

1.   Balance on the board any way you can.
2.   Can you balance with your feet apart?
3.   Can you balance with your feet together?
4.   Can you balance with your arms out from the sides?
5.   Can you balance with your arms at your sides?
6.   Can you balance with your eyes closed?
7.   Can you squat down and balance?
8.   Can you squat half-way down and balance?
9.   Can you balance with a beanbag or eraser on your head?
10. Can you balance and catch a ball?
11. Can you toss a ball while balancing?
12. Can you throw at a target while balancing?
13. Can you balance on one foot?
14. Can you bounce a ball while balancing?
15. Can you touch various body parts while balancing?
16. Can you step from one balance board to another?
17. Can you balance with a partner on another board while holding hands?
18. Can you toss and catch a ball while balancing?
19. Can you turn around on the board?

Balance Blocks Balance blocks may be cut to various sizes depending on the age and ability level of the children; they should be about 12 inches long and made out of 4 feet by 4 feet, 2 feet by 2 feet, or 2 feet by 4 feet sections of board. They should be placed on a surface that is not slippery.

1.   Can you balance on both feet?
2.   Can you balance on one foot?
3.   Can you touch various body parts while balancing?
4.   Can you balance at various levels?
5.   Can you balance and catch a ball?
6.   Can you balance and bounce a ball?
7.   Can you balance and toss and catch a ball to yourself?
8.   Can you balance with a partner?
9.   Can you turn around while balancing?
10. Can you find new ways to balance?

Coffee-Can Stilts Coffee can stilts are easily made from metal coffee containers and  a length of rope. They offer a new dimension to stability because the center of gravity is raised, thus making balancing more difficult

1. Can you walk in various directions (forward, sideways, and backward)?
2. Can you step over a low object?
3. Can you step under objects?
4. Can you walk at various levels (high, low, and medium)?
5. Can you walk at various speeds?
6. Can you hop on one foot?
7. Can you jump forward?
8. Can you have races on the coffee can stilts?
9. Can you move a disk forward while walking on the stilts?

Barrels Barrels may be obtained from a janitorial supply company or oil distributor. They make an excellent piece of equipment for enhancing dynamic balance abilities and serve as containers for storing equipment. However, they must be closely supervised.

1. Can you sit on the barrel and balance?
2. Can you balance on your stomach, back, or knees?
3. Can you stand on the barrel and balance?
4. Can you balance at different levels?
5. Can you touch various body parts while balancing?
6. Can you walk on the barrel, moving it forward or backward?
7. Can you stand on the barrel and bounce and catch a ball?
8. Can you and a partner balance on the barrel in any of the above ways?

Wands Wands can be easily made from ¾-foot dowling cut to 4-foot lengths. A variety of balance principles may be illustrated with wands as well as numerous challenging activities.

1. Can you balance the wand on the floor horizontally, then vertically? Which is easiest, or hardest? Why?
2. Can you balance your wand vertically, clap your hands, and grab it before it falls to the ground?
3. Can you run around your wand while it is balancing and catch it before falling to the ground?
4. Can you balance the wand horizontally on a variety of body parts (palm of hand, finger, foot, and forehead)?
5. Can you balance your wand vertically on a variety of body parts?
6. What do your eyes do when balancing the wand? Where do they look?
7. Can you move about while balancing your wand on various body parts?
8. Can you balance your wand while moving from a standing to a sitting position?
9. Who can balance their wand the longest?
10. Can you balance your wand either horizontally or vertically and transfer it from one body part to another?

Balance Ropes When placed on the floor, ropes can serve as a simple means of developing knowledge about balancing without any fear on the part of the child. When balancing on ropes the children should perform in their bare feet in order to enhance the tactile stimulation. The

ropes may be placed in a variety of configurations and you may wish to heighten the interest by developing an appropriate story play such as one about a high-wire walker at the circus.

1. Can you walk in various directions (forward, backward, and sideways?
2. Can you walk at various levels (high, medium, and low)?
3. Can you walk and step over objects?
4. Can you walk and step under objects?
5. Can you step from one rope to another?
6. Can you jump from one rope to another?
7. Can you walk the rope with your eyes closed?
8. Can you find new ways to walk and balance on the rope?

Inner Tubes Inner tubes may be obtained from tire-salvage stores. Use large truck tubes or airplane inner tubes if possible. Be sure to secure the valve and stem of each inner tube prior to use in order to avoid any safety hazards.

1. Can you walk around the tube?

Inner tubes are an excellent means for developing dynamic balance abilities.

2. Can you move in different directions, levels and at different speeds while walking around the tube?
3. Can you jump up and down on the tube (spot carefully)?
4. Can you jump onto the tube, jump into the center, jump back on, and then off the opposite side?
5. Can you repeat the above activity using different variations?
6. Can you sit on the tube and bounce?
7. Can you balance on the tube while someone is bouncing it?
8. Can you do a knee bounce on the tube? From a standing position near the tube bounce, on the knees, returning to a controlled standing position. Repeat three or four times.
9. Can you do a feet bounce? From a standing position on the tube, bounce on both feet, bending the knees slightly. To obtain height, raise the arms forward and upward. Do this at first with a spotter holding the wrist. Do in a series.
10. Can you do a seat drop? Stand 1−2 feet away from the tube with your back to the tube. Kick your legs out, landing on your seat supported by the hands near hips. Bounce back to a standing position.
11. Can you bounce with a partner? Partners, holding hands, stand on top of the tube facing each other. Partners bounce on both feet all the way around the tube to the right and then to the left.

Beanbags Although generally thought of as a manipulative piece of equipment, beanbags serve as an excellent piece of equipment for enhancing stability abilities. Among the numerous possibilities for activity are the following:

1. What does it feel like? What is inside?
2. Can you drop it and pick it up without moving your feet?
3. Can you drop it and pick it up without bending your knees?
4. Can you drop it so you must stretch to pick it up? Without moving your feet?
5. Can you move it around your body without dropping it?

6. How many ways can you balance while the beanbag is on one part of your body, then on another part?
7. Can you keep it balanced while you are moving around the room?
8. Can you move the beanbags from one place to another and not drop it?
9. Can you move it with other parts of your body?
10. Can you move it from your feet to your hands?
11. Can you move it from your feet to your head, then shoulder?
12. Can you balance your beanbag on a body part and exchange it to the same body part on your partner without using your hands?

ACTIVITIES WITH LARGE EQUIPMENT

At the preschool and elementary-grade levels the use of large equipment is often limited. The cost of commercially purchased apparatus often makes it prohibitive for nursery and elementary schools to purchase traditional gymnastic equipment such as side horses, parallel bars, and turning bars. There are, however, a number of pieces of equipment particularly beneficial to young children. Some may be hand made but others must be purchased commercially. Among these pieces of equipment are the balance beam, benches, bounding board, trampoline, horizontal ladder, and "Lind climber." The following is a compilation of numerous activities utilizing large equipment appropriate for use with preschool and elementary-grade children.

Objectives

1. To enhance fundamental stability abilities on a variety of large equipment.
2. To enhance dynamic balance abilities on a variety of large equipment.

Movement Experiences

Balance Beam The balance beam is an extremely useful piece of equipment. It may be purchased commercially or made in a variety of ways for only a few dollars.

1. Walking on a single beam:
   a. Walking forward and backward with arms at different positions (held forward, sideways, overhead, behind back, on head, etc).
   b. Side-step with hands in various positions. Use for closing steps, crossing front and rear, alternating crossing.
   c. Walk forward, backward, using follow steps.
   d. Move forward with one step for halfway; complete the trip with another step.
   e. Perform dip walks from one end of the beam to the other.

The balance beam is a versatile piece of equipment.

f.   Walk forward and backward to middle of the beam, kneel on one knee; straighten leg forward until the heel is on the beam and knee is straight. Rise and walk to the end of the beam.

g.   Hop forward and backward on right or left foot the full length of beam. Variations: hop the length of the beam, then turn around and hop back. Hop to the middle of the beam, turn around on same foot, and hop backward to the end of the beam.

h.   Walk to the middle of the beam balance on one foot, and walk backward to the end of the beam.

i.   Walk to the middle of the beam left sideways, turn around and walk to the other end right sideways.

j.   With arm clasped behind the body to the rear, walk forward to the middle, turn around once, and walk backward the remaining distance.

k.   Place an eraser at the middle of the beam, walk out to it, kneel on one knee, place the eraser on top of the head, rise, turn around, and walk backward to the end of the beam. Variations: kneel on one knee, pick up the eraser, and place it on the beam behind you, rise, and continue to the end. Walk beam left sideways, pick up the eraser, place it on the right side of the beam, turn around, and walk right sideways to the end of the beam.

l. Walk the beam backward with an eraser balanced on the back of each hand. At the center, turn around and walk backward to the end of the beam.

m. Walk to the middle of the beam, do a right-side or left-side support, rise, and walk to the end.

n. Walk to the middle of the beam, do a balance standing on one foot, arms held sideways with the trunk and free leg held horizontally.

o. Hold the wand 15 inches above the beam. Balance an eraser on the head, walk forward, backward, and sideways right or left, stepping over the wand.

p. Have the wand held at a height of 3 feet. Walk forward and backward with hands on the hips, and pass under it.

q. Fold a piece of paper at a right angle so it will stand on the beam at the middle. Walk to the paper, kneel, do a right-side or left-side support, pick it up with teeth, rise, and walk to the end of the beam.

r. Walk the beam forward, backward, and sideways, left or right, with the eyes closed.

s. Stand on the beam (feet side by side, one foot in advance of the other, on right or left foot) with the eyes closed.

t. Partners start at opposite ends, walk to the middle, pass each other, and continue to the end of the beam.

2. Partners on two parallel beams:
   a. Walk forward, inside hands joined. Walk backward.
   b. Walk sideways with both hands joined.
   c. Walk sideways with both hands joined, using grapevine step.
   d. Alternate crossing feet behind and in front while stepping.
   e. Toss and catch a ball while balancing on the beam.

3. Throwing, catching, bouncing:
   a. Roll a volleyball or playground ball across the beam.
   b. Bounce the ball across
   c. Dribble the ball across. Bend low for short dribbles.
   d. Pass and receive from a partner at the head of the beam.
   e. Hit the ball back to a partner.

Benches Many schools have benches as part of their standard equipment. They may be used in a number of ways to enhance stability abilities.

1. Can you walk on the bench:
   a. Forward, backward, sideways?
   b. On hands and feet (cat walk)?

    c. Duck walk?
    d. Using beanbag on the head for balancing?
    e. Bounce and toss a ball?
    f. Pass a partner without touching each other?
  2. From a lying position, can you:
    a. Pull your body along, with your arms while in a prone position?
    b. From a back-lying position, balance with the body crosswise to the bench?
    c. From the above balance position, roll lengthwise along the bench?
  3. From a sitting position on the bench can you:
    a. Swing on the seat?
    b. Sitting astride, reach as far sideways as possible to touch the floor without falling off?
    c. Support your weight on your hands?
  4. Can you vault over the bench?
  5. Can you do a forward roll on the bench?
  6. Can you do a backward roll to a straddle seat on the bench?
  7. Can you find some more ways to move and balance on the bench?

Horizontal Ladder An old wooden ladder makes an ideal piece of equipment for enhancing stability abilities. Here are some appropriate activities for use with young children.

  1. From a position on the side supports can you:
    a. Walk forward?
    b. Walk backward?

    c. Bounce a ball between the rungs while walking?
    d. Walk forward on one support?
    e. Walk backward on one support?
    f. Walk sideways on one support using a step-close-step, or crossover step?

2. From a position on the rungs can you:
    a. Walk forward?
    b. Walk sideways using a follow step?
    c. Walk sideways using a crossover step?
    d. Walk backwards?

3. From a position between the rungs can you:
    a. Walk forward?
    b. Walk sideways using a follow step?
    c. Walk sideways using a crossover step?
    d. Walk backwards?

Horizontal Ladder North American children are often weak in the upper arms and
(suspended) shoulder girdle. Practice in activities on a suspended horizontal ladder are excellent for developing these groups of muscles. The following is a list of suggested activities that may be performed on a horizontal ladder, turning bar, or parallel bars.

1. Can you grab hold of one of the rungs with your thumbs around the bar and hang for 5 seconds?
2. Can you swing forward and backward?
3. Can you swing and drop off at the end of your swing? Where is it best to drop off?
4. Can you travel like a monkey from one end of the ladder to the other:
    a. Using a follow grasp?
    b. Using an alternating grasp?
5. Can you do a chin-up (palms facing child) or pull-up (palms facing away)?

6. Can you hook your knees on one bar and with your hands on the other do several pull-ups?
7. Can you hang by your knees?
8. Can you pull your knees and legs between your arms and turn over to a stand?
9. Can you "skin the cat" (same as above but return to the original hanging position without letting go)?
10. Can you get yourself up to the top of the bars and then jump off?
11. Can you travel from one end of the ladder to the other and pass a partner traveling in the opposite direction?

Bounding Board A bounding board may be easily constructed with plywood and blocks of wood measuring 4 inches by 4 inches. It provides an opportunity for young children to experience alterations in the force of gravity. Here are some activities appropriate for preschool and primary-grade children:

1. Can you bounce on both feet?
2. Can you bounce on one foot?
3. Can you bounce with right foot, left foot combinations?
4. Can you bounce with quarter, half, and full turns?
5. Can you bounce from one board to another?
6. Can you begin at one end and bounce forward, backward, or sideways?
7. Can you bounce while visually fixating on an object?
8. Can you bounce and toss a ball?
9. Can you bounce while bouncing a ball?
10. Can you bounce and catch a ball?
11. Can you bounce and toss at a target?

Trampoline The trampoline is an expensive piece of equipment and rather limited in its use due to the fact that only one person at a time can be performing on it. It also requires *close supervision*. It can, however, be very beneficial in enhancing stability abilities.

Careful supervision on the trampoline is essential to its' safe use.

1. Can you mount on the trampoline:
    a. Climbing up?
    b. Rolling forward?
    c. Vaulting up?
2. Can you walk around on the trampoline (get the "feel" of it)?
3. Can you bounce:
    a. In the center?
    b. Fixating on an object out in front without looking at the bed?
    c. Controlling your bounce?
    d. Moving the arms and legs in rhythmical coordination?
    e. Making a turn (quarter, half, three-quarters)?
    f. Touching various body parts?
    g. Tucking your knees up?
    h. Stopping on command by bending at the knees and hips?

   3. Can you perform stunts on the trampoline with:
  - **a.** Knee drop?
  - **b.** Hands and knees drop?
  - **c.** Seat drop?
  - **d.** Front drop?
  - **e.** Back drop?
  - **f.** Back roller?
  - **g.** Swivel hips?
  - **h.** Combinations of these?

   4. Can you toss and toss and catch a ball while bouncing?

SUMMARY

There are many stability skill themes that are possible through either isolation or a combination of movements. If we isolate the theme of bending for example, the following might be representative of the exploratory, discovery, and combination experiences utilized.

Theme: Bending

A. Exploratory Experiences

The teacher suggests or challenges but refrains from setting a "correct" model for performance.

1. Have straight and curved line drawings taped to walls or cones—the figure will have one or a combination of angles and/or curves that the children will mimic.
2. A similar idea might be to use pictures of objects such as trees, triangles, rocket ships, and so forth.
3. Utilize mats and small apparatus that the children can shape their bodies around and which can serve as obstacles to the direct reaching of an object.
    - (a) A cardboard box with holes in the sides might be used to cause children to reach through and bend the arm(s) in various positions in pursuit of objects within the covered box.
    - (b) The placement of a hoop or tire on the floor with a beanbag inside might lead a child to utilize his or her feet in retrieving the object.
    - (c) Obstacle course set-ups can also be incorporated here.

B. Discovery Experiences

The teacher places qualifications or limitations on movements as the children explore, discover, and share their experiences.

1. The teacher manipulates a rope or hinged stick and asks the children to mimic the figures with their bodies. The teacher with the children points out the different solutions. (Some children will use their entire body and some will use only their limbs or parts of their body).

2. The teacher qualifies the body position to be used. Bending movements can be performed with the children on their stomachs, backs, sides, and all fours.

3. The teacher qualifies the elements of movement to be utilized such as force, time, level, and flow. Bending movements can be performed slowly, rapidly, tightly, loosely, forward, sideways, and so forth.

C. Combination Experiences

1. *Indirect:* The teacher continues to qualify or limit movements so that previous movements become progressively more difficult to perform.

    (a) The teacher asks the children to combine several movements to create their own combinations.

        (1) "Can you bend two, three, or four body parts at once?"

        (2) "In how many different directions can you bend your body parts?"

    (b) The teacher may also utilize rhythm patterns or music to guide bending movements.

        (1) "Bend a different way each time you hear the drum."

        (2) "Bend your knees and walk in place to the music."

        (3) "Bend your arms on the heavy beat and straighten your arms on the light beat" (increase or decrease the tempo).

2. *Direct:* The teacher suggests, demonstrates, or drills the child in the desired skill form to be used.

    (a) The teacher combines several fundamental movements into a series of movements or a routine.

    (b) The teacher demonstrates a routine with regard to movement pattern form.

The exploratory, discovery, and combination experiences often incorporated in a lesson do *not* necessarily mean that the child's learning will not be directly guided by the teacher. Depending on the personalities of the teacher and the child, the established level of communication between the two, and safety factors it may be quite appropriate for the teacher to utilize direct rather than indirect teaching. Conversely, indirect teaching is quite appropriate in a typically direct teaching situation. The two approaches must be used to *complement* one another in attempting to communicate effectively with the learner to enhance understanding of the movement and to stimulate thinking concerning one's own interpretation of movement.

Five

SKILL THEME
INTEGRATION

CHAPTER 19

Integrating Rhythmic Activities

Rhythm plays an important role in the daily lives of children. Responding to rhythm is one of the strongest and most basic urges of childhood. It is basic to the life process itself, as evidenced by the rhythmical functions of the body as in breathing, heart beat, and the performance of any movement in a coordinated manner. *Rhythm, therefore, is the measured release of energy made up of repeated units of time.*

Children begin developing their rhythmic abilities during infancy, as seen in the infant's cooing response to the soft rhythmical sounds of a lullabye, and by his/her attempt to make pleasurable rhythmic sights, sounds, and sensations last. As children grow they continue to explore their environment. An internalized time structure is developed and refined. This ability to respond rhythmically is developed and refined through practice and experience. As a result rhythmic activities play an important role in the preschool and elementary-grade program.

One avenue by which rhythmic abilities may be developed and refined is through movement. Rhythm is a basic component of all coordinated movement and as such the two may be effectively combined to enhance both of these interdependent areas. Movement activities designed to enhance rhythmic abilities of young children include creative experiences that are both imitative and interpretative in nature. They also involve auditory rhythmic experiences that include finger plays, rhymes, and singing rhythms. This chapter will examine the role of rhythmic movement activities in enhancing fundamental rhythmic abilities.

The general objectives of the movement experiences contained in the following pages are: (1) to enhance children's fundamental locomotor and nonlocomotor abilities, (2) to enhance the child's ability to respond to variations in tempo, accent, intensity, underlying beat, and rhythmic pattern, (3) to enhance children's ability to imitate and interpret through creative rhythmic movement, and (4) to develop and refine children's auditory rhythmic abilities through participation in finger plays, nursery rhymes, poems, and singing rhythms.

RHYTHM, MUSIC, AND MOVEMENT

Rhythm is an element of movement. It is a distinctive and essential quality inherent in all coordinated movement. To be rhythmic there must be a presentation of a formed pattern in motion, sound, or design. Rhythm, music, and/or dance must possess the following qualities in order to be rhythmic. First, there must be a regulated flow of energy that is organized in both duration and intensity. Second, the time succession of events must result in balance and harmony. Third, there must be sufficient repetition of regular symmetrical groupings in order to be rhythmical in nature.

A close parallel of rhythmics exists between music and movement. Rhythmic structure in music is allied with rhythmic structure in dance movements and, with rare exception, children love both. They enjoy the melodic rhythmic succession of beats characteristic of music and the opportunity to express this through movement.

As children listen to music they respond to its rhythm in a variety of ways. They kick and laugh, jump and clap. They wiggle and giggle, twirl and skip. Sometimes they listen and relax, or simply burst into song and dance. They begin, in their own crude way, to make their own music. They hum, sing, and play a variety of improvised instruments in an effort to make music. The formation of a rhythm band utilizing a variety of homemade pieces of rhythmic equipment is an important first opportunity for young children to organize their efforts into an expressive whole. All children have music as a part of their being, and it is incumbent on the teacher to help each bring out his/her interest and to explore his/her own potential. Rhythmical music and movement is a vital part of the school program for preschool and primary-grade children, but how much depends on the teacher. You may not feel particularly adept at singing or playing a piano but you can:

1. Play chords on a guitar.
2. Use a tape recorder.
3. Use records.*
4. Use a small xylophone.
5. Use a set of simple bells.
6. Use a drum.

*Please refer to the end of this chapter for a list of selected record references listing appropriate record companies.

Elements of Rhythm

Through listening and responding to music children begin to develop a knowledge and understanding of the elements of rhythm. Moving rhythmically is an excellent means by which children can begin to internalize the concepts of:

1. *Accent*—The emphasis given to any one beat (usually the first beat of every measure).
2. *Tempo*—the speed of the movement, music, or accompaniment.
3. *Intensity*—the loudness or softness of the movement or music.
4. *Underlying beat*—the steady, continuous sound of any rhythmical sequence.
5. *Rhythmic pattern*—a group of beats related to the underlying beat.

Participation in a variety of locomotor and nonlocomotor activities stressing the elements of rhythm serves as a means of practicing performance in a variety of fundamental movement skills while learning about the elements of rhythm. For example, practice with running, jumping, and skipping to different tempos, intensities, and accents serves as a means of enhancing knowledge of fundamental elements of rhythm as well as developing skill in the movements themselves.

ACTIVITY IDEAS FOR ENHANCING CREATIVE RHYTHMIC ABILITIES

We often talk about creativity, but just what is it? When one creates something external, symbols or objects are manipulated in order to produce unusual events uncommon to the individual and/or environment. To create means to bring into existence, to make something out of a word or an idea for the first time, or to produce along new or unconventional lines. Generally speaking, we have not been trained to use our imagination to apply knowledge we already have and to extend it into creative behavior. Creativity hinges on the need for freedom to explore and experiment. It relies on a flexible schedule that permits time to explore, stand back and evaluate the results, and then continue on with the idea or project. Rhythm and dance constitute one avenue for enhancing creative expression.

Creative rhythmic activities require a flexible teacher and classroom techniques oriented toward creativity. The teacher needs to encourage the children to develop faith in themselves and others. The teacher must not leave creativity to chance, but must: (1) encourage curiosity, (2) ask questions that require thought, (3) reorganize original creative behavior, (4) be respectful of questions and unusual ideas (show them that their ideas have value), (5) provide opportunities for learning in creative ways, and (6) show a genuine interest in each child's efforts.

As humans we have the unique capacity to think and act creatively—an ability that makes it possible to reach out for the unknown. All persons have the potential capacity to create, although some seem to have more innate ability than others.

Highly creative individuals tend to possess characteristics such as openness to new experiences, esthetic sensitivity, and imagination. However, all children should be encouraged to develop their creative ability to its fullest. In order to develop they must have many opportunities to create and thus expand their insight, skill, and confidence.

Dance as an art experience is concerned with creativity. Even the beginner should be encouraged to make imaginative responses and to self-direct activity. The creative response can be attained through the process of exploration and improvisation, as well as through composition problems that provide opportunities for the children to think, feel, imagine, and create. Creative growth depends on experience and time to develop. Children must have the opportunity to progress from the simple to the complex and the demands of each creative rhythmic endeavor must be related to the developmental level of the individual.

Children are born with a natural drive for movement for it is a primary means by which they learn about their expanding world. They gradually expand their horizons through the cultivation of their inner impulses and urges for movement and learn to *think, act,* and *create* as they move. Creative rhythm is one avenue through which these desirable abilities can be developed and expanded in young children. Creative rhythmic experiences provide a means by which children can rhythmically *imitate* and *interpret* through movement.

Music and movement ideas that are used in creative rhythms must relate to the child's world in order to initiate spontaneity. The teacher serves as an essential catalyst in helping children develop and expand their powers of creativity and self-expression. As a result he or she should take the time necessary to carefully plan and execute lessons in creative rhythms.

Imitative Rhythms

Through imitative rhythms the children express themselves by trying to "be something." The teacher should be careful, however, to see to it that the children realize the movement potential of their own bodies prior before they are introduced to imagery as a part of the rhythmic lesson. In their own minds the children take on the identity of what they are imitating. They interpret this identity with expressive movements to the accompaniment of a suitable rhythm. They are encouraged to explore and express themselves in various original movements as they react to the rhythm. There are three general approaches to imitating rhythms. In the first the teacher begins with a rhythm and lets the children decide what each one would like to be based on the characteristics of the rhythm. This approach is one of "what does this rhythm make you think of?" In the second method the teacher selects a piece of music and has the children make a choice of what they would select to imitate. All of the children imitate the same thing. Each child creates the selection as he or she wishes. If the choice were a "giant," each child would interpret his own individual concept of a giant. The third approach begins with a selection for imitation and thus choosing an appropriate rhythm for movement. Listening to the musical accompaniment is important in all three approaches, as the children must "feel" the character of the music. The music (ranging from clapping or a drum beat to piano music or a recording) must be appropriate for the identity to be assumed in order to be effective; otherwise the movement becomes artificial. The movements of the children should also be in time with the music and reflect a basic understanding of the elements of rhythm.

Objectives

Practice in creative imitative rhythmic activities with children will contribute to their ability:

1. To think and act out creative movement sequences in response to rhythmic accompaniment.
2. To imitate the function of animate and inanimate objects through creative rhythmical movement.
3. To move efficiently through space in a controlled rhythmical manner.
4. To think and act creatively.

Movement Experiences

Imitating Living Creatures. There are many living creatures that children will enjoy imitating. These imitations may be done to the beat of a drum, piano, record, or without any form of accompaniment.

1. Animals:

a.	Elephant	f.	Snake	k.	Fish
b.	Giraffe	g.	Rabbit	l.	Bird
c.	Bear	h.	Kangaroo	m.	Kitten
d.	Lion	i.	Puppy		
e.	Seal	j.	Duck		

2. People:

a.	Firefighter	e.	Soldier	i.	Cowpoke
b.	Letter carrier	f.	Airplane pilot	j.	Carpenter
c.	Doctor	g.	Mountain climber		
d.	Sailor	h.	Ballet dancer		

3. Imaginary people and animals:

a.	Martian	e.	Giant	i.	Troll
b.	Goblin	f.	Fairy	j.	Monster
c.	Elf	g.	Pixie		
d.	Dwarf	h.	Dragon		

Imitating Things in Nature. Young children are rapidly expanding their knowledge and understanding of the world of nature. There are numerous things in nature that they will enjoy imitating and through these experiences will increase their knowledge and nature vocabulary.

1. Weather conditions:
    a. Wind   e. Hail   j. Storm
    b. Rain   f. Hurricane   k. Sun
    c. Snow   g. Tornado
    d. Sleet   h. Clouds

2. Climatic conditions:
    a. Hot   d. Cool   h. Autumn
    b. Cold   e. Sunny   i. Winter
    c. Warm   g. Summer   j. Spring

3. Miscellaneous:
    a. Smoke   e. Sun   i. Mineral
    b. Fire   f. Star   j. Soil
    c. Wave   g. Flower
    d. Moon   h. Water

Imitating Objects. There are several play objects and machines that children enjoy imitating.

1. Play objects:
    a. Swing   e. Ball   i. "Slinky"
    b. Slide   f. Pull toy   j. Silly putty
    c. Seesaw   g. Yo-yo
    d. Merry-go-round   h. Frisbee

2. Modes of transportation:
    a. Rowboat   d. Car   g. Bicycle
    b. Snowmobile   e. Canoe   h. Motorcycle
    c. Truck   f. Rocket   i. Train

3. Machines:
    a. Elevator   d. Crane   g. Pneumatic drill
    b. Tractor   e. Cement mixer   h. Lawn mower
    c. Bulldozer   f. Old-fashioned coffee grinder i. Record player

Imitating Events. As the world of children is expanding, so is their exposure to special events outside the home. The following is a list of suggested activities and events that may be imitated at strategic times during the year.

1. The circus:
    a. Clown   e. High-wire walker   i. Barker
    b. Acrobat   f. Trapeze artist   j. Ringmaster
    c. Juggler   g. Lion tamer
    d. Trained animal   h. Marching bandmember

Imitating objects is an aspect of creative rhythms.

2. Sporting events (in slow motion, imitate the movements found in the following athletic events):

a.	Soccer	**e.**	Volleyball	**i.**	Tennis
b.	Football	**f.**	Track and field events	**j.**	Bowling
c.	Baseball	**g.**	Swimming and diving	**k.**	Ice hockey
d.	Basketball	**h.**	Fencing	**l.**	Field hockey

Interpretative Rhythms

Interpretative movements are the second form of creative rhythms. In interpretative rhythms the children act out an idea, a familiar event, or an ordinary procedure. They also express feelings, emotions, and moods through movement. The quality and direction of the interpretative movements rely on the mood, intelligence, and personal feelings of the children. In interpretative movement the teacher creates the atmosphere for the children to express themselves. There are three general approaches to this also. In the first the teacher begins with an idea, story, or other basis. As the story progresses, suitable rhythmic background can be used. Recordings, a piano selection, percussion rhythms, or even a rhythm band can be used. The teacher provides the verbal background and directions for the drama; however, the story can unfold without this.

The second approach begins with a piece of music, generally a recording, and develops an idea to fit the music. The piece of music selected should have sufficient changes in tempo and pattern to provide different kinds and qualities of background. A general idea or plan of action can be selected and fitted to the music. An idea such as "going to the fair" may be selected and an adaptable recording chosen.

In the third approach the children express moods or feelings. A piece of music may be played and the children act out how the music makes them feel. An alternative method is simply to give cue words that denote specific moods (happy, sad, etc.) and have the children express these words through movement.

Objectives

Practice in creative interpretative rhythmic activities with children will contribute to their ability:

1. To think through and act out creative movement sequences in response to rhythmic accompaniment.
2. To interpret moods, feelings, and ideas and to express them through creative rhythmic moves.
3. To solve rhythmic problems creatively through expressive movement.
4. To move efficiently through space in a coordinated rhythm.
5. To think and act creatively.
6. To "feel" auditory and visual symbols, and to be able to express these feelings through movement.

Movement Experiences

Interpreting Action Words. Numerous verbs provide opportunities for creative movement. Try several during the first few minutes of the lesson. The following represent only a few of the numerous possibilities:

1.	Bang	8.	Blow	15.	Dart
2.	Crack	9.	Bump	16.	Zoom
3.	Spin	10.	Tingle	17.	Bop
4.	Pop	11.	Grab	18.	Zip
5.	Twinkle	12.	Grumble	19.	Boom
6.	Glow	13.	Punch	20.	Pluck
7.	Bubble	14.	Float		

Interpreting Feelings and Moods. Children experience many feelings and moods during the course of their day. They will enjoy openly expressing them through expressive movement. Musical accompaniment may be used in order to enhance the experience.

1.	Happiness	8.	Love	15.	Bravery
2.	Sadness	9.	Hate	16.	Shyness
3.	Confusion	10.	Friendship	17.	Boredom
4.	Pride	11.	Jealousy	18.	Interest
5.	Disappointment	12.	Fear	19.	Laughter
6.	Gladness	13.	Hurt	20.	Tears
7.	Gaiety	14.	Surprise		

Interpreting Art Through Movement. Art is an experience that may, through guided discovery, be successfully interpreted through movement. Various lines, forms, colors, and textures may be expressed through creative movement. Remember that the children should be encouraged to express how these things make them feel. Guessing games may be played with one group trying to guess what the other is imitating. Discuss the various art forms with the children before they show you their interpretation.

1. Line:
   a. Straight   d. Dotted
   b. Curved   e. Dashed
   c. Zig-zagged   f. Broken

2. Form:
   a. Circle   d. Rectangle
   b. Square   e. Hexagon
   c. Triangle

3. Color:
   a. Red   d. Blue   g. Purple   j. Orange
   b. White   e. Yellow   h. Pink
   c. Green   f. Black   i. Brown

4. Texture:

a.	Smooth	**e.**	Hard	**i.**	Scratchy
b.	Slippery	**f.**	Soft	**j.**	Slick
c.	Bumpy	**g.**	Furry		
d.	Rough	**h.**	Silky		

Interpreting Action Sequences. There is an innumerable number of action sequences that children enjoy interpreting. The following is a list of only a few of the possibilities that may be explored.

1. Move through molasses
2. Shoo the flies away
3. Float in water
4. Hit the punching bag
5. Grow like a flower
6. Sway like a tree in the breeze
7. Build a house
8. Fight a fire
9. Rocket to the moon
10. Ride a bumpy road

Interpretating Pendular Movements. Have the children think of objects that swing. Let them move (clock, golf club, baseball bat, swing, etc.) to each one. Use an object that has a pendular motion so they can keep time. Encourage them to swing with their eyes closed and then open to see if they are still in time with the beat. Encourage the children to also swing individual parts of their body one at a time.

Interpreting Special Holidays. Discuss the meaning of various special holidays with the children, encouraging them to share their experiences with the class.

1. Christmas
2. Hanukah
3. Halloween
4. Easter
5. Valentine's Day
6. Flag Day
7. Thanksgiving
8. Fourth of July
9. Summer vacation
10. Snow days

ACTIVITY IDEAS FOR ENHANCING AUDITORY RHYTHMIC ABILITIES

Children should experience creative movement responses through as many different sensory modalities as possible. Singing rhythms, finger plays, and nursery rhymes offer opportunities for combining movement and socialization to rhythmic patterns.

Singing rhythms are appealing to children because they: (1) tell a story, (2) develop an idea, (3) have pleasing rhythmic patterns, (4) stimulate use of one's imagination, or (5) have dramatic possibilities. Singing plays an important role in the life of children. They love repetition and will sing over and over again the songs they know. They enjoy hearing the same old songs and learning new ones. Children also like to respond to songs through movement. When responding to activity songs, they will usually join in the singing. This singing is important for it helps to internalize the rhythm of the song itself. When simple songs are utilized, children are given a variety of opportunities for repetition of movement and a chance to be creative and express themselves dramatically.

Singing and accompanying rhythmic responses are complex physical activities. Doll and Nelson have stated that: "They demand exacting functions of the small muscles. Well-planned rhythmic movements give one facet of the musical experience to the large and small muscles, generating a musical response throughout the total being."[1]

Young children need and enjoy singing rhythms and rhymes. Singing rhythms, finger plays, and rhymes are made up of actions that the children do as they sing or chant a particular song or repeat a particular rhyme. There may be a great deal of variation in the action patterns used in singing rhythms and finger rhymes. It will depend on how the children follow and interpret the actions suggested by the auditory cues, their willingness to express themselves freely, and the teaching cues used by the teachers.

The incorporation of action patterns with various songs, rhymes, and finger plays will do much to enhance young children's auditory rhythmic abilities. Developing and reinforcing an internal sensitivity to tempo, accent, intensity, and rhythmic pattern will be by-products of successful participation in singing rhythms, rhymes, and finger plays that require a movement response.

The importance of developing the ability to express internally perceived rhythm motorically cannot be overemphasized. It is through the development of temporal awareness that children establish a meaningful and effective time structure. To see why the ability to interpret auditory rhythmic patterns is important, we need only look at how children first learn the alphabet or a new song. The "sing-song" rhythmic cadence used to recite the alphabet or song seems to make it easier to recall and retain. As adults we find it much easier to recall and remember the words to an old "long-forgotten" song than those uttered by your instructor just yesterday. For example, listening to the melody of an old Beatles tune ("She Loves You," "I Want to Hold Your Hand," etc.) will often trigger recollection of the words that accompany the tune. This would not be possible or would be considerably more difficult if our auditory rhythmic abilities were not adequately developed and refined. Hence from the standpoint of preschool and primary-grade children, practice and participation in singing, rhythms, rhymes and poems are

[1] Edna Doll and Mary Nelson, *Rhythms Today,* Morristown, N. J.: Silver Burdette, 1977, p. 4.

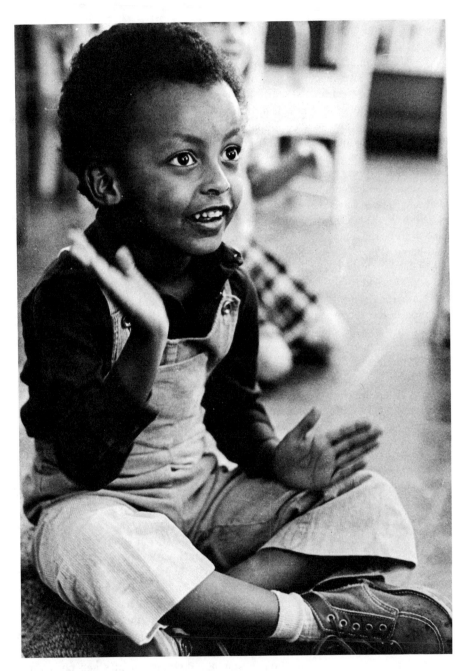

Singing rhythms and rhymes are enjoyed by young children.

important. Incorporation of the medium of movement serves as a means of making these experiences more enjoyable and increasing the number of sensory modalities involved.

The following pages present numerous examples of finger plays, rhymes, and singing rhythms that may be effectively used with young children. Finger plays are generally most appropriate for preschool children, along with most nursery rhymes. Singing rhymes are generally initiated during kindergarten through the second grade.

Finger Plays

Finger plays and nursery rhymes are generally the first verses committed to memory by preschool children. Finger plays are generally quite short and easy to learn. Many of them have been handed down from generation to generation. The small muscles of the hands and fingers are less well developed in preschool children than their other muscles. Practice in finger plays does much to aid in increasing their finger dexterity. They also provide children with an opportunity to begin using movement to interpret specified rhythmical verses.

Objectives

Practice in finger play activities will contribute to children's:
1. Auditory rhythmic abilities
2. Fine motor dexterity
3. Auditory memory abilities
4. Ability to combine rhythmical auditory and movement sequences into a coordinated whole
5. Ability to utilize movement to interpret specified rhythmical sequence

Movement Experiences

Here Is the Beehive

Here is the beehive. (fold hands)*
But where are the bees? (puzzled look)
Hiding inside, where nobody sees. (peek inside)
They're coming out now. They're all alive. (show surprise)
One, two, three, four, five. (raise fingers one at a time)
Bzzzzzzzzzzzzzzzzzzz.

*The words in parentheses indicate the suggested action pattern.

This Little Clown

This little clown is fat and gay. (hold up thumb)
This little clown does tricks all day. (hold up forefinger)
This little clown is tall and strong. (hold up middle finger)
This little clown sings a funny song. (hold up ring finger)
This little clown is wee and small. (hold up little finger)
But he can do anything at all.

I'm a Little Teapot

I'm a little teapot short and stout.
Here is my handle. (place hand on waist, forming handle)
Here is my spout. (form spout with the other arm)
When I get all steamed up then I shout: (hiss)
Tip me over and pour me out. (pour the ''tea'' out the ''spout'')

Over the Hills

Over the hills and far away (pounding motion of hands)
We skip and run and laugh and play. (clap hands)
Smell the flowers and fish the streams, (sniff a flower—cast a line)
Lie in the sunshine and dream sweet dreams. (sleep, cheek on hand)

Row, Row, Row

Row, row, row your boat (rowing motion with both hands)
Gently down the stream. (forward waving motion, one hand)

Merrily, merrily, merrily, merrily, (clap hands in rhythm)
Life is but a dream. (sleep)

Dig a Little Hole

Dig a little hole, (dig)
Plant a little seed, (drop seed)
Pour a little water, (pour)
Pull a little weed. (pull up and throw away)
Chase a little bug (chasing motion with hands)
Height-ho, there he goes! (shade eyes)
Give a little sunshine, (cup hands, lift to the sun)
Grow a little rose. (small flower, eyes closed, smiling)

Ten Fingers

I have ten little fingers (extend the 10 fingers)
They all belong to me.
I can make them do things,
Would you like to see?
I can open them up wide, (spread fingers apart)
Shut them up tight, (clench fists)
Put them out of sight, (place hands behind back)
Jump them up high, (raise hands)
Jump them down low, (lower hands)
Fold them quietly, and sit (fold them in lap)
Just so!

Little Fish

I hold my fingers like a fish, (hold hands back-to-back with fingers spread, wave
hands to the side as in swimming, continue to
and fro)
and wave them as I go,
Through the water with a swish,
So gaily to and fro.

Bunny

Hippity, hoppety, hop, hop, hop, (raise hands to side of head)
Here comes a little bunny, (children hop on both feet)
One ear is down, one ear is up, (press fingers of one hand against palm)
Oh, doesn't he look funny?

If I Were a Bird—1

If I were a bird, I'd sing a song (entwine the two thumbs and so that palms of the
                                    hands are facing inward)
and fly about the whole day long, (flutter the hands)
And when the night came, go to rest (fold the hands and go to sleep)
up in my cozy little nest.

If I Were a Bird—2

If I were a bird, I'd sing a song, (raise both arms, waving them as a bird flying)
And fly about the whole day long.
And when the night came, go to rest, (place both hands together on one side of face,
                                       like sleeping)
Up in my cozy little nest.
Oh look and see out—airplanes (raise both arms in horizontal positions, as an
                               airplane)
Away up in the sky.
Watch us gliding through the air, (fly about, as an airplane)
                    This is how we fly.

Two Little

Two little eyes that open and close, (children point to parts of the body indicated
                                      by the verses)
Two little ears and one little nose,
Two little lips and one little chin,
Two little cheeks with the rose shut in,
Two little elbows so dimpled and sweet,
Two little shoes on two little feet.
Two little shoulders so chubby and strong,
Two little legs, running all day long.

Flowers

See the blue and yellow blossoms, (hold both hands above the head with fingers
                                   touching, spread hands apart,
                                   drop one hand)
In the flower bed.
The daisy spreads its petals wide,
The tulip bows its head.

Left and Right

This is my right hand, raise it up high, (raise right hand high)
This is my left hand, I'll touch the sky. (raise left hand high)
Right hand, left hand, whirl them 'round, (whirl hands before you)
Left hand, right hand, pound, pound, pound. (pound left fist with right)
This is my right foot, tap, tap, tap, (tap right foot three times)
This is my left foot, pat, pat, pat, (tap left foot three times)
Right foot, left foot, run, run, run, (run in place)
Right foot, left foot, jump for fun. (lift right foot, and down;
                               lift left foot, and down;
                               jump up and down)

Nursery Rhymes and Poems

There are numerous nursery rhymes and poems that have been passed from generation to generation that we are all familiar with. The following rhymes and poems may be less familiar but are equally suitable for adding action sequences. Nursery rhymes are particularly enjoyed by preschool and kindergarten-age children.

Objectives

Practice in nursery rhymes and poems that incorporate action sequences will contribute to children's:

1. Auditory rhythmic abilities
2. Listening skills
3. Auditory memory abilities
4. Ability to combine rhythmical auditory sequences effectively with coordinated action patterns
5. Ability to utilize movement to interpret specific rhythmical sequence

Movement Experiences

My Hands

I raise my hands up high
Now on the floor they lie
Now high, now low
Now reach up to the sky.

I spread my hands out wide
Now behind my back they hide
Now wide, now hide
Now I put them at my side.

I give my head a shake, shake, shake,
Now, not a move I make
Now shake, shake, shake
Not a move I make
Now my whole self I shake

The Noble Duke of York

The noble Duke of York
He had ten thousand men
He marched them up a hill
And marched them down again
So when you're up, you're up
And when you're down, you're down
And when you're only half way up
You're neither up nor down. (children stand and sit in response to the words
                                            "up"

Choo-choo

"Choo-choo" we hear the train
"Choo-choo" it goes again
It pulls a heavy load all day. (pull self while sliding; use arm and feet movements)

Windy Weather

Like a leaf or a feather
In the windy, windy weather
We will whirl around
And twirl around
And all sink down together.

Funny Clown

I am a funny clown
I move like a funny clown
I jump, I skip and run.
I stop and have a lot of fun.

My Little Puppy

My little puppy's name is Rags,
He eats so much that his tummy sags.
His ears flip flop, his tail wig wags,
And when he walks, he zigs and zags.

How Creatures Move

The lion walks on padded paws,
The squirrel leaps from limb to limb
While flies can crawl straight up a wall,
And seals can dive and swim.
The worm, he wiggles all around,
The monkey swings by his tail,
And birds may hop upon the ground
Or spread their wings and sail
But boys and girls have much more fun;
They leap and dance and walk and run.

Jack-In-the-Box

Jack-in-the-box
All shut up tight,
Not a breath of air,
Not a peep of light,
How tired he must be
All in a heap
I'll open the box
And up he'll leap.

Stormy Days

On stormy days
When the wind is high
Tall trees are brooms
Sweeping the sky.

They swish their branches
In buckets of rain
And swish and sweep it
Blue again.

Follow the Leader Rhymes

Who feels happy? Who feels gay?
All who do clap your hands
   this way.
Who feels happy? Who feels gay?
All who do tap your feet
   this way.
Who feels happy? Who feels gay?
All who skip around this way.
(Add other activities as desired.)

I'll touch my hair, my eyes,
I'll sit up straight, then
   I'll rise
I'll touch my ears, my nose, my chin
Then quietly I'll sit down again.

The elephant walks just so
Swaying to and fro—
He lifts up his trunk to the trees
Then slowly gets down on his knees

Tip-toe, tip-toe, little feet,
Tip-toe, tip-toe, little feet,
Now fast, now slow
Now very softly—
Tip-toe, tip-toe little feet
(Add other activities as desired.)

Shall we go for a walk today?
A walk today, a walk today?
(Repeat—use—pick flowers,
smell flowers:

Shall we pick flowers today, etc.
Shall we smell flowers today, etc.)

(Use any other ideas to incorporate bending, jumping, etc. to the above verses.)

Drawing Numerals in Space

A line straight down and that is all (repeat twice)
To make the numeral 1
Around and down and to the right (repeat twice)
To make the numeral 2
Curve around and curve again (3)
Down, across, than all the way down (4)
Down, curve around, a line at the top, (5)
Curve down, and all the way around (6)
A line across and then slant down (7)
Curve around and then back up (8)
Curve around and then straight down (9)
A straight line down and circle around (10)

(Have the children sit or stand and perform the actions of the words as they are sung through.)

Head, Shoulders, Baby

Head, shoulders, baby, 1, 2, 3. (repeat)
Head, shoulders, head, shoulders, head, shoulders, baby, 1, 2, 3.
Chest, stomach, baby, 1, 2, 3. (repeat)
Chest, stomach, chest, stomach, chest, stomach, baby, 1, 2, 3.
Knees, ankles
Ankles, knees
Stomach, chest
Shoulders, head

Miss Mary Mack

Teacher: Miss Mary Mack
Pupils: Mack, Mack
Teacher: All dressed in black
Pupils: Black, black
Teacher: With silver buttons
Pupils: Buttons, buttons

Teacher: She asked her mother
Pupils: Mother, Mother
Teacher: For fifteen cents
Pupils: Cents, cents
Teacher: To see the elephants
Pupils: Elephants, elephants
Teacher: Jump the fence
Pupils: Fence, fence
Teacher: They jumped so high
Pupils: High, high
Teacher: They touched the sky
Pupils: Sky, sky
Teacher: And they never came down
Pupils: Down, down
Teacher: Till the Fourth of July
Pupils: ly, ly.

(Standing in a circle, the children sing the song and respond to the beat by jumping.)

Singing Rhythms

A singing rhythm is a dance in which the children sing verses to a song that provides cues as to how to move. The children will first need to learn the words to the song. If musical accompaniment is used they should listen to it often until they have a general grasp of the words. The action phase of the activity should be added lastly.

Objectives

Practice in singing rhythmic activities will aid children in the development of:

1. Auditory memory skills
2. Listening skills
3. Auditory rhythmic abilities
4. Fundamental movement abilities

Movement Experiences

Bingo

Desired outcomes	1.	To develop auditory memory and sequencing abilities.
	2.	To perform rhythmic clapping to a prescribed rhythmic pattern.
Formation	Single circle facing the center.	

Number of participants   Any number.

Song There was a farmer who had a dog,
And Bingo was his name
B-I-N-G-O, B-I-N-G-O, B-I-N-G-O
And Bingo was his name-O

Procedures   Begin by singing whole song and then repeating the song, dropping the "o" in Bingo, substituting a clap. Next time drop the "g" and substitute two claps for the missing letters. Continue until each letter of Bingo is dropped and the whole word is clapped. (This may be done in a circle, standing, or sitting.)

Variations   Select a "Bingo" and let him or her perform the actions of a dog while the others are singing.

Did You Feed My Cow?

Teacher: Did you feed my cow?
Pupils: Yes, yes, yes.
Teacher: Could you tell me how?
Pupils: Yes, yes, yes.
Teacher: What did you feed her?
Pupils: Corn and hay.
Teacher: What did you feed her?
Pupils: Corn and hay.

Teacher: Did you milk her good?
Pupils: Yes, yes, yes.
Teacher: Did you milk her like you should?
Pupils: Yes, yes, yes.
Teacher: Well, how did you milk her?
Pupils: Squish, squish, squish.
Teacher: How did you milk her?
Pupils: Squish, squish, squish.
Teacher: Did my cow get sick?
Pupils: Yes, yes, yes.
Teacher: Was she covered with ticks?

Pupils: Yes, yes, yes.
Teacher: How did she die?
Pupils:
Teacher: How did she die?
Pupils: Um um um!

Teacher: Did the buzzards come?
Pupils: Yes, yes, yes.
Teacher: Did the buzzards come?
Pupils: Yes, yes, yes.
Teacher: How did they come?
Pupils: Flop! Flop! Flop!
Teacher: How did they come?
Pupils: Flop! Flop! Flop!

Little Red Caboose

Desired outcomes	**1.** To reinforce awareness of "red" as a color word, and the functions of a train.
	2. To perform brisk walking movements to a prescribed rhythmic pattern.
Formation	Single line with both hands on the shoulders of the person in front.
Number of participants	Ten to 15 per line.

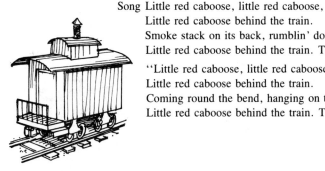

Song Little red caboose, little red caboose,
    Little red caboose behind the train.
    Smoke stack on its back, rumblin' down the track,
    Little red caboose behind the train. Toot!"

"Little red caboose, little red caboose,
    Little red caboose behind the train.
    Coming round the bend, hanging on the end,
    Little red caboose behind the train. Toot!

Procedures	While singing the song, groups of children can form a line with hands on the shoulders or waist of the child ahead. As some of them sing and move in time with the music, others chant the words "choo, choo, choo, choo."
Variations	Make up other verses to the song about trains as they rumble down the tracks.

Mulberry Bush

Desired outcomes	1. To perform rhythmic pantomining motions in time to the song.
	2. To skip and move in other ways in time to the music.
Formation	Single circle facing in with one child at the center of the circle.

Song Here we go round the mulberry bush, the mulberry bush, the mulberry bush,
Here we go round the mulberry bush so early in the morning.

This is the way we wash our clothes, we wash our clothes, we wash our clothes
This is the way we wash our clothes, so early in the morning.

(Continue with:)
This is the way we hang our clothes.
This is the way we iron our clothes.
This is the way we fold our clothes.
This is the way we rake the leaves.
This is the way we sweep the floor.

Number of participants	Any number.
Procedure	Children may form a circle; one child designated as the mulberry bush stands in the center. Let them skip around the circle holding hands as they sing the chorus, and stopping to perform the action of the verses.
Variation	Make up other words to the songs, such as when doing a circus unit. (the words might be, "this is the way the elephant walks," "this is the way the seals clap," etc.)

Ten Little Jingle Bells

Desired outcomes	1. To reinforce counting skills and increase small-muscle dexterity.
	2. To perform galloping and pantomining skills to a pre-scribed rhythmic pattern.
Formation	Double row of 10 children in each row behind the leader (horse).
Number of participants	Twenty-one children.

Song Ten little jingle bells hung in a row,
Ten little jingle bells helped the horse go.
Merrily, merrily over the snow
Merrily, merrily sleighing we go.

One little jingle bell fell in the snow
Nine little jingle bells helped the horse go.
Merrily, merrily over the snow
Merrily, merrily sleighing we go.

(Continue subtracting bells until one is left.)

One little jingle bell fell in the snow (sing slowly)
No little jingle bells help the horse go.
Slowly, so slowly the bells are all gone.
We'll get some new ones and put them right on.

Procedures

One child may be the horse and 10 children the jingle bells in a double row behind the horse. One jingle bell drops off during each verse until only the horse is left. They should carry sleigh or jingle bells and ring them as they move to the rhythm.

Variations

Have two or three teams of horses so that full participation of all class members is going on.

Lobby Loo

Desired outcomes

1. To reinforce left-right concepts of directional awareness through a rhythmic activity.
2. To perform turning, skipping, jumping, and shaking movements.

Formation

Single circle, all facing center with hands joined.

Number of participants

Any number.

Song Here we dance looby loo
    Here we dance looby light
    Here we dance looby loo
    All on a Saturday night.

1. "I put my right hand in
   I take my right hand out
   I give my right hand a shake, shake, shake
   And turn myself about."
2. "I put my left hand in, etc . . . ."
3. I put my right foot in, etc . . ."
4. I put my left foot in, etc . . ."
5. I put my head way in, etc . . ."
6. I put my whole self in, etc . . ."

Procedures

On the verse part of the dance, the children stand still facing the center and follow the directions of the words. On the words "and turn myself about," they make a complete turn in place and get ready to skip around the circle. On the last verse, the children jump forward and then backward, shaking themselves vigorously, and then turning about.

Variation

This is an excellent activity to help children with left—right concepts. Be sure to use it as such.

Blue Bird

Desired outcomes	1. To remember a song and melody and to be able to perform pantomime movements while singing it. 2. To be able to walk in time to a prescribed rhythmic pattern.
Formation	Single circle facing inward.
Number of Participants	About 10 per circle.

Song   Blue bird, blue bird, in and out my windows,
         Blue bird, blue bird in and out my windows,
         Oh! Johnny, I am tired.

         Take a boy (girl) and tap him (her) on the shoulders
         (repeat two more tir ˢ).

Procedures

The boys and girls form a circle facing inward, with hands joined raised to form arches. One child (the blue bird) stands outside the circle. Sing the words of the song as the bird goes in and out of the arches.

The child who has been tapped becomes the new bluebird while the former one takes the vacant place in the circle. Repeat until every one has been the bluebird. (You may need more than one circle.)

Let the children form a chain of bluebirds until all of the children become birds and there are no windows left.

Ten Little Indians

Desired outcomes	To enhance rhythmical expression and pattern.
Formation	Single circle facing inward.
Number of participants	Ten per group.

Song

First verse: 1 little, 2 little, 3 little Indians,
            4 little, 5 little, 6 little Indians,
            7 little, 8 little, 9 little Indians,
            10 little Indian boys.

Second verse: 10 little, 9 little, 8 little Indians,
              7 little, 6 little, 5 little Indians,
              4 little, 3 little, 2 little Indians,
              1 little Indian boy.

Simple folk dances are often enjoyed by first and second graders.

Procedures	The children stand in a circle facing the center. Each child is given a number from 1 to 10. As the first verse is sung, the children squat when their number is called. During the second verse they stand when their number is called. The song is repeated with the children hopping and whopping, Indian fashion, counterclockwise during the first verse and clockwise during the second verse.

Farmer in the Dell

Desired outcomes	To enhance auditory memory and rhythmical sequencing.
Formation	Single circle facing inward.
Number of participants	Sixteen to 20 per circle.
Song	

First verse: The farmer in the dell,
The farmer in the dell,
Heigh-ho the dairy, oh,
The farmer in the dell.

Second verse: The farmer takes a wife—
(repeat first verse except for farmer in the dell.)

Third verse: The wife takes a child—
Fourth verse: The child takes a nurse—
Fifth verse: The nurse takes a cat—
Sixth verse: The cat takes a mouse—
Seventh verse: The mouse takes the cheese—
Eighth verse: The cheese stands alone—

Procedures

The children form a circle, holding hands with one child (that is, the farmer) in the center of the circle. The children walk or skip counterclockwise as they sing the song. As they sing the second verse, the farmer chooses somebody to be his wife, and during the singing of the third verse, the wife chooses somebody to be her child. Each time a new verse is sung, a child is chosen to play the role of the character about whom they are singing. The last child selected always chooses the next child. When the children finish the last verse, the "cheese" chases the children about the room. The child tagged becomes the farmer for the next time the dance is performed.

How Do You Do, My Partner?

Desired outcomes
To develop an understanding of rhythmical sequencing and enhance spatial awareness.

Formation
Single circle facing inward.

Number of participants
Any number.

Song
How do you do, my partner?
How do you do today?
Will you dance in a circle?
I will show you the way.

Chorus: Tra-la-la-la-la-la.

Procedures
One child is stationed in the middle of the circle. He faces a member of the circle and shakes hands while the children sing the song. As the song ends, the two skip around the circle as everyone sings, "Tra-la-la-la-la-la." When the chorus ends, the two face new partners and the song begins again. Continue this procedure until all children are dancing.

Round and Round the Village

Desired outcomes
To develop an understanding of rhythmical sequencing and enhance spatial awareness.

Formation
Single circle facing inward with one child on the outside.

Number of participants
Ten to 20.

Song

    Chorus: Go round and round the village,
              Go round and round the village,
              Go round and round the village,
              As we have done before.

First verse: Go in and out the windows—

Second verse: Now stand and face your partner,—

Third verse: Now follow me to London—

Procedures

The children stand in a circle with hands joined and one child stands outside the circle. The children walk counterclockwise singing the chorus (the child outside the circle skips clockwise). After the chorus, the children stop and raise their arms to make "windows" while singing the first verse. The child on the outside of the circle goes in and out of the windows. As the circle sings the second verse, the child selects a partner. The partners skip around on the outside of the circle while the other children sing the third verse. Repeat this procedure until all children have a partner.

I See You

Desired outcome

To enhance rhythmic sequencing abilities.

Formation

Double circles facing inward, one behind the other.

Number of participants

Any number.

Song

    First verse: I see you, I see you
              Tra la, la-la, la.
              I see you, I see you
              Tra la, la-la, la.

    Second verse: You see me and I'll see you,
    You swing me and I'll swing you,
    You see me and I'll see you,
    You swing me and I'll swing you.

Procedures

The children form a circle with the girls standing behind the boys with their hands on the boys' shoulders. They then proceed to play "peek-a-boo" over the boys' shoulders on the first verse in tempo with the verse on each "see" and each "tra-la," "la-la," and "la." On the second verse, the boys face their partners, hook elbows, and skip around in a circle. The boys then change places with their partners and play "peek-a-boo" as the song begins again.

A Hunting We Will Go

Desired outcome | To enhance rhythmical sequencing and body awareness.

Formation | Two parallel lines facing one another.

Number of participants | Six to eight per line.

Song A hunting we will go,
  A hunting we will go,
  We'll catch a fox and put him in a box
  And then we'll let him go.

Procedures

The head couple holds hands and slides down the line with eight fast steps and back again as the song is sung the first time. As the song is repeated, they lead a "parade" of all of the couples skipping in a circular pattern to the foot of the set. The head couple then forms an arch while the other children take the hand of the person across from them and walk through the arch and back to their places. The entire verse is sung while doing this. The dance is repeated until all have had an opportunity to be the head couple.

Did You Ever See a Lassie?

Desired outcome | To develop an understanding of rhythmical sequencing.

Formation | Single circle facing inward.

Number of participants | Ten to 12 per circle.

Song

Chorus: Did you ever see a Lassie, a Lassie, a Lassie.
Did you ever see a Lassie go this way and that?
Go this way and that way, go this way and that way;
Did you ever see a Lassie go this way and that?

Procedures

The children join hands and form a circle. One child is placed in the center of the circle and is designated to be a Lassie (or Laddie). The other children are also given character names such as farmer, soldier, fireman, cowboy, and so on. When the verse is sung, the child in the center performs various movements to the rhythm of the song and the children in the circle try to imitate these movements. Each time the verse is sung another name is substituted for Lassie and the above procedure is repeated.

Jolly Is the Miller

Desired outcome	To enhance fundamental rhythmical sequencing abilities.
Formation	Double circle facing counterclockwise.
Number of participants	Twenty-one to 25.
Song	Oh, jolly is the miller who lives by the mill The wheel turns round with a right good will. One hand in the hopper and the other in the sack The girl steps forward and the boy steps back.
Procedures	The children form a double circle facing counterclockwise and hold their partner's hand. One child is placed in the center of the inner circle (that is, the miller). The children move counterclockwise as they sing the song. They change partners on the words "the girl steps forward . . ." At this time the "miller" attempts to get a partner and the child left without a partner becomes the "miller."

SUGGESTED RECORDS

Capon, Jack and Rosemary Hallum, *Get Ready to Square Dance*, Educational Activities, Inc., Box 392, Freeport, New York (AR68).

Congdon, Paul, *Fun Dances for Children*, Kimbo Records, Deal, New Jersey, Box 246 (KEA1134).

Durlacher, Don, *Up-Beat Square Dances*, Educational Activities, Inc., Box 392, Freeport, New York (HYP35).

Glass, Henry "Buzz", *Dances Without Partners*, Educational Activities, Inc., Box 392, Freeport, New York (AR32, AR33, AR46).

Glass, Henry "Buzz," and Rosemary Hallum, *Around the World in Dance*, Educational Activities, Inc., Box 392, Freeport, New York (AR542).

Hallum, Rosemary, and Henry "Buzz" Glass, *America Dances!*, Educational Activities, Inc., Box 392, Freeport, New York (AR57, AC57).

Herman, Michael, *First Folk Dances*, RCA Victor, New York LPM6625.

International Folk Dances, Educational Activities, Inc., Box 392, Freeport, New York (HYP22).

Janiak, William, *Everyday Skills for Early Childhood and Special Education*, Kimbo Records, Deal, New Jersey, Box 246 (KIM7016-7021).

Lewis, Vivian, Peter Werner, and Herbert Drummond, *Soul Folk Dances*, Educational Activities, Inc., Box 392, Freeport, New York (AR573).

Marches, Educational Activities, Inc., Box 392, Freeport, New York (HYP-B11).

Palmer, Hap, *Creative Movement and Rhythmic Exploration*, Educational Activities, Freeport, New York (Box 392, AR533).

———, *Folk Song Carnival*, Educational Activities, Freeport, New York (Box 392, AR524).

———, *Holiday Songs and Rhythms*, Educational Activities, Freeport, New York (Box 392, AR538).

————, *Homemade Bank,* Educational Activities, Freeport, New York, Box 392 (AR545).

————, *Mod Marches,* Educational Activities, Freeport, New York, Box 392 (AR527).

————, *Simplified Folk Songs,* Educational Activities, Freeport, New York, Box 392 (AR518).

Pexton, Boyd M., *Contemporary Tinikling Activities,* Educational Activities, Inc., Box 392, Freeport, New York (KEA8095).

Seyler, Anita, *We Move to Poetry,* Bridges, 310 W. Jefferson, Dallas, Texas 75208.

Zeitlin, Patty and Marcia Pearce, *Won't You Be My Friend?* Bridges, 310 W. Jefferson, Dallas, Texas, 75208 (AR544).

Music for Creative Movement, Bridges, 310 W. Jefferson, Dallas, Texas, 75208 (2 volumes, (LP6070, LP6080).

Rhythmic Activity Songs for Primary Grades, Bridges, 310 W. Jefferson, Dallas, Texas 75208 (4 volumes, LP1055, LP1066, LP1077, LP1088).

Singing Action Games, Bridges, 310 W. Jefferson, Dallas, Texas 75208 (HYP507).

Action Songs and Sounds, Bridges, 310 W. Jefferson, Dallas, Texas 75208 (HYP508).

20

Integrating
Perceptual – Motor
Activities

Every man, woman, and child is constantly being bombarded with stimuli from the environment. The ability to recognize these stimuli, absorb them into the flow of mental processes, and store them for future use is referred to as perception. Being able to absorb, assimilate, and react to the incoming data when needed falls into the area of perceptual – motor ability. Because the very essence of physical education is movement, perceptual – motor skills can easily be introduced, practiced, and refined in a well-organized and sensitive program. Indeed the physical education program is not the sole place where this type of learning can occur. Programs of this type can and should be carried out by the classroom teacher as well. The need for programs of perceptual – motor learning are important, and they should be viewed as an essential part of the curriculum of every child.

The physical education curriculum affords a natural teaching base for perceptual – motor skills because in reality all voluntary movement is perceptual – motor in nature. Interaction with our environment is a perceptual as well as a motor process. There is a dependency of voluntary motor processes on perceptual information. Conversely the perceptual stimuli received by the organism rely on the development of one's voluntary movement abilities.

What we have, then, is a process of stimulation and reaction that is essential to human life. This characteristic must be learned and the best time and place for this learning to occur is when children are *young*. During the early years, children are open to a wide variety of new and different situations that can enhance their perceptual – motor abilities.

Perceptual—motor activities help children achieve a *general* stage of readiness that helps prepare them for academic work. These activities provide a foundation for future perceptually and conceptually based learnings. Through a program of perceptual—motor skill development children can develop and refine their movement abilities as well as their perceptual—motor abilities.

Learning disabilities in academics are sometimes linked to perceptual—motor problems. Integrating and organizing information is related to visual and motor capabilities. If these capabilities are below normal the child *may* experience problems in the classroom that may or may not be permanent. Introduction to a program of perceptual—motor training, however, *may* contribute to the improvement of the condition. Perceptual—motor programs and activities are not intended as a panacea for remediation of all learning disabilities or developmental lags. They should, however, be viewed as important *contributors* to the remediation of perceptual problems. The opportunities afforded by a well-organized, well-taught physical education program geared to the individual's needs and capabilities provide an ideal avenue for helping children with perceptual and motor deficiencies as well as those who do not display any problem. Programs that stress the development of fundamental locomotor, manipulative, and stability abilities have a direct affect on enhancing the perceptual—motor components of: (1) body awareness, (2) spatial awareness, (3) directional awareness, and (4) temporal awareness.

ACTIVITY IDEAS FOR ENHANCING BODY AWARENESS

Children are continually exploring the movement potentials of their bodies. They are in the process of gaining increased information about the body parts, what the body parts can do, and how to make them do it. The teacher of young children can assist in this exploratory process by structuring informal learning experiences that maximize children's opportunities for using a variety of body parts in a multitude of activities. The following is a compilation of some activities that will be helpful in enhancing body awareness.

Objectives

Through participation in body awareness activities the children will learn:

1. The location of the various parts of the body.
2. The names of these parts.
3. The relationship of one body part to another.
4. The importance of a single body part in leading movement.
5. How to move the body more efficiently.
6. To be aware of the body and its parts at all times.
7. To be able to contract and relax specific muscles.

Movement Experiences

Locating the Large Body Parts

1. Have the children find the location of their large body parts. Have them see how quickly and accurately they can touch each part as you name it. See how quickly can they touch their:
    a.   Head
    b.   Neck
    c.   Chest
    d.   Waist
    e.   Stomach
    f.   Hips
    g.   Legs
    h.   Elbows
    i.   Shoulders
    j.   Back
    k.   Spine
    m.   Front

2. Repeat the above activity, this time reversing the procedure. That is, point to the body parts and have the children name them. The body parts may be as general or as specific as you wish, depending on the children's abilities.
3. Have the children find out how large their body parts are. For example:
    a.   Move your hand down the length of your arm. Where does it start, and where does it stop?
    b.   Place two hands around your waist . . . how big is it? . . . how can you move at the waist? Try bending forward, backward, and sideward . . . can you twist at the waist?
4. Help the children discover all about the sides of their bodies. For example, you may request that they:
    a.   Move one hand down the sides of their bodies.
    b.   Find the side of the head . . . shoulder . . . chest . . . waist . . . hip . . . knee . . . ankle . . . foot.
    c.   Repeat the same procedure on the opposite side of the body.

Locating the Small Body Parts

1. While the children are standing, the teacher may have the children
    a.   Put their elbows together.
    b.   Put their feet apart.
    c.   Touch one elbow.
    d.   Put their knees together.
    e.   Touch their noses.
    f.   Touch their toes with their arms crossed.

    g. Touch one knee and one foot.
    h. Place their palms together.
    i. Touch their heels.
    j. Touch their eyelashes, eyebrows.
2. Use other body parts in place of or in addition to those mentioned above.

Move and Listen

1. Have the children perform a locomotor task but have them stop and position themselves on your command. For example, you may have them moving about the room and tell them to stop on:

    a. One foot
    b. Both feet
    c. One hand
    d. Seat and both feet
    e. Feet and fingers
    f. Head, hands, and feet
    g. Hands and knees
    h. Back
    i. One foot and one hand
    j. One foot, two hands, and head

2. Permit the children to choose their own way of stopping and positioning themselves on your command of "freeze."

Partner Practice

1. Have the children move around the floor to a different person each time and touch the following body parts with their hands to another person as directed by the teacher:

a.	Spine	**f.**	Arms	**k.**	Toes	**p.**	Back
b.	Ears	**g.**	Elbows	**l.**	Hands	**q.**	Knees
c.	Neck	**h.**	Legs	**m.**	Fingers	**r.**	Hips
d.	Chin	**i.**	Ankles	**n.**	Chest	**s.**	Feet
e.	Shou[.]ders	**j.**	Wrists	**o.**	Stomach	**t.**	Heels

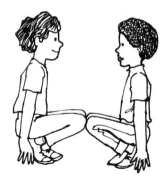

2. Repeat the above activity with the children using the body parts you named to touch the corresponding body part of another child.

Body-Part Differentiation

1. Hip movement with bending at the knee:
    a. Draw the knees up to the chest, then thrust them out straight while on the back.
    b. Do the same thing as above, but with continuous circular thrusting movements.
    c. While lying on the stomach, draw both knees up under the stomach and then extend them both outward.
    d. While on the stomach bend one knee and draw it up alongside the body, on the floor, until it is in line with the hip.
2. While they are lying on their backs have the children:
    a. Lift one leg and lower it.
    b. Move the leg out to the side along the floor, then return it to the midposition beside the other leg.
    c. Swing the leg out to the side and back.
    d. Rotate the leg back and forth on the heel.

     e.   Lift one leg and cross it over the other leg and touch floor if possible.

     f.   Swing one leg over the other.

     g.   Lift the leg and rotate it at the hip, making circles in the air with the foot.

     h.   Place an object between the child's knees and tell him to hold it tightly.

3. Repeat the above activities while on the stomach.

4. While they are standing have the children perform the following shoulder movements:

     a.   Move a hand up alongside the body, extend it over the head, and lower it in the same way.

     b.   Extend an arm out at the side, then lower it.

     c.   Extend an arm over the head, then down.

     d.   Extend an arm out in front, then lower it.

     e.   Extend an arm out in front, then move it from the center out to the side and then back again.

     f.   Hunch the shoulders up and down with the arms at the sides, then swing them forward and backward.

     g.   Swing the arms in a circle in front of the body.

     h.   Swing the arms in a full circle at the side.

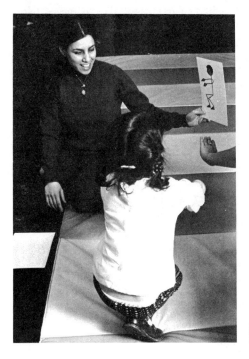

Imitating body positions is an excellent learning experience.

      i.   Extend the arms out at the sides and swing them in circles of various sizes.

      j.   Move just the shoulders forward and backward.

      k.   Move the shoulders in a circle.

5. While they are seated have the children perform the following hand and finger movements:

      a.   Make a fist.

      b.   Spread the fingers apart, then move them back together.

      c.   Bring the tip of the thumb and all of the fingers together.

      d.   Bring the tip of the thumb and the "pointer" finger (forefinger) together.

      e.   Extend the fingers and thumb to maximum and then relax.

      f.   Move the thumb across the four fingers and back.

      g.   Touch each fingertip with the tip of the thumb. Begin with the "pointer" finger and move to the little finger then back.

      h.   Grasp a ball in one hand, then lift one finger at a time.

      i.   Close the hand to a fist, and then release one finger at a time.

      j.   Extend the hands, then lower one finger at a time to form a fist.

Where Can You Bend?

1. Permit the children to experiment with a still dowel and with a jointed "Barbie" doll to see where the body parts bend. If possible, a paper skeleton or a real one, and a dentist's jaw could be used to graphically portray the body parts that bend.

2. Encourage the children to move the following joints in as many ways as possible:

      a.   Jaw

      b.   Neck

      c.   Shoulders

      d.   Elbow

      e.   Wrist

      f.   Fingers

      g.   Waist

      h.   Hip

      i.   Knee

      j.   Ankle

      k.   Toes

3. Experiment with what movement is like *without* one of the above items at a time.

Paired Parts

1. Have the children touch one body part to another. The following is a list of examples:

      a.   Touch your ear to a shoulder.

     b. Touch your cheek to a shoulder.
     c. Touch your shoulder to a knee.
     d. Touch your nose to a knee.
     e. Touch your elbow to a thigh.
     f. Touch your thigh to a knee.
     g. Touch your knee to an ankle.
     h. Touch your toe to a knee.
     i. Touch your toe to the chin.

2. There are numerous other possibilities for touching paired parts. Have the children explore them.

Rhymes for Enhancing Body Awareness. The following is a compilation of several rhymes that may be used to enhance body awareness. A variety of body action can easily be set to these rhymes.

1. Caterpillar

Caterpillar crawling around
Where green and juicy leaves are found
Soon a silk cocoon you'll spin
Winding threads 'til you're within
When the spring comes by and by
Flutter out a butterfly.

2. Hands

Hands on your shoulders
Hands on your knees
Hands behind you—if you please
Touch your tummy, now your toes
Now your head, now your nose,
Hands up high in the air,
Now down to your side, then touch your hair.
Hands up as high as before
Now clap your hands, $1-2-3-4$
And now—if you please, sit on the floor.

3. You're a tree

You're a tree, and so am I
With branches reaching to the sky
Our trunk is wrinkly, rough, and brown
Our feet planted deep within the ground
But our leaves the colors of pumpkins and berries
Are preparing to fly as gaily dressed fairies
Who love to play on a windy day
(And that's a secret I've been told)
We swing and sway in a gentle breeze
But winter nears so the wind is cold
And we shiver and shake, shudder and sneeze
And look! What's happened to all our leaves
What lovely costumes the fairies wear
As they glide donned in leaves through the air

Down, downy
Slowly
down downy
Where they'll leave their gowns
To paint the ground. . . .

4. Jack-in-the box

Down in the box, still as still can be
Lift up the lid, what do you see?
Jumping jacks, jumping jacks, high as we go!
Jumping jacks, jumping jacks, this is how we go!

(or)

Jack-in-the-box is out of sight
When the cover is fastened tight
Lift the lock and up he goes,
Jack-in-the-box with his hopping toes!

5. Monkey on a string

I can climb so very high,
I can almost reach the sky,
I can climb most anything
I'm a monkey on a string!

6. Snowman

We're building a snowman big and round
And when the sun shines
He'll melt to the ground.

Finger Plays for Enhancing Body Awareness. The following is a compilation of several finger plays that contribute to the development of body awareness.

1. Eensy weensy spider

Eensy weensy spider
Went up the water spout
Down came the rain
and washed the spider out
Out came the sun
and dried up all the rain
So the eensy weensy spider
Crawled up the spout again.

2. Where is thumbkin?

Where is thumbkin?
Where is thumbkin?

Here I am
How are you today sir?
Very fine, I thank you
Run a way
Run a way

(Repeat for pointer)
(Repeat for tall man)
(Repeat for ring man)
(Repeat for pinkie)

3. Two little firefighters

Two little firefighters sleeping in a row.
Ding dong goes the bell down the pole they go.
Off on their engines red they go-go go-go-go.
Fighting the blazing fire so-o so-o so.
When all the fire is out home sooooo slooooow.
Back to bed they go—all in a row.

4. Three blue pigeons

Three blue pigeons, sitting on a wall
Three blue pigeons, sitting on a wall
One flew away, OHHHHH!
Two blue pigeons sitting on a wall
Two blue pigeons sitting on a wall
Another one flew away, OHHHH!
One blue pigeon sitting on a wall
One blue pigeon sitting on a wall
And one came back hooray!
Two blue pigeons sitting on a wall
(etc.)

5. In a cabin

In a cabin in the woods
Little man by the window stood
Saw a rabbit hopping by,
Knocking at his door.
Help me, help me, help me he cried!
Else the hunter shoot me dead
Little rabbit come inside
Happy we will be!

6. Five little squirrels

Five little squirrels sat upon a tree
The first said, "What do I see?"
Second said, "I smell a gun."
Third said, "Come on! Let's run."
Fourth said, "Let's hide in the shade."
Fifth said, "I'm not afraid."
Bang, bang! Went the hunter's gun.
And, away they ran, everyone.

Put-Together People

1. Have the children make a life-sized figure by crushing single pieces of newspaper and stuffing them into long underwear. After the underwear is completely stuffed, dress the figure and have the children each draw a head and features from a paper bag. The hands and feet may be made with gloves and an old pair of shoes. The stuffed figure may be representative of a particular time of the year or theme.

   a. Cut out the body parts of a "person" using construction paper or poster board. Have the children assemble the legs, arms, head, and torso of the figures. Hook the pieces together with brads, or tape the pieces together to complete the figure.

b. Cut out the body party parts of two or more "people." Give each child in the group one body part. See if they can assemble the figure. The same activity may be repeated as a relay.

c. Using a doll with movable joints, have the children bend it into various positions and then see if they can reproduce these positions with their bodies.

d. Giants: The children sit in a circle around two giant paper cut-out parts of two bodies, one a boy, the other a girl. Two children are chosen to compete in putting the parts together; the one completing the giant figure first is the winner.

Mirror Activities

1. One child stands in front of a full-length mirror. The other children give directions to locate his body parts. The child can only look at his reflection in the mirror when touching the designated part. Upon making a mistake, the child giving the last instruction takes the mirror position.

2. Repeat the above activity but having the mirror child using both hands to touch his body.

3. Repeat the above activities but indicating the right or left parts of the body in the mirror reflection.

4. The teacher serves as the mirror. The children imitate the movements of the "mirror."

ACTIVITY IDEAS FOR ENHANCING SPATIAL AWARENESS

Objectives

Through practice in spatial awareness activities the children will:

1. Learn how much space their bodies occupy.

2. Be able to project their bodies into external space.

3. Be able to locate objects in space from a personal frame of reference (egocentric localization).
4. Be able to locate objects in space independent of one another (objective localization).
5. Improve their fundamental movement abilities.
6. Enhance their efficiency of movement.

Movement Experiences

Big and Small

1. Have the children find a place on the area where they are free from contact with others. Ask them to make themselves as small as possible. Point out that as small "balls," each child takes up very little room and so does not bother his neighbor.

2. Now have the children make themselves as big as possible. Now point out that as they get bigger so do their neighbors. This means that each needs more room for himself and to keep from bumping someone else. The children become familiar with their spatial relationships to others.
3. The children can be asked to assume different shapes such as a "tree," "rock," or "telephone pole." Have the children assume the new positions at varying rates of speed. Assuming the shapes of letters and numbers may also be performed.

Maze Walk

1. Children walk through a maze of chairs and tables without touching.
   a. Walk between objects
   b. Step over ojbects
   c. Crawl under objects
   d. Walk around objects
   e. Step on objects
2. Perform the maze activities using a variety of locomotor activities.
   a. Jumping

    b. Hopping
    c. Skipping
    d. Crawling

Rope Walking

   1. Place ropes in various patterns and geometric shapes on the floor. Have the children walk the rope forward.

    a. Wavy lines
    b. Circle
    c. Square
    d. Triangle
    e. Step over and through objects

   2. Repeat the activities as above but do them moving forward while blindfolded. Have children tell you about the shape of the line they are walking on.

Back Space

   1. Walk a rope placed on the floor going backward. Place the rope in various patterns.
   2. Throw objects backward to a visualized goal.

3. Sit down on an object without visually monitoring it.
   a. Chair
   b. Beanbag chair
   c. Inner tube
   d. Trampoline
4. Walk backward through a simple obstacle course that the child has had an opportunity to visually memorize.
5. Count the number of steps to a point on the floor while walking forward. Repeat while walking backwards and see how close the children come to the predetermined point.

Obstacle Course

1. Use tasks such as:
   a. "Footsteps" placed on the floor

   b. Carpet squares on the floor
   c. Climbing and sliding ropes
   d. Crawling over and under and through objects
   e. Stepping into shoe boxes
2. Map.
   a. Follow yarn line through the obstacle course.

Body Space

1. Outline the children's bodies on a sheet of newsprint while they are lying on their backs. Have the children:
   a. Cut out their bodies
   b. Color their bodies
   c. Dress their bodies
   d. Hang their bodies up
   e. Compare sizes

2. Gross motor activities:
   a. Have the children roll over and see how much space they occupied.
   b. Have the children spread out and see how much space they can occupy.
   c. Have the children see how little space they can occupy.
   d. Have them crawl under a table and other objects of different heights and see how well they fit without touching.
   e. Count steps, jumps, and so on taken to go from one point to another.

Other Space

1. Using empty milk cartons:
   a. Compare different-sized milk cartons (half pint to gallon containers).
   b. Compare the water-holding capacity of the containers. Compare size by pouring from carton to carton.
   c. Fill different-sized containers with sand. Compare the weights of the containers.
   d. Compare the volumes of sand held by each container.

Near and Far

1. Egocentric localization:
   a. Have the children estimate the distance from where they are standing to a specific point by the number of steps that it will take to get there.
   b. Measure the distance in steps. Compare estimates.
2. Objective localization:
   a. Have the children estimate the distance between two independent points, for example, the doll house and the carpentry bench.
   b. Step off the distance and compare.

Twister Activities

1. Have the children first play the game individually in order to develop free body control.
2. Have them play the game with a partner.

Map Activities

1. Map reading:
   a. Place a large map of the classroom, school, commmunity, or state on the floor. Give them a route to follow indicating specific points that they must visit before proceeding to the next point.
   b. Give each child a map with clues to the "treasure." Indicate in precise terms where they should go and the procedures to be followed. (Second grade and up).

Miscellaneous Spatial Awareness Activities

1. Locomotor movements:
   a. Crawling
   b. Leaping
   c. Jumping
2. Axial movements:
   a. Bending
   b. Rising

Exploring space in an important means of developing spatial awareness.

          c. Stretching
          d. Reaching
          e. Twisting
          f. Falling
     3. Following objects:
          a. Following colors
          b. Following arrows
          c. Following words
          d. Tunnel crawling
     4. Exploring space:
          a. Self-space
          b. Common space
          c. Moving at different levels
          d. Moving in different floor patterns

ACTIVITY IDEAS FOR ENHANCING DIRECTIONAL AWARENESS

Directional awareness is of considerable concern to the classroom teacher and children who are beginning formal instruction in reading. Directional awareness involves both an internal and external sensitivity for sidedness. Activities designed to enhance directional awareness may have an influence on perceptual readiness for reading.

Objectives

Practice in movement activities that emphasize the directional aspect of the task will:

     1. Contribute to the development of laterality (i.e. internal awareness of direction).
     2. Contribute to the development of directionality (external projection of laterality).
     3. Aid in establishing readiness for reading.
     4. Contribute to the development of fundamental movement abilities.
     5. Enhance one's ability to move efficiently through space.

Movement Experiences

Clock Games

     1. Make a clock on a chalkboard about 18 inches in diameter. Instruct the children to place their right hand on one of the numbers and their left hand on a second number, holding a piece of chalk in each hand. Ask them to

SPECIAL ORDER
UNIVERSITY BOOKSTORE
UNIVERSITY OF NORTHERN COLORADO
GREELEY, CO 80639   (303) 351-2136

CUSTOMER NAME	Lois Mueller
ADDRESS	1411 10th Ave #2 Greeley
	DATE 7/7 19
	PHONE 352-4767
	ZIP CODE 80631

AUTHOR		**PUBLISHER**
Gillsun G L		Rush Mefi
TITLE		
Developmental Measurement & Evaluation		
Children		
ISBN#		
0-02-340230-6		
CLERK	**QUANTITY**	**EDITION/PAPER OR CLOTH?**
ML		**PRICE**

If available, would you accept a used book?   Yes ☐   No ☐

WE CANNOT GUARANTEE PRICES FOR ANY BOOKS.
PUBLISHERS CHANGE PRICES WITHOUT NOTICE.

move their left hand to a different number and their right hand to a different number on your command. Both hands should move at the same time and arrive at their goals at the same time.

2. Variations:
   a. Toward the center: Place hands on the circumference of circle and bring both to center. Place hands on 1 and 5 and bring to 0, then 6 and 2 to zero.
   b. Away from center: Begin with both hands on 0 and move out to specified numbers.
   c. Parallel movements: Put the left hand on 7 and right hand on 0, then move the left hand to 0 and right hand to 3. Change directions.
   d. Crossed midline movements. Place the left hand on 7 and right hand on 1, then move both hands to 0. Change directions.
   e. Left to right: Place the left hand at 7 and right hand at 0, then move the left hand to 0 and right hand to 1.

Directional Swinging-Ball Activities

1. Attach a ball to a string. Move it in different directions and in different orientations to the child.
   a. Tap it, then catch it.
   b. Swing it with one hand, then the other, then both.
2. Swinging activities:
   a. Swing ball to the left and to the right.
   b. Swing ball forward and backward.
   c. Swing ball in circles around the child.
   d. Swing ball in circles in front of the child.
   e. Swing ball in different planes above the child as he lies on his back.
   f. While he is on his back, swing ball from left to right, then from head to toe.
3. Striking activities: repeat the above activities but using striking motions.

Directional Commands

1. The following are some examples of patterns in which children may move in order to enhance directional awareness. The number of possibilities is limitless. Use your imagination:
   a. Run forward 10 steps and walk backward five steps.
   b. Put your feet together and jump to one side.
   c. Hop forward three times on one foot, then backward three times on the other foot.
   d. Move sideways across the room.
   e. Have the child move close to you and then move far away.
   f. Move from the front of room to the rear of room, going over one object and under another object.
   g. Stand near the desk.
   h. Stand far away from the pencil sharpener.
   i. Point to the wall nearest you and walk to that wall.
   j. Place the closest chair between the desk and the wall.
   k. One child sits and another stands. Have the standing child move in front of, to the side of (etc.) the sitting child.

Over, Under, and Around

1. Long jumping rope
   a. Two people hold a jump rope and place the rope on the floor. The child runs and jumps over it. The rope is raised slightly for each succeeding jump. Game ends when the child hits the rope.
   b. Go under a high rope which is then lowered slightly each try.
   c. Walk over instead of running and jumping.
2. Place several objects around the gym such as jump ropes, walking boards, mats, chairs, tires, ladder, or any large equipment. Children follow the leader and imitate as he moves around the obstacles.
   a. Could be played in the classroom as leader moves around room.
   b. Place objects on the floor and permit each child to go around the objects in his or her own direction and name the direction in which he went.
   c. Give verbal commands for the direction of each obstacle.
   d. Blindfold the children. Have them work with a "seeing" partner who gives directional commands (no tactile clues) on how to get to the object.

Directional Walking-Board Activities

1. Walk forward.
2. Walk backward—discourage looking back.
3. Walk sideways—slide one foot over, then bring the other one to meet it.

4. Turn on the board:
   a. Walk forward, turn, and walk sideways.
   b. Walk forward, turn, and return, walking forward.
   c. Walk backward, turn, and return walking backward.
   d. Vary combinations.
5. Step over and under objects placed on the board.
6. Walk across the board carrying heavy objects.

Directional, Unilateral, Bilateral, and Cross-lateral Activities

1. Bilateral movements:
   a. Lie flat on the floor on your back with your arms at your sides and your feet together.
      i. Move feet apart as far as you can, keeping the knees stiff.
      ii. Move the arms along the floor until the hands come together above the head, keeping elbows stiff.
      iii. Move the arms and legs at the same time.
2. Unilateral and cross-lateral movements:
   a. Lie flat on the floor on your back with your arms at your sides and your feet together.
      i. Move the right leg only to an extended position and return it.
      ii. Repeat the above with the left leg only, right arm only, and left arm only.
      iii. Move the right leg and right arm together.
      iv. Move the left arm and leg together.
      v. Move the right arm and the left together.
      vi. Move the left arm and the right leg.

Directional Throwing Activities

1. Use beanbag and a wastebasket:
   a. Set a basket in front of the child and have him throw at it.
   b. Vary the basket's orientation to the right or left and throw at it.

2. Use ball to roll at a bowling pin.
   a. Vary the location of the bowling pin or the child.
   b. Vary the distance of the roll.
3. From a prone position, or a supine position, have the child throw a beanbag:
   a. Upward
   b. Forward
   c. Backward
   d. To each side

Directional Chalkboard Activities

1. Dot-to-dot. Teacher makes two dots, child connects, teacher makes a third dot and child connects, and so on. (Do not cross child's midline here.)
2. Dot-to-dot, but cross child's midline.
3. Draw double circles and change directions after completion and/or in the middle of drawing.
4. Draw "lazy-eight" figures. With one hand, then the other; one direction, then reverse.
5. Draw vertical lines, up–down, down–up.
6. Draw horizontal lines, left-right, right-left.
7. Draw horizontal lines and vertical lines simultaneously.
8. Draw a square, then alter size, direction, and starting point.

Directional Ladder Activities

1. *Walking:* Looking straight ahead, the child walks the length of the ladder.
   a. Walk forward in the spaces.
   b. Walk backward in the spaces.

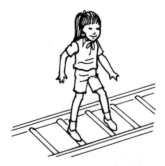

   c. Walk sideways in the spaces. Walking sideways may be done by:
      i. Leading with the left foot
      ii. Leading with the right foot
      iii. Continually crossing the lead foot in front

      iv. Continually crossing the lead foot in back
   d. Walk the rungs (forward, backward, sideways).
2. *Crawling:* The ladder is turned on its side, and to secure it, the teacher sits on the top side. The children crawl in and out of the spaces.
   a. Crawl forward.
   b. Crawl backward.
   c. Do not touch the rungs if possible.

Twist-Board Activities

1. The child places his feet about shoulder width apart on the board and bends his knees slightly. He may twist by:
   a. Moving both of his arms to one side and then to the other side.
   b. Swinging one arm forward and up, and swinging the other arm backward and down.
2. The child puts his left arm behind his back and uses his right arm to simulate a one-arm breast stroke. This will cause the child to turn completely around.
3. Repeat step (2), and change arm positions (right arm behind back, left arm moving).
4. While twisting, the child:
   a. Crosses his arm in front of his chest.
   b. Extends his arms (hands clasped):
      i. In front of his body
      ii. Behind his body
      iii. Over his head

Directional Creeping and Walking Activities

1. Creeping
   a. Creep in a homolateral pattern (left hand with left knee, right hand with right knee) while looking at target placed at eye level.
   b. Creep in a cross-lateral pattern (left hand with left knee, right hand

with right knee) looking first at eye-level target, then at the forward hand.

    c. Creep in a homolateral pattern while looking at the hand that goes out in front.

    d. Creep forward, backward, and to the side using the above patterns.

2. Walking:

    a. Walk in a homolateral pattern (left hand points to left toes while right arm is stretched behind the child, then right hand points to right toes).

    b. Cross-lateral walking.

    c. Mid-air change—begin with the left arm forward and the left foot forward, with the weight evenly distributed on both feet. Right arm should be straight out in back. On command "change" each child jumps up in the ari, reversing the position of arms and legs. The eyes should fixate on a target at all times and the child should land on the take-off spot.

    d. Mid-air change—cross-lateral movement (left arm and right leg forward).

Directional Ball Activities

1. Use one hand, then repeat the skills with the other hand:

    a. Tap a swinging ball.

    b. Bounce and catch a ball with one hand.

    c. Dribble a ball with one hand.

    d. Bounce and catch with alternating hands.

    e. Throw in various directions.

    f. Catch from different directions.

2. Use one foot, then repeat the skills with the other foot.

    a. Kick a ball with alternate feet, using the toe.

    b. Kick a ball with alternate feet, using the instep.

    c. Trap a ball with one foot, then the other.

    d. Trap a ball with one knee, then the other.

ACTIVITY IDEAS FOR ENHANCING TEMPORAL AWARENESS

Temporal awareness involves the development of a time structure within the body. Eye-hand coordination and eye-foot coordination refer to the child's ability to coordinate movements and are the end result of a fully established time structure within the child. This "clock mechanism" helps children to better coordinate the movements of their bodies with the various sensory systems.

Objectives

Through temporal awareness movement activities children will learn:

1. *Synchrony,* which is the ability to get the body parts to work together smoothly.
2. *Rhythm,* which is the process of performing many synchronous acts in a harmonious pattern or succession.
3. *Sequence,* which is the proper order of actions required to perform a skill.
4. Eye-hand coordination and eye-foot coordination, which are the end result of synchrony, rhythm, and sequence being efficiently integrated.

Movement Experiences

Ball Activities

1. Stationary ball:
   a. Contact it with an open hand.
   b. Contact it with an implement.
   c. Kick at it.
   d. Contact it with various body parts.
2. Swinging ball:
   a. Contact it with an open hand as a fist.
   b. Alternate left and right hands.
   c. Contact it with various body parts.
   d. Contact it with various implements moving from shorter to longer levers (spoon, table tennis paddle, tennis racket, squash racket, baseball bat).
   e. Catch the swinging ball with both hands.
   f. Catch the swinging ball with one hand.
   g. Visually track the ball as it swings, without moving the head.
   h. Visually track the ball and point at it as it swings.

Rhythmic Training

1. On the signal have each child find his own "personal space." Have them make a low, balanced shape, keeping one hand free to tap on the floor along with the beat of the drum. When the drum changes beat and pattern, the children must do the same.
2. Remaining balanced, have the children tap with a foot, elbow, and heel. Have a body part move in the air, following the drum. Use different tempos in each position. Keep the tempo even. Don't accelerate or decelerate.

My Beat. This activity, called "My Beat," enables the children to make and follow their own tempo and sequence.

1. Each child makes his or her own accompaniment and sets his or her own beat. They can make noises with their mouths or slap a hand against their bodies. Once they have established even beats, have them explore their personal space (the area around them) while moving to the beat.
2. Have each child explore around the room while moving to the beat. Let them move to a different tempo.

Free Flow

1. Ask the children to perform a relaxed, smooth swinging motion with their bodies. The motion can take them anywhere around the play area. (Stress spatial awareness to them to avoid collisions.) Have them perform a controlled swing so that it can be stopped on command. Make sure that when they stop a movement they are in complete balance and control.
2. Introduce physical obstacles that the children must successfully negotiate so as to improve body control and movement.

Moving-Target Toss

1. Have the children line up facing the target. Use an inflatable toy punching clown that will right itself after being pushed down. Use a barrel, waste basket, or pot and attempt to toss an object at it while it is moving from a reclining position to its normal upright position.
2. Suspend a hoop from a rope. Start it swinging in a pendular motion. Have children throw beanbags through the swinging hoop.
3. Roll a hoop or tire along the floor. Toss objects through it.

Balloon-Volleying Activities

Keep a balloon up in the air:

    a.   Use a volleying motion.
    b.   Hit it underhand.
    c.   Hit it above the head.
    d.   Use it below the waist.
    e.   Use various body parts tohit the balls.
    f.   Weight the balloon slightly and repeat the above activities.

Miscellaneous Large-Motor Temporal Activities

1. Move in different ways to a beat.
2. Jump rope to a beat.
3. Bounce a ball to a beat.
4. Pass a ball rhythmically.

5. Partners make their own beat and move to it.
6. Perform movements in sequence.
7. Accelerate and decelerate movement.
8. Create and absorb force.
9. Perform tossing and catching activities.
10. Perform kicking and trapping activities.
11. Perform dodging activities.

Miscellaneous Fine-Motor Temporal Activities

1. Bead stringing
2. Jacks
3. Pick-up sticks
4. Lacing and sewing cards
5. Clay modeling
6. Cutting
7. Coloring and pasting
8. Finger painting
9. Nuts and bolts
10. Sewing
11. Weaving
12. Zipping, snapping, and buttoning
13. Carpentry activities
14. Puppets
15. Chalkboard activities
16. Tracing
17. Pouring skills

SUGGESTED RECORDS

Brazelton, Ambrose, *Clap, Snap and Tap,* Kimbo Records, Deal, New Jersey, Box 246 (EA48).

Capon, Jack and Hallum, Rosemary, *Perceptual-Motor Rhythm Games,* Educational Activities, Inc., Box 392, Freeport, New York (11520, AR50, AC50).

Cratty, Bryant, J., *Physical Development for Children,* Kimbo Records, Deal, New Jersey, Box 246 (EA-PD).

Glass, Henry "Buzz", *Learning By Doing, Dancing, and Discovering,* Educational Activities, Inc., Box 392, Freeport, New York (11520, AR76).

Hallum, Rosemary and Glass, Henry "Buzz", *Individualization in Movement and Music,* Educational Activities, Inc., Box 392, Freeport, New York 11520 (AR49, AC49).

Hissam, Harold, *Coordination Skills,* Educational Activities Inc., & Kimbo Educational Records, P.O. Box 392, Freeport, New York 11520 (KEA 6050).

Lee, Karol: *Music for Movement Exploration,* Educational Activities, Inc., Box 392, Freeport, New York 11520 (KEA 5090).

Lewandowski, Diane, Ken Iversen, Herman Baldassarre, and Robert Marciante, *Limb Learning,* Educational Activities, Inc., Box 392, Freeport, New York 11520 (KEA 1145).

Palmer, Hap, *Creative Movement and Rhythmic Exploration,* Educational Activities, Inc., Box 392, Freeport, New York 11520 (AR/AC 533).

Palmer, Hap, *Easy Does It,* Educational Activities, Box 392, Freeport, New York 11520 (AR/AC 581).

Palmer, Hap, *Homemade Band,* Educational Activities Box 392, Freeport, New York 11520 (AR/AC 545).

Palmer, Hap, *Mod Marches,* Educational Activities, Inc., Box 392, Freeport, New York 11520 (AR/AC 527).

Palmer, Hap, *Getting to Know Myself,* Educational Activities, Freeport, New York, Box 392.

Riccione, Georgiana, *Developmental Motor Skills for Self-Awareness,* Kimbo Records Deal, New Jersey, Box 246 (KIM 9075).

21

Integrating Visual, Tactile and Auditory Perception Activities

Movement is one of the primary modes by which children develop and refine their perceptual world, and it may be used effectively by the classroom teacher and motor development specialist as a means of enhancing these abilities. The movement activities contained in this chapter may be described as "motor-perceptual" rather than "perceptual-motor," as in the previous chapter, although the differences are subtle and of no significant consequence when actually dealing with children. The activities contained in this chapter are movement activities designed to enhance the functioning of specific perceptual modalities, whereas the activities in earlier chapters are movement activities designed to enhance *both* perceptual *and* motor abilities.

In this chapter we will examine the contribution of movement experiences to the development of visual perception, auditory perception, and tactile perception. The olfactory and gustatory modalities have not been included because of their limited role in the education of children.

ACTIVITY IDEAS FOR ENHANCING VISUAL PERCEPTION

The visual apparatus is complete and functional at birth. Visual abilities develop rapidly during the early years of life and are crucial to effective functioning in a world that is visually oriented. The process of maturation and gaining experience both contribute to the development of highly sophisticated visual perceptual abilities. It has been estimated that up to 80 percent of all information we take in and utilize comes from the visual modality. As a result it becomes abundantly clear that the development and refinement of accurate visual perception is extremely important. The following pages contain a variety of movement experiences that have been found helpful in developing three aspects of visual perception crucial to effective functioning in school and the world, namely depth perception, form perception, and figure-ground perception.

Depth Perception

Depth perception is the ability to judge relative distances in three-dimensional space. Teachers working with depth perception activities need to consciously plan many and varied spatial and dimensional cues to serve as reference points for judgment of distance.

Objectives

    1. To enhance the ability to accurately judge distances and depth.
    2. To increase the ability to utilize external clues in determining depth distance and size.
    3. To enhance the ability to move efficiently in three-dimensional space.
    4. To enhance fundamental movement abilities.

Movement Experiences

Bowling When rolling a ball toward an object, line the lane moving toward the target with Indian clubs or markers of some type.

Targets A box within which balls land in various lengths and depths can be used as a target for throwing, striking, and kicking a light ball. Target throwing with all types of objects and at various distances is helpful.

The videotape machine is an excellent aid to visual perceptual development.

Hoops Hula hoops arranged in three-dimensional formations, plywood boxes with shapes cut out of the sides, pipes, and logs are good for tactile realization of depth.

Jumping Jumping from heights, over objects, and from one object to another develops perception of depth and distance. Use jumping from various heights on an angled balance beam or steps to the floor.

Balance Beam Place a balance beam diagonally toward the wall. Have the children find the point where they can reach and touch the wall while walking on the beam. Tape several points onto the balance beam. Show the children one piece of tape; remove it and have the children walk and stop where they think the tape was.

Boxes Place boxes of various heights in the center of a room. Attach objects at various heights to the wall. Instruct the children to select the box that will best assist them in retrieving the object they want.

Form Perception

Form perception or the ability to recognize shapes, forms, and symbols is necessary for academic success. Young children may be able to identify shapes correctly, but because of distortions of their visual memory, are often unable to reproduce them. Perception of shape constancy becomes crucial to children's ability to recognize shapes. They must learn that two- and three-dimensional forms belong to certain categories of shapes, regardless of size, color, texture, mode of representation, or the angle seen by the perceiver. Recognition of similarities and differences is the first step in identifying shapes and forms. Object discrimination is the second.

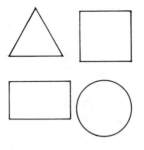

Three and 4-year olds rely on shape or form rather than color for identification of objects. At 5 years of age, color is generally a more important tool than form for identification of an object. At age 6-7 years, color and form are both important.

Objectives

1. To recognize and reproduce basic shapes.
2. To perceive differences in shapes and pieces of a puzzle.
3. To match similar symbols.
4. To recognize and reproduce basic forms and to use them in generalized situations (for example, to be able to see that a square and a triangle can form a house).
5. To be able to draw forms that exist in the environment and that can be seen in isolation of one another.

Movement Experiences

Shape Walking Walk simple geometric shpes placed on the floor.
1. Have the children walk a rope that is placed in various geometric shapes. Walking barefoot will enhance the tactile clues.
2. Walk a masking tape line and "feel" the shape with your toes.
3. Present a simple geometric shape to the children. Permit them to visually monitor it while they attempt to walk out the shape on the floor. They should strive to arrive back at the starting point when they complete the shape.
4. Repeat the above activity but do not permit visual monitoring of the displayed form.
5. Name a shape and have the children walk it out, returning to the starting point when they have completed the shapes.

Tracing Trace around geometric shapes with the fingers.
1. Use three-dimensional shapes.
2. Use templates.
3. Trace shapes drawn on a sheet of paper.
4. Reproduce the shapes by tracing over them.
5. Have the children complete incomplete geometric shapes drawn for them.

Making Things Make a variety of things utilizing various shapes.
1. Make a collage of geometrical shapes.
2. Use various-shaped blocks to build a familiar object.
3. Draw a picture of a person composed entirely of different geometric shapes.
4. Make shapes using toothpicks, straws, or tongue depressors.

Body Shapes Have the children use their bodies to make a variety of shapes.
1. Have the children form various shapes, letters, and numerals with their bodies.

2. Have the children from part of a shape with their bodies. Ask one to help complete the shape he or she thinks the others are forming.

Shape Tag Play tag using selected shapes as free places.

Stepping Shapes Spread various shapes on the floor around the room. Have the children step only on certain shapes. Make and play a game of twister using shapes as the focal point.

Matching Shapes Play matching games using various shapes and sizes. Sort objects according to shape.

Beanbag Toss Throw beanbags on targets with different-shaped holes cut out. Points are scored for throwing through the various shapes.

Shadow Pantomime Hang a sheet with a light in front of it in a closet with the door open. Have child imitate physical activities while the others guess what they think is being done.

Figure–Ground Perception

Visual figure–ground perception is the ability to select a limited number of stimuli from a mass. These particular stimuli (auditory, tactile, olfactory, kinesthetic, visual, and/or gustatory) form the figure. The others form a dim field. This figure is the center of attention. When the attention shifts, the former figure fades into the background. We can only perceive something in its relation to its field.

In teaching children who have not fully developed their figure-ground perception, attempt to limit the number of stimuli in the background and progress by adding gradually. For example, practice dribbling the "red" ball *not* on the red-and-black tiled floor, but on a posterboard (white or light solid color) or sheet to simplify contrasting the figure of attention and the background. Do not place the children in a milieu of posters, streamers, and other attention-grabbers.

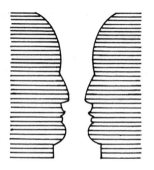

1. To be able to focus attention on the object of regard.
2. To be able to move efficiently through the visual field.
3. To be able to locate objects located in field of vision.
4. To improve eye-hand and eye-foot coordination.

Movement Experiences

Discrimination Discriminate between various objects in a room. Find objects that are difficult to locate.

Sorting Sort according to size, shape, color, texture, number, thickness, and length.

Attention Practice shifting attention by selecting designated objects from a box or bag.

Ladder Maze Place a ladder on a floor of a solid design, on one with a diagonal design, and on one with various other designs. Have the children step between the rungs without touching them.

Target Toss Use targets to focus attention. Throw beanbags at selected parts of the target. For example, you may use a large chosen target and throw at various body parts.

Egg-Shell Walk Place a path of egg-shell halves on the floor. Cross that path with other paths of various materials, such as rope, tape, and paper. Have the children step only on the egg shells.

Rope Walk Walk on a rope winding through a myriad of objects.

Paddle Balance Have the children balance a ball on a paddle or board.

Rope Maze Form a maze on the floor of rope paths. Have identical clues at each end of the same rope. Send the children to find the match of the clue they are given.

Candyland Play a life-sized version of "Candyland" (by Parker Brothers) where the children spin for colors and take their places on the appropriate color on the "board."

Tetherball "Tetherball" is a good game for developing one's ability to concentrate on one figure through a field.

Find Hidden Objects Use *Highlights* magazine for pictures with concealed objects that the children can find.

Finger Fixation Have the children hold their right and left forefingers about a foot apart and a foot from their eyes. They then look quickly from one finger to the other. They must be sure to "land" each time. If they have difficulty they can be helped by having another person move their own finger in the same way the eyes are to move.

Pencil-Wall Fixation The children hold a pencil erect about 10-12 inches in front of their nose. They then look from pencil to numbers on a calendar (or picture on the wall) and back again for several "round trips." They must move their eyes quickly and fixate on each object.

Paper-Punch Picture Punch holes in a picture until the children are no longer able to obtain meaning from the pictures. Pictures of many objects are harder to perceive than pictures of only one subject.

ACTIVITY IDEAS FOR ENHANCING AUDITORY PERCEPTION

The development of auditory perceptual abilities has not received the attention by authors and practitioners that the visual modality has. Auditory perception, however, is nonetheless important, particularly with young children. Their inability to read makes their formal education primarily one of: (1) listening to auditory clues, (2) discriminating between sounds, and (3) applying meaning to them.

Auditory perception is enhanced when children attend to verbal directions, translate music into movement, and interpret the "feel" of various sounds through movement. The use of musical instruments aids in developing the auditory abilities. The following pages contain numerous activities for developing and reinforcing listening skills, auditory discrimination, and auditory-memory abilities.

Listening Skills

It is important for children to hear and remember what is said, but it is also crucial that they first *listen* to what is being said. Learning to listen is basic to auditory perception. Many children have been conditioned to "tune out" certain auditory clues. Take, for example, the child engrossed in a television program who somehow manages not to hear the pleas of mother or father to come to dinner. We are all familiar with children who "never listen." Learning to listen to auditory clues can be developed through a variety of activities. Games that involve an awareness and identification of sound sources enhance listening abilities. Activities that require the following of simple directions are also helpful, as well as activities that require a motoric response to a verbal command.

Objectives

1. To develop an awareness of sound sources.
2. To be able to identify various familiar sounds.

3. To develop the ability to listen to auditory clues in the immediate environment.
4. To respond appropriately to auditory commands.
5. To be able to respond efficiently, through movement, to auditory clues.
6. To enhance the ability to discriminate between various auditory clues.

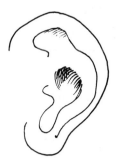

Movement Experiences

Traditional Games Many traditional games that children have played down through the years involve a considerable amount of listening skills:

1. Simon Says
2. Mother May I
3. Red Rover
4. Red Light

Hot and Cold Hide an object somewhere in the room while "it" is not looking. "It" attempts to find the object by moving around the room and listening to the loudness or softness of the class's clapping. As he or she approaches the object the clapping becomes louder. As he or she moves away from it the clapping becomes softer.

Clap Clap The class is spread out around the room. One child is told to clap her hands twice when "it" says "clap clap." "It" points to the person who she thought did the clapping.

Poems Read a poem to the class requesting them to fill in the rhyming words.

Music Listen to music that has a variety of fast and slow sections. Request that they move about the room in time to the music. If space does not permit active movement, simply have the children raise their hands when they hear the fast part or the slow part.

Bounce Bounce Have a small group of children sit down with their backs toward you. Drop a utility ball from waist height and let it bounce. Children should count the number of bounces that the ball makes.

Active Animals Use a variety of rhythm instruments to depict the sounds of moving animals while telling a story containing the names of several animals. Whenever the animal's name is mentioned the child with the corresponding instrument makes its sound. For example:

1. Drum for a lumbering elephant
2. Sandpaper blocks for a slithering snake
3. Triangle for birds
4. Xylophone-for caterpillar
5. Rhythmic sticks for galloping horses

Hands One child is blindfolded and must guess what another child is doing with her hands. She may, for example, be clapping, snapping, rubbing, scratching the desk, or tapping the chalkboard.

Echo The teacher claps out a simple rhythmic pattern using slow or fast beats, even or uneven beats, and the children respond by moving around the room to the appropriate beat.

Listening Walk The children and teacher take a walk around the neighborhood for the purpose of listening to and identifying different sounds. Sounds may be categorized as:

1. Human sounds (walking, talking, etc.)
2. Animal sounds (running and cries of cats, dogs, birds, etc.)
3. Machinery sounds (noise of cars, buses, power mowers, trucks, etc.)
4. Nature sounds (wind, rustling of trees, leaves, etc.)

It Is I Play this game when the children know one another fairly well. One child sits in a chair with his back to the class. Another child comes up behind the seated child and knocks three times on the back of the chair. The seated child asks, "who is knocking at my door?" and the other child replies, "it is I." The seated child tries to guess who is knocking by identifying the child's voice. The teacher sets the number of guesses permitted.

Tape Recorder Sounds Use a tape recorder to record many familiar and easily distinguished sounds, such as a car horn, paper tearing, breathing, crying, clock ticking, sneezing, and so forth. Make a list of the sounds in their proper order so that you know what they are. Have the children try to identify the sounds.

Voice Recording Record several children's voices on the tape recorder and have them attempt to identify their classmates' voices and their own.

Freeze and Melt The teacher or a student says word "freeze" while the class is moving about the room. They immediately stop what they are doing and cease all movement (of the body and the mouth). When the word "melt" is called out they resume moving around the room. This is an effective activity for the teacher to introduce first as a game and to later incorporate in the classroom as a means of getting the immediate attention of the class.

Marching Performing a variety of marching activities in which the children must respond to verbal commands is excellent for helping older children learn to listen. Marching is also helpful in developing directional awareness.

Auditory Discrimination

Auditory discrimination is similar to visual figure-ground perception. It is the ability to detect one specific tonal quality and frequency within a whole complexity of sound stimuli. Individuals tend to initiate movement toward the direction from which the sound cue emerges (directional awareness). Auditory rhythm is an aspect of discrimination and is the ability to identify a regulated series of sounds interspersed by regulated moments of silence in repeated patterns.

The following is a list of general teaching hints for children experiencing difficulty in auditory discrimination.

1. Speak slowly, distinctly, and on the child's level.
2. Speak in natural volume. Extra volume can confuse the child's ability to discriminate what you say.
3. Speak so that the child can see your lips (for severe disabilities).
4. Maintain eye—to—eye contact.
5. Deliver brief, simple directions.

6. Control the environment.
7. Use situations with verbal responses, physical responses, and both responses.
8. Avoid repeating directions whenever possible.
9. Use a blindfold for emphasis on developing auditory sensations.

Objectives

1. To be able to respond to sounds or verbal commands.
2. To be able to react independently to verbal commands without visually monitoring others.
3. To be able to listen to a command and then carry it out without verbal repetition.
4. To enhance fundamental rhythmic abilities.
5. To be able to distinguish between similar sounds.
6. To be able to distinguish between dissimilar sounds.

Movement Experiences

Close Your Eyes Ask the children to close their eyes as you clap your hands several times. As the children to "clap just as I did." Vary this procedure by clapping in different rhythms.

1. You may also use two drums, having children imitate drum beats.
2. Repeat the activity with stamping, clapping, and snapping fingers.
3. Begin with even beats and progress to syncopated rhythm.

Tape Recorder Using a tape recorder, encourage children to say their names, imitate animals, and sing songs. The tape recorder may teach sounds not easily found in the child's environment. Encourage children to discuss and name the various sounds.

Musical Instruments Select several rhythm-producing instruments such as a drum, a triangle, a sand block, or a wooden block. Children watch as you make a sound on each. Ask the children to close their eyes and listen carefully. Strike a sound on one of the instruments such as a drum, and have the children open their eyes and tell you which instrument you played. Next have the children close their eyes as the teacher plays two instruments. Have the children tell you which instrument was played first, and which one was played last.

What Does It Sound Like? Using familiar noises have the children differentiate between loud and soft, fast and slow, first and last, high and low.

What Is It? Place a number of objects on a table. Tap these objects in order to familiarize the children with the sound produced. Have the children put their heads down. Tap an object and ask, "what is it?" After the children have become familiar with the objects, tap several of them and ask which you tapped first, second, and so on.

Where Is the Bell? Seat the children in a circle. Have one child leave the room. Give one of the children in the room a bell small enough to hide in his hand. Ask the child who left the room to come back in. When the child has returned, have all of the children stand and shake their fists above their heads. You may use more than one bell when the children become accustomed to the game.

Keep Off A stretched canvas piece is needed to be strung taut in a rectangular frame, about 3½ feet off the floor. The child is beneath. The teacher tosses a beanbag onto the canvas. By the sound of its landing, the child can hear where to bump it to hit it off the canvas.

Wall Targets Throwing blindfolded, the children listen to hear their beanbag hit a target made out of a resounding material.

Bounce Off Various textures and materials are situated as targets around the gym. They are used as rebound targets for the children throwing balls to hear the difference in sounds the bounces make.

Match the Cans Take 10 cans. Fill five with five different materials and duplicate these with the last five cans. Mix up the order and ask the child to match the cans by sound.

Auditory Memory

Auditory memory is the ability to retain auditory clues. Since much of the child's world involves the auditory modality, a great deal of information must be stored and

retained. The folliwng activities are designed to encourage retention of auditory clues.

Objectives

1. To enhance the ability to remember auditory clues.
2. To enhance the ability to readily remember directions.
3. To develop listening skills.
4. To enhance comprehension of what is heard.
5. To increase the ability to move efficiently to a series of auditory clues.

Movement Experiences

A Trip to the Zoo Begin a story about a trip to the zoo and all the animals that you will see. Give each child the name of an animal to imitate. When you name that animal in the story the child with the name of that animal acts out his or her interpretation.

Perform the same activity, having the children repeat the actions of the animal mentioned along with those that preceded it.

Story Telling Tell a familiar story (such as *Green Eggs and Ham, Cat in the Hat,* or *Jack in the Beanstalk*), having the children supply the repetiitve phrases at the proper place in the story.

Action Rhymes Sing a familiar "action" rhyme such as *Head, Shoulders, Knees, and Toes.* Omit a word from the song such as "head" and have the children touch that body part instead of naming it.

Instrument Playing Using the same idea as above play a simple pattern of notes on an xylophone several times. After the pattern is well known, omit a note and have the children fill it in.

Silly Hat Using an old hat (a beanbag will do), give the children a series of silly things to do. Start with two directions and gradually increase the numbers and complexity of the instructions.

Horse Race Using children as the "horses," conduct a horse race. Put a number on each child. Begin the race using only two or three "horses." Have them race (gallop) to a designated point and declare a winner indicating the number of the "horse" and its place (i.e., "number three came in first, and number eight came in second").

Have the remainder of the group tell you the order of the finish, using the horse numbers only. Increase the number of horses to four or more after practice with having the children recall the first three, four, or five "horses" to cross the finish line.

The Winner Is. . . . Repeat the above activity but declaring the ribbon winners. For example, "the horse that came in first wins the blue ribbon. Which number was it? The horse that came in second wins the red ribbon. Which number was it?" and so forth. You may then want to continue with "what color ribbon did number four win?" and so forth.

Lost and Found Pretend that several children in class lost an article of clothing. Have the children recall the names of those missing something.

ACTIVITY IDEAS FOR ENHANCING TACTILE PERCEPTION

The development of the sense of touch serves as a means of enhancing children's knowledge of the world about them. It is the modality by which they come into actual physical contact with their world. As with the visual and auditory channels, the tactile modality is developed through experience with objects in the environment. Tactile discrimination is the first and most basic aspect of tactile perception and involves the development of an awareness of the "feel" of things. Tactile memory involves the ability to associate tactile impressions with known objects.

The tactile modality is often neglected in the education of young children and is assumed to develop "naturally." It has been the experience of the author, however, that touch plays an important role in developing a more accurate sense of body-awareness. Children should learn to direct their tactile movements in such activities as climbing a ladder, crawling through a tunnel, tracing a maze blindfolded, or walking on a slippery surface.

Tactile Discrimination and Matching

Tactile discrimination is the earliest form of tactile development and involves developing an awareness of things through touch. Young children developing their tactile discrimination abilities are also in the process of developing a corresponding vocabulary of words such as hard, soft, spongy, rough, smooth, bumpy, coarse, slick, and sticky. The ability to distinguish form through tactile clues also begins to develop. Differentiating between circles, squares, and triangles as well as large and small objects develops, along with the ability to sort and match objects tactilely.

Objectives

1. To develop an awareness of tactile sensations.
2. To be able to discriminate between tactile clues.

Cutting a variety of different textured materials enhances tactile perception as well as fine motor coordination.

3. To be able to sort objects according to tactile characteristics.
4. To be able to match objects according to feel.

Movement Experiences

Collections Make collections of several types of objects and describe how they "feel."

1. Cloth (nylon, cotton, velvet, fur, burlap, dotted swiss, leather, wool, corduroy, etc.)
2. Balls (ping-pong, rubber, cork, styrofoam, steel, fringe balls, beach balls, golf balls, bowling balls, etc.)
3. Seeds (to pine cones, black walnuts, chestnuts, buckeyes, acorns, coconuts, sumas, beans, pods, etc.)
4. Minerals (shale, sandstone, gypsum, granite, marble, limestone, etc.)
5. Sandpaper (assorted grades of sandpaper ranging from coarse to very fine)
6. Food wrap (aluminum foil, waxed paper, plastic wrap, butcher paper, cellophane, brown paper bags, etc.)
7. Household staples (salt, sugar, flour, pepper corns, rice, macaroni, etc.)
8. Kitchen items (blunt scissors, butter spreader, various-sized spoons, fork, spatula, rubber scraper, cookie cutter, etc.)
9. Miscellaneous (plastic, metal, aluminum, steel, glass, tin, etc.)

Textured Paintings Make textured paintings using glue to secure such things as rice, sawdust, tissue paper, small stones, seeds and pods, popcorn, and sand.

Collages Make collages using a wide variety of textures.

Creative Movement Discriminate between various textures through movement. Have the children feel a texture such as silk and interpret it by moving the way it feels. Use a variety of textures that exhibit characteristics such as:

1. Bumpy
2. Smooth
3. Coarse
4. Prickly

Mystery Bag Place familiar but similar objects in a sack such as a toy car, boats, and trucks. Have a child reach in the bag, without looking, and describe to the class how one object feels. Children guess what object is being held.

Repeat the above activity but have the child reaching in guess what the object is after describing it to the class.

Tag an Object Place several different objects on the floor (use as many different objects as there are children). Blindfold each child (four to eight at a time works well) and whisper the name of the object they are to locate. On the signal "go," send them around the area trying to locate their object. They may remove their blindfold when they think they have located the proper object.

Repeat the same activity using several geometric shapes.

Geometric Shapes Blindfold a child. Hand the child one geometric shape at a time and have him tell all about it and name the shape.

Shape Trace Using your finger trace a geometric shape on the child's back. The child then tells about the shape and names it if possible.

Heavy and Light Sort a variety of objects into two categories of heavy and light. The same may be done with rough–smooth, soft–hard.

Sandpaper Sort Using different grades of sandpaper, sort them according to texture blindfolded.

Repeat the above activity but sort according to size, shape, texture. Perform first while visually monitoring, then with a blindfold.

Touch Tag Play a game of tag in which you tell the children to touch something "soft," "hard," "smooth," "wide," "sharp," and so forth. The last child touching that type of object sits in the "mush pot" for one turn (avoid excluding children in games of this nature).

Search Place several different objects in a large cloth bag. Have the children reach in without looking and find, by touch, the correct object described such as:

1. "Find something you eat with."
2. "Find something you wear."
3. "Find something you write with."

Tactile Memory

Tactile memory activities are similar to discrimination and matching activities but involve a greater degree of sophistication. Memory activities require the child to discriminate nonvisually between familiar and unfamiliar objects and to apply verbal labels to these tactile clues.

Objectives

1. To remember what objects feel like.
2. To be able to identify tactilely unfamiliar objects by touch.
3. To be able to identify tactilely familiar objects.

Movement Experiences

Where Is It? Using a textured drawing of a familiar figure (kitten, donkey, Santa Claus), have the children locate its various body parts while blindfolded.

Guess Who? Have the children form a circle. "It" is blindfolded, turned around twice, and placed in the center of the circle. He then steps forward until he touches another child and attempts to determine who it is. He feels the child's clothing, hair, face, and so forth in an effort to determine who it is. Three guesses are permitted, then a new child is "it."

Put in Order Scatter several objects on the floor. Blindfold the children and tell them the type of object they must locate. Begin with three types. Have them locate the objects and place them in order. For example, tell them to find something round, then something hard, then something smooth.

Memory Ball Secure several different types of ball from the gymnasium (football, basketball, baseball, softball, soccerball, volleyball, kick ball, tennis ball, and whiffle ball). Place the balls on the floor and have the children, blindfolded, locate and name the various balls and tell what they are used for.

Sandpaper Numbers and Letters Blindfold the children and have them distinguish between various numbers and letters by touch. Older children can solve simple addition or subtraction problems using the numbers or spelling words.

SUGGESTED RECORDS

Berman, Marcia and Patty Zeitlin, with Ann Barlin, *Rainy Day Dances, Rainy Day Songs,* Educational Activities, Box 392, Freeport, New York 11520 (AR 570).
————, *Body Jive,* Educational Activities, Inc., Box 392, Freeport, New York 11520 (AR 96, AC 96).
————, *Clap, Snap, and Tap,* Educational Activities, Box 392, Freeport, New York 11520 (AR 48).
————, *Get Fit While You Sit,* Educational Activities, Inc., Box 392, Freeport, New York 11520 (AR 516).
————, *Only Just Begun,* Educational Activities, Box 392, Freeport, New York 11520 (KEA 5025).
Finger Games, Bridges, 310 W. Jefferson, Dallas, Texas 75208 (HYP506).
Gallina, Jill and Michael Gallina, *Hand Jivin',* Educational Activities, Box 392, Freeport, New York 11520, (AR 95, AC 95).
Glass, Henry "Buzz", *It's Action Time—Let's Move!,* Educational Activities, Box 392, Freeport, New York 11520 (AR 79).
Glass, Henry "Buzz" and Rosemary Hallum, *Rhythm Stick Activities,* Educational Activities, Box 392, Freeport, New York 11520 (AR 55).
Hallum, Rosemary, *Fingerplay Fun,* Educational Activities, Box 392, Freeport, New York 11520 (AR 529).
Johnson, Laura, *Simplified Lummi Stick Activities,* Educational Activities, Box 392, Freeport, New York 11520, (K 2015).
Kaplan, Dorothy, *Perceptual Development Through Paper Folding,* Bridges, 310 W. Jefferson, Dallas, Texas 75208 (LP9010).
Lummi Stick Fun, Kimbo Records, Deal, New Jersey, Box 246 (KIM2000).
Riccione, Georgiana *Fun Activities for Fine Motor Skills,* Kimbo Records, Deal, New Jersey, Box 246 (KIM9076).
Smith, Les and Gabe DeSantis, *Roomnastics,* Educational Activities, Box 392, Freeport, New York 11520 (KEA 1131).
Williams, Linda and Donna Wemple, *Sensorimotor Training in the Classroom,* Volume 1, Educational Activities, Box 392, Freeport, New York 11520 (AR 532).
Williams, Linda and Donna Wemple, *Sensorimotor Training in the Classroom,* Volume II, Educational Activities, Box 392, Freeport, New York 11520 (AR 566).

INDEX